WHO WANTS TO BE A MILLIONAIRE

THE BUMPER QUIZ BOOK II

WHO WANTS TO BE A MILLIONAIRE

THE BUMPER QUIZ BOOK II

BOXTREE

First published 2001 by Boxtree
an imprint of Pan Macmillan Ltd
20 New Wharf Road London N1 9RR
Basingstoke and Oxford

Associated companies throughout the world

www.panmacmillan.com

ISBN 0 7522 6141 X

1 3 5 7 9 8 6 4 2

A CIP catalogue record for this book is available from the British Library.

Designed by seagulls
Printed by Mackays of Chatham plc

CONTENTS

How to play

Did you pull your hair out in the hotseat of your armchair over the teasers in *Who Wants To Be A Millionaire? The Quiz Book*, *The Ultimate Challenge* and the first *Bumper Quiz Book*? Then brace yourselves because *The Bumper Quiz Book II* is sure to test you to your absolute limits! The question masters have been busy crafting another 2,000 new and exclusive tantalizers in this second bumper edition. You can make it personal and challenge yourself, or invite some friends round and pit your wits against each other to win the game.

FOR 1 PLAYER

As on *Who Wants To Be A Millionaire?*, the aim of the game is to reach £1 Million. Before you can even think about the cash, you must first correctly answer a question from the Fastest Finger First section. You have just 30 seconds to put the letters in the correct order. When time's up, follow the page reference at the foot of the page to find out if you can take your place in the hotseat and begin your climb for the cash!

Once in the hotseat

Start with a question worth £100 and once you have decided on your final answer (and you are absolutely sure . . .) follow the page reference at the foot of the page to find out if you've won that amount. If your answer is correct, you can play to win £200 and so on up the Money Tree. The page where each money level begins is listed in the answer section.

As on the programme you have three Lifelines to help you on your way to £1 Million. These are, of course, optional but each of them can only be used once, so only use them when you really need to.

50:50

This option takes away two incorrect answers leaving the correct answer and one incorrect answer remaining. A page reference at the bottom of each page will direct you to the relevant section.

Phone-A-Friend

If you have a telephone handy (and a willing friend!) ring him/her up to help you out. You have thirty seconds (no cheating, now ...) to read the question to your Friend and for them to tell you what they think the answer is. If there's someone else around, ask if they can time it for you.

Ask The Audience

This works in exactly the same way as on *Who Wants To Be A Millionaire?* except we've asked the Audience so you don't have to! Simply follow the page reference at the bottom of each page to find out what the Audience thought. In the end, however, the final decision is yours.

If you answer incorrectly, you are out of the game. £1,000 and £32,000 are 'safe havens' so if you answer a question incorrectly and you have not reached £1,000 then not only are you out of the game but you won't have won a penny! If you have reached one (or both) of these havens and you answer a question incorrectly, then you are out of the game but you will have won the value of the previous haven you have reached. If at any point during the game you are unsure of an answer and don't want to risk being out of the game if you answer incorrectly, you can 'stick' at the amount you have won so far and that will be your final score. As you play, use the score sheets at the back of the book to keep a running record of the amount you have won and the Lifelines you have used.

FOR 2–5 PLAYERS

Players should take it in turns at being 'Chris Tarrant' and posing questions to the other contestant/s. The rules are the same as for a single player (see pages 6–7). If someone reaches £1 Million, that person is the winner and the game is over. Otherwise, whoever has won the most money when everyone else is out is the winner.

Are you ready to play? Good. With all that money at stake, we're sure we don't need to tell you to think very carefully before you give your final answer. Good luck and be sure to remember at all times the motto of *Who Wants To Be A Millionaire?* – it's only easy if you know the answer!

FASTEST FINGER FIRST

FASTEST FINGER FIRST

1

Put these British swimmers in the order they won Olympic gold.

- A: Duncan Goodhew
- B: Anita Lonsbrough
- C: Adrian Moorhouse
- D: David Wilkie

2

Starting with the earliest, put these athletes in the order they were born.

- A: Roger Bannister
- B: Daley Thompson
- C: Harold Abrahams
- D: Darren Campbell

3

Put these men in the order they first won the Formula 1 World Drivers' Championship.

- A: Nigel Mansell
- B: Damon Hill
- C: Jacques Villeneuve
- D: Michael Schumacher

4

Starting with the most recent, place these actors in order by the year of their birth.

- A: Charles Laughton
- B: Ralph Fiennes
- C: James Mason
- D: Albert Finney

5

Put these Scottish rulers in the order they reigned.

- A: James VI
- B: Macbeth
- C: Mary
- D: Robert the Bruce

Answers on page 491

6

Starting with the most recent, place these groups in the order they were formed.

- A: Shadows
- B: Simple Minds
- C: Simply Red
- D: Sugababes

7

Beginning with the earliest, put these authors in order by the year of their birth.

- A: Irvine Welsh
- B: Daphne du Maurier
- C: Zadie Smith
- D: Thomas Hardy

8

Starting with the most recent, place these albums in order of their year of release.

- A: Definitely Maybe
- B: Abbey Road
- C: Dark Side of the Moon
- D: The Joshua Tree

9

Put these words in alphabetical order.

- A: Grey
- B: Glisten
- C: Gulf
- D: Going

10

Place these London landmarks in reverse alphabetical order.

- A: Nelson's Column
- B: Buckingham Palace
- C: Hyde Park
- D: Eros

Answers on page 491

11

Starting with the earliest, place these TV sitcoms in the order they were first shown on British TV.

A: Rising Damp
B: The Army Game
C: Only Fools and Horses
D: The Vicar of Dibley

12

Put these comedies in the order they were first seen on British television.

A: Absolutely Fabulous
B: Alas Smith and Jones
C: Bless This House
D: Dad's Army

13

Starting with the smallest, place these animals in order of average mature adult size.

A: Hippo
B: Beaver
C: Lion
D: Grasshopper

14

Place these historical events in chronological order.

A: Storming of the Bastille
B: Battle of Bannockburn
C: Hillary's ascent of Everest
D: Death of Queen Victoria

15

Starting with the earliest, place these singers in the order they first had a UK number one single.

A: Geri Halliwell
B: Vera Lynn
C: Sandie Shaw
D: Lisa Stansfield

Answers on page 491

16

Put these songs in the order they were British UK number one singles for Michael Jackson.

A: Billie Jean
B: Black Or White
C: Earth Song
D: One Day In Your Life

17

Beginning with the closest, place these parts of Britain in order of distance from the equator.

A: Aberdeen
B: London
C: Manchester
D: Portsmouth

18

Put these names in alphabetical order of their last letter.

A: Hilary
B: Joanne
C: Michael
D: Nicholas

19

Starting with the earliest, place these US presidents in the order they took office.

A: Richard Nixon
B: Dwight Eisenhower
C: Thomas Jefferson
D: Jimmy Carter

20

Put these James Bond films in the order they were first released.

A: Moonraker
B: Dr No
C: On Her Majesty's Secret Service
D: The Living Daylights

Answers on page 491

21

Starting with the most recent, place these prime ministers in the order they took office.

A: Benjamin Disraeli
B: Harold Macmillan
C: Spencer Perceval
D: Herbert Asquith

22

Put these words in order to form the title of a 1983 film.

A: Return
B: Jedi
C: The
D: Of

23

Starting with the most recent, place these films in order according to the year of their initial release.

A: The War of the Worlds
B: Aliens
C: Logan's Run
D: The Matrix

24

Starting with the first, place these tennis scores in the order they would appear in a single game.

A: Love - 15
B: Deuce
C: 30 - 15
D: Fifteen all

25

Put these words in order to make a common proverb.

A: Cat
B: Curiosity
C: Killed
D: The

Answers on page 491

26

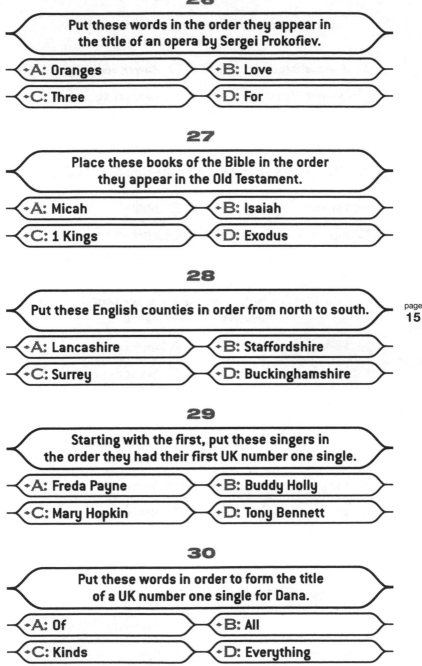

Put these words in the order they appear in the title of an opera by Sergei Prokofiev.

- A: Oranges
- B: Love
- C: Three
- D: For

27

Place these books of the Bible in the order they appear in the Old Testament.

- A: Micah
- B: Isaiah
- C: 1 Kings
- D: Exodus

28

Put these English counties in order from north to south.

- A: Lancashire
- B: Staffordshire
- C: Surrey
- D: Buckinghamshire

29

Starting with the first, put these singers in the order they had their first UK number one single.

- A: Freda Payne
- B: Buddy Holly
- C: Mary Hopkin
- D: Tony Bennett

30

Put these words in order to form the title of a UK number one single for Dana.

- A: Of
- B: All
- C: Kinds
- D: Everything

Answers on page 491

31

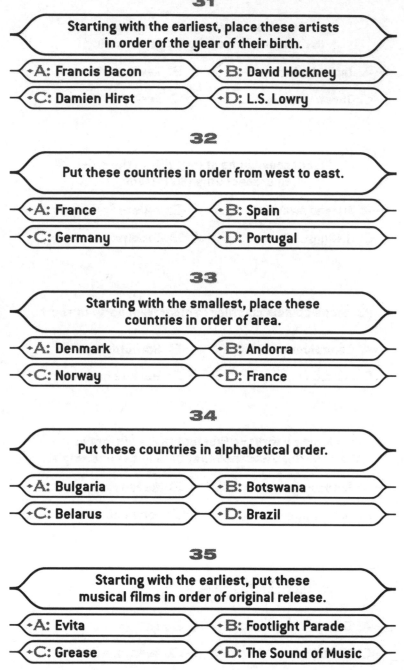

Starting with the earliest, place these artists in order of the year of their birth.

- A: Francis Bacon
- B: David Hockney
- C: Damien Hirst
- D: L.S. Lowry

32

Put these countries in order from west to east.

- A: France
- B: Spain
- C: Germany
- D: Portugal

33

Starting with the smallest, place these countries in order of area.

- A: Denmark
- B: Andorra
- C: Norway
- D: France

34

Put these countries in alphabetical order.

- A: Bulgaria
- B: Botswana
- C: Belarus
- D: Brazil

35

Starting with the earliest, put these musical films in order of original release.

- A: Evita
- B: Footlight Parade
- C: Grease
- D: The Sound of Music

Answers on page 491

36

Starting with the first, put these women in the order they died.

- A: Janis Joplin
- B: Marilyn Monroe
- C: Queen Victoria
- D: Ginger Rogers

37

Put these films starring Tom Cruise in order of original release.

- A: Far and Away
- B: Days of Thunder
- C: Risky Business
- D: Cocktail

38

Put these actresses in the order they were born.

- A: Demi Moore
- B: Julie Christie
- C: Anna Chlumsky
- D: Ruby Keeler

39

Starting with the fewest, put these countries in order by the number of letters in their name.

- A: Morocco
- B: Malawi
- C: Mali
- D: Madagascar

40

Place these capital cities in alphabetical order.

- A: Berne
- B: Canberra
- C: Madrid
- D: Jakarta

Answers on page 491

41

Put these members of the group ABBA in alphabetical order.

A: Anni-Frid
B: Agnetha
C: Benny
D: Björn

42

Starting with the earliest, put these films starring Jim Carrey in order of original release.

A: Liar Liar
B: The Mask
C: The Truman Show
D: Me, Myself and Irene

43

Put these men in the order they married Elizabeth Taylor.

A: John Warner
B: Larry Fortensky
C: Eddie Fisher
D: Michael Wilding

44

Put these words in order to form the title of a 1984 film starring Michael Caine.

A: On
B: Rio
C: It
D: Blame

45

Put these words in order to form the title of a number one album for Chris Rea.

A: The
B: To
C: Hell
D: Road

Answers on page 491

46

Beginning with the earliest, place these characters in the order they made their first TV appearance.

- A: Ali G
- B: Alan Partridge
- C: Dame Edna Everage
- D: Anthony Aloysius Hancock

47

Starting with the first, put these Grand Slam tournaments in the order Andre Agassi first won them.

- A: French Open
- B: Wimbledon
- C: US Open
- D: Australian Open

48

Put these American cities in order from west to east.

- A: San Diego
- B: Miami
- C: Philadelphia
- D: New Orleans

49

Starting with the furthest left, put these letters in the order they appear on a standard UK keyboard.

- A: S
- B: F
- C: K
- D: H

50

Put these numbers in reverse alphabetical order.

- A: Twelve
- B: Thirteen
- C: Fourteen
- D: Fifteen

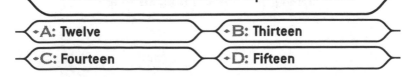

Answers on page 491

51

Starting with the eldest, put the children of Tony Blair in order of age.

A: Euan
B: Leo
C: Kathryn
D: Nicky

52

Put these words in order to form the title of a UK number one single for T'Pau.

A: In
B: Hand
C: Your
D: China

53

Starting with the furthest west, put these African capitals in order.

A: Khartoum
B: Accra
C: Dakar
D: Addis Ababa

54

Put these chemical elements in alphabetical order.

A: Bismuth
B: Beryllium
C: Bromine
D: Barium

55

Put these words in the order they occur in the title of Björk's 1995 hit song.

A: So
B: It's
C: Quiet
D: Oh

Answers on page 491

56

Starting with the earliest, put these films in the order they were first released.

- A: High Sierra
- B: High Society
- C: High Plains Drifter
- D: High Noon

57

Starting with the least, put the four home countries in order according to their population.

- A: England
- B: Northern Ireland
- C: Scotland
- D: Wales

58

Put these German numbers in order from nine to twelve.

- A: Elf
- B: Zwölf
- C: Neun
- D: Zehn

59

Starting with the earliest, put the last four Poets Laureate in order.

- A: John Betjeman
- B: Ted Hughes
- C: Andrew Motion
- D: Cecil Day Lewis

60

Place these cities in alphabetical order.

- A: Stoke-on-Trent
- B: Salford
- C: Sheffield
- D: Southampton

Answers on page 491

61

Put these vegetables in reverse alphabetical order.

- A: Parsnip
- B: Pepper
- C: Potato
- D: Pea

62

Starting with the first, put these US Presidents in the order they were assassinated.

- A: James Garfield
- B: John F. Kennedy
- C: William McKinley
- D: Abraham Lincoln

63

Put these words in order to form the title of a Robbie Williams album.

- A: You're
- B: Sing
- C: Winning
- D: When

64

Put these English counties in order from south to north.

- A: Cumbria
- B: Devon
- C: Lincolnshire
- D: Oxfordshire

65

Starting with the earliest, put these films for which Katharine Hepburn won Best Actress Oscars in order.

- A: On Golden Pond
- B: Guess Who's Coming to Dinner
- C: The Lion in Winter
- D: Morning Glory

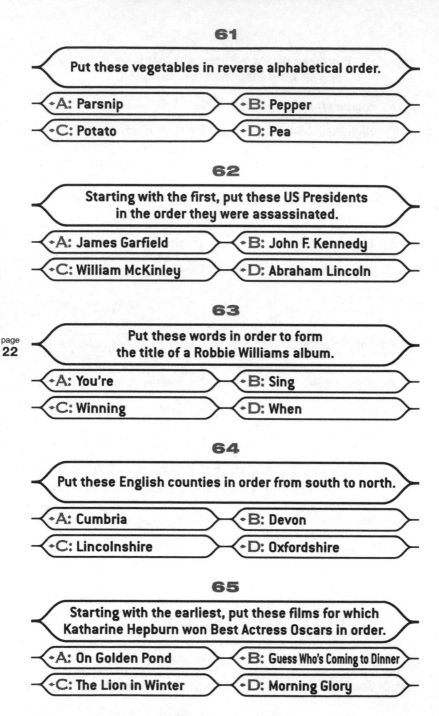

Answers on page 491

66

Put these words in order to form the title of a hit single for Olivia Newton-John.

A: Hopelessly
B: To
C: Devoted
D: You

67

Beginning with the most recent, place these films in order of their original year of release.

A: Rogue Trader
B: Bonnie and Clyde
C: Ned Kelly
D: Buster

68

Starting with the first, put these 'Ages' in the order they occurred in the Earth's history.

A: Bronze Age
B: Ice Age
C: Stone Age
D: Iron Age

69

Put these items of office stationery in alphabetical order.

A: File
B: Stapler
C: Pencil
D: Tippex

70

Starting with the earliest, put these London landmarks in order according to when they were built.

A: Tower of London
B: Canary Wharf
C: Buckingham Palace
D: Millennium Dome

Answers on page 491

71

Starting with the earliest, put these stage musicals in the order they were written.

- A: Sunset Boulevard
- B: Cats
- C: Evita
- D: Hair

72

Put these TV characters in the order they first entered the UK singles charts.

- A: Teletubbies
- B: Orville the Duck
- C: Zig and Zag
- D: Roland Rat

73

Starting with the lowest total, put these in order.

- A: One set of sextuplets
- B: Two sets of quins
- C: Three sets of triplets
- D: Four sets of twins

74

Put these words in the order they occur in the title of the fairy tale.

- A: The
- B: Killer
- C: Jack
- D: Giant

75

Starting with the earliest, put these films in the order of their first release.

- A: North to Alaska
- B: South Pacific
- C: East of Eden
- D: West Side Story

Answers on page 491

76

Starting with the fewest, put these amounts in a standard pack of playing cards in order.

- A: Number in a suit
- B: Number of suits
- C: Number of court cards
- D: Number of jokers

77

Put these people in the order they became 'Blue Peter' presenters.

- A: Anthea Turner
- B: Janet Ellis
- C: Mark Curry
- D: Simon Groom

78

Place these dinosaurs in alphabetical order.

- A: Brontosaurus
- B: Velociraptor
- C: Stegosaurus
- D: Triceratops

79

Starting at the left, put these vowels in the order they appear on the top line of letters on a keyboard.

- A: E
- B: I
- C: O
- D: U

80

Put these Dan Aykroyd films in the order they were made.

- A: Driving Miss Daisy
- B: Ghostbusters
- C: Pearl Harbor
- D: The Blues Brothers

Answers on page 491

81

Starting with the smallest, put these creatures in order, according to their mature size.

- A: Lobster
- B: Whale
- C: Dolphin
- D: Prawn

82

Put these women in the order they first won a Wimbledon singles title.

- A: Martina Hingis
- B: Lindsay Davenport
- C: Martina Navratilova
- D: Jana Novotna

83

Starting with the first, put these football clubs in the order Gary Lineker played for them.

- A: Leicester
- B: Grampus Eight
- C: Barcelona
- D: Tottenham Hotspur

84

Put these words in the order they appear in the title of a Beatles album.

- A: Band
- B: Club
- C: Hearts
- D: Lonely

85

Starting with the closest, put these fielders in the order for a spin bowler, according to their distance from the cricket stumps.

- A: Deep extra cover
- B: Wicket-keeper
- C: Mid wicket
- D: Short leg

Answers on page 491

86

Starting with the earliest in the year, place these quarter days in order.

- A: Lammas
- B: Whitsunday
- C: Candlemas
- D: Martinmas

87

Put these actresses in the order they first won an Oscar for Best Supporting Actress.

- A: Tatum O'Neal
- B: Geena Davis
- C: Rita Moreno
- D: Juliette Binoche

88

Starting with the first, put these states in the order they were admitted to the Union.

- A: Georgia
- B: Kentucky
- C: Iowa
- D: Mississippi

89

Used as Womble names, put these places in order from north to south.

- A: Wellington
- B: Cholet
- C: Tomsk
- D: Orinoco

90

Starting with the earliest, put these actors in order of birth.

- A: Errol Flynn
- B: Howard Keel
- C: Robin Williams
- D: Buster Keaton

Answers on page 491

91

Put these African countries in order from west to east.

A: Libya
B: Egypt
C: Mauritania
D: Algeria

92

Put these words in the order they appear in the title of a Thomas Hardy novel.

A: Crowd
B: Far
C: From
D: Madding

93

Starting with the closest, put these lines of latitude in order of their distance from the South Pole.

A: Tropic of Capricorn
B: Arctic Circle
C: Antarctic Circle
D: Tropic of Cancer

94

Starting with the fewest, put these in order, according to how many wheels they normally have.

A: Motorcycle
B: Unicycle
C: Bus
D: Tricycle

95

Put these English coastal resorts in order from north to south.

A: Great Yarmouth
B: Felixstowe
C: Hastings
D: Scarborough

Answers on page 491

96

Starting with the earliest, put these TV sitcoms in order of first transmission.

- A: One Foot In The Grave
- B: Only Fools and Horses
- C: Open All Hours
- D: On The Buses

97

Put these words in order to form the title of a 1985 film starring Michael J. Fox.

- A: Future
- B: Back
- C: To
- D: The

98

Starting with the earliest, put these films starring Johnny Depp in order of release.

- A: Sleepy Hollow
- B: Donnie Brasco
- C: Edward Scissorhands
- D: What's Eating Gilbert Grape

99

Starting with the earliest, put these pop duos in the order they had their first UK top ten single.

- A: Eurythmics
- B: Proclaimers
- C: Ant and Dec
- D: Righteous Brothers

100

Put these words in order to form the title of a 1952 musical film.

- A: In
- B: Rain
- C: Singin'
- D: The

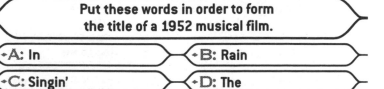

Answers on page 491

FASTEST FINGER FIRST

101

Starting with the oldest, put these Brontë family members in order of age.

- A: Charlotte
- B: Emily
- C: Anne
- D: Branwell

102

Starting with the earliest, put these Madonna albums in order of release.

- A: Erotica
- B: True Blue
- C: Ray of Light
- D: Like A Prayer

103

Put these words in order to form the name of a US rock group.

- A: Peppers
- B: Hot
- C: Chili
- D: Red

104

Starting with the earliest, put these popular singers in order, according to the year they died.

- A: Elvis Presley
- B: Frank Sinatra
- C: Buddy Holly
- D: Freddie Mercury

105

Starting with the earliest, put these battles involving Horatio Nelson in order.

- A: Battle of Calvi
- B: Battle of the Nile
- C: Battle of Trafalgar
- D: Battle of Santa Cruz

? Answers on page 491

106

Put these four islands in order of area from largest to smallest.

A: Anglesey
B: Isle of Wight
C: Lindisfarne
D: Skye

107

Starting with the earliest, put these UK runners in order, according to when they won their Olympic golds.

A: Allan Wells
B: Linford Christie
C: Chris Brasher
D: David Hemery

108

Put these Asian cities in order from south to north.

A: Bangkok
B: Kuala Lumpur
C: Hong Kong
D: Tokyo

109

Put these British actresses in the order they were born.

A: Peggy Ashcroft
B: Maggie Smith
C: Emma Thompson
D: Julie Walters

110

Starting with the longest, put these athletic events in order of distance.

A: 110 metres hurdles
B: 800 metres
C: 3,000 metres steeplechase
D: 20,000 metres walk

Answers on page 491

111

Put these playwrights in the order they were born.

- A: Euripides
- B: William Shakespeare
- C: Tom Stoppard
- D: Oscar Wilde

112

Put these dances in alphabetical order.

- A: Tango
- B: Waltz
- C: Jive
- D: Foxtrot

113

Starting with the smallest, place these bodies of water in order of size.

- A: Loch Ness
- B: North Sea
- C: Atlantic Ocean
- D: Mediterranean Sea

114

Put these religious leaders in the order they were born.

- A: Buddha
- B: Saint Peter
- C: Muhammad
- D: John Wesley

115

Put these parts of a car in their usual order from front to back.

- A: Boot
- B: Headlight
- C: Sunroof
- D: Wing mirror

Answers on page 491

116

Starting with the earliest, put these films in order, according to when they won the Best Picture Oscar.

A: Annie Hall
B: Ben Hur
C: Casablanca
D: Midnight Cowboy

117

Put these countries in alphabetical order.

A: Panama
B: Paraguay
C: Pakistan
D: Papua New Guinea

118

Put these men in the order in which they presented BBC's 'Match of the Day'.

A: David Coleman
B: Jimmy Hill
C: Gary Lineker
D: Des Lynam

119

Starting at the extremity, put these parts of the hand in their correct order.

A: Knuckles
B: Nails
C: Wrist
D: Palm

120

Put these films in the order they were first released.

A: All About Eve
B: All the President's Men
C: All That Jazz
D: All Quiet on the Western Front

Answers on page 491

FASTEST FINGER FIRST

121

Put these violinists in order of their year of birth.

A: Nigel Kennedy
B: Paganini
C: Vanessa-Mae
D: Yehudi Menuhin

122

Put these men in the order in which they first won the Olympic 100 metres title.

A: Donovan Bailey
B: Linford Christie
C: Carl Lewis
D: Allan Wells

123

Starting with the fewest, put these colours in order, according to how many vowels are in each word.

A: Turquoise
B: Maroon
C: Aquamarine
D: Vermillion

124

Put these stages of a couple's relationship in chronological order.

A: Decree absolute
B: Decree nisi
C: Engagement
D: Marriage

125

Put these bridge bids in order from lowest to highest.

A: Four spades
B: One club
C: Three hearts
D: Two diamonds

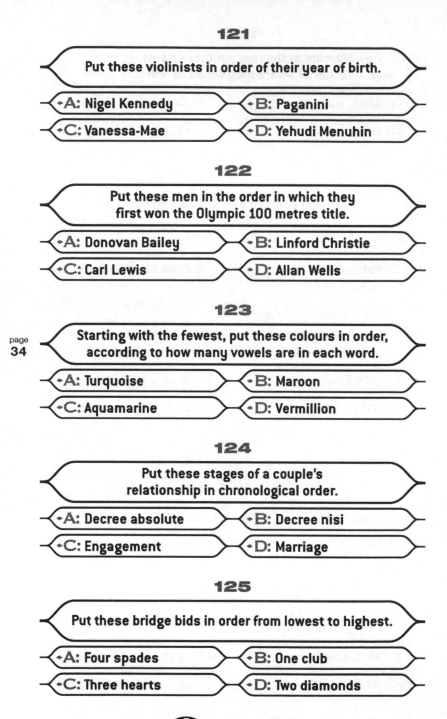

Answers on page 491

126

Starting at the top, put these items in order of where they would be worn.

A: Beret
B: Bra
C: Briefs
D: Brogue

127

Put these actresses in the order they were born.

A: Sharon Stone
B: Meryl Streep
C: Barbra Streisand
D: Gloria Swanson

128

Starting with the northernmost, put these inlets in clockwise order.

A: Bude Bay
B: Cardigan Bay
C: Firth of Forth
D: Moray Firth

129

Put these Italian cities in order from north to south.

A: Florence
B: Milan
C: Naples
D: Palermo

130

Put these skiers in the order they first won Winter Olympic gold.

A: Franz Klammer
B: Ingemar Stenmark
C: Hermann Maier
D: Alberto Tomba

? Answers on page 491

131

Starting with the earliest, put these actors in the order they died.

A: Harold Lloyd
B: Oliver Hardy
C: Charlie Chaplin
D: Stan Laurel

132

Put these parts of the leg in order from highest to lowest.

A: Ankle
B: Calf
C: Knee
D: Thigh

133

Put the answers to these sums in order from lowest to highest.

A: 3 plus 2
B: 12 minus 9
C: 16 divided by 4
D: 2 multiplied by 1

134

Put these Eddie Murphy films in the order they were first released.

A: Beverly Hills Cop
B: Doctor Dolittle
C: 48 Hrs
D: Trading Places

135

Starting with the earliest, put these groups in the order they first entered the UK singles charts.

A: Modern Romance
B: Lighthouse Family
C: REM
D: New Seekers

Answers on page 491

136

Put these actors in alphabetical order of their surnames.

A: Goldie Hawn
B: Nigel Havers
C: Nigel Hawthorne
D: Rita Hayworth

137

Starting with the highest, put these ranks of Anglican clergy in order.

A: Archbishop
B: Archdeacon
C: Bishop
D: Deacon

138

Put these artistic styles and movements in the order they began.

A: Baroque
B: Cubism
C: Impressionism
D: Pop Art

139

Put these characters in the order their names appear in the song 'Widdicombe Fair'.

A: Bill Brewer
B: Peter Gurney
C: Harry Hawk
D: Jan Stewer

140

Starting with the closest, put these capitals in order according to their distance from London.

A: Rangoon
B: Reykjavik
C: Rabat
D: Riyadh

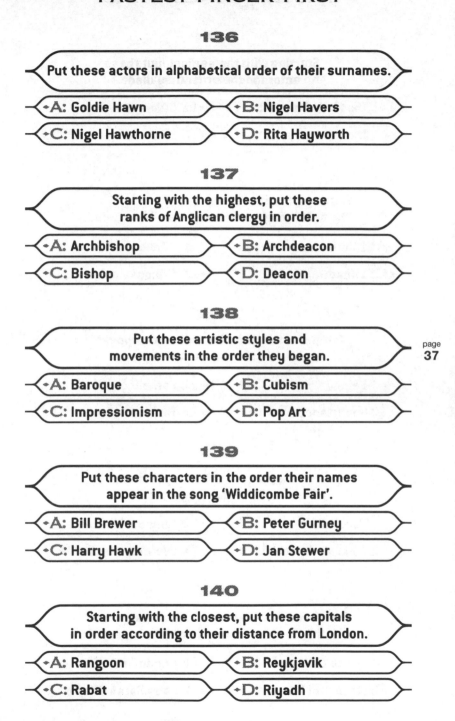

Answers on page 491

141

Put these Disney feature films in the order they were first released.

- A: The Little Mermaid
- B: Cinderella
- C: The Rescuers
- D: Pinocchio

142

Starting with the earliest, put these books in the order they occur in the New Testament.

- A: 1 Corinthians
- B: 1 Peter
- C: 1 Timothy
- D: 1 Thessalonians

143

Put these words in the order they appear in the title of an Oscar Wilde play.

- A: Being
- B: Earnest
- C: Importance
- D: The

144

Starting with the earliest, put these golfers in the order they were born.

- A: Nick Faldo
- B: Tony Jacklin
- C: Colin Montgomerie
- D: Lee Westwood

145

Put these four grandchildren of the Queen Mother in order from oldest to youngest.

- A: Prince Charles
- B: Prince Andrew
- C: Viscount Linley
- D: Lady Sarah Chatto

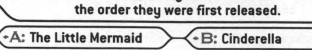

Answers on page 491

146

Put these words in order to give the name of a popular Italian tourist attraction.

A: Leaning
B: Of
C: Pisa
D: Tower

147

Starting with the earliest, put these TV soaps in the order they were first broadcast.

A: Brookside
B: Waterfront Beat
C: Hollyoaks
D: Grange Hill

148

Put these films directed by Robert Altman in the order they were made.

A: Nashville
B: Popeye
C: Short Cuts
D: M*A*S*H

149

Put these countries on the Greenwich meridian in order from north to south.

A: Spain
B: Algeria
C: Ghana
D: England

150

Starting with the furthest west, put these shipping forecast areas along the south coast in order.

A: Wight
B: Plymouth
C: Portland
D: Dover

Answers on page 491

15	£1 MILLION
14	£500,000
13	£250,000
12	£125,000
11	£64,000
10	£32,000
9	£16,000
8	£8,000
7	£4,000
6	£2,000
5	£1,000
4	£500
3	£300
2	£200
1 ◆	£100

1 ◆ £100

1

Which of these describes someone with a stout body?

A: Portly
B: Ginly
C: Vodkaly
D: Rumly

2

What is the proper name for a 'conker'?

A: Horse chestnut
B: Cow toenut
C: Bull headnut
D: Ram donut

3

Which people historically come from Scandinavia?

A: Spaniards
B: Apache
C: Vikings
D: Maoris

4

Which of these animals is native to Australia?

A: Polar bear
B: Koala
C: Llama
D: Panda

5

What is the ring of dirt left behind in the bath when all the water has drained out?

A: Scumline
B: Tidemark
C: Dirtlevel
D: Grimestain

6

Which of these is a thief who breaks into buildings by climbing to upper storeys?

A: Dog snatcher | B: Cat burglar
C: Horse thief | D: Cattle rustler

7

Which people formed the crew of a ship flying the 'skull and crossbones' flag?

A: Merchant sailors | B: Medieval explorers
C: Pirates | D: Atlantic rowers

8

What does a jukebox play?

A: Cards | B: Ball
C: Records | D: Truant

9

According to the rhyme, what were made by a Queen and stolen by a Knave?

A: Savoury quiche | B: Tarts
C: Custard creams | D: Cornish pasties

10

Which of these are soft shoes for wearing indoors?

A: Snippers | B: Skippers
C: Slippers | D: Strippers

50:50 Go to page 443 Go to page 467 ? Answers on page 492

1 ◆ £100

11

Which of these is foolish talk about nonsensical ideas?

- A: Flip-flop
- B: Claptrap
- C: Tex-Mex
- D: Zigzag

12

What is sold from a 'box office'?

- A: Boxes
- B: Boxing gloves
- C: Boxer shorts
- D: Tickets

13

Which of these would a DIY practitioner screw on to a bolt?

- A: Striker nut
- B: Wing nut
- C: Half-back nut
- D: Goalkeeper nut

14

What partners 'cheese' in the phrase which confirms that two things just don't go together?

- A: Chains
- B: Chalk
- C: Chintz
- D: Chilblains

15

If potato is the 'bubble', what is the 'cabbage', in the traditional British dish of leftovers?

- A: Squelch
- B: Squidge
- C: Squeak
- D: Squirt

50:50 Go to page 443 Go to page 467 ? Answers on page 492

1 ◆ £100

16

Which of these pet names refers to a horse?

A: Bunny
B: Dobbin
C: Neddy
D: Jumbo

17

According to the proverb, you can lead a horse to water but you can't make it... what?

A: Drink
B: Swim
C: Paddle
D: Wash

18

Which of these is a firework named after a saint?

A: Bernadette rocket
B: Bridget sparkler
C: Catherine wheel
D: Theresa candle

19

What is traditionally distributed by the British sovereign on Maundy Thursday?

A: Easter eggs
B: Hot cross buns
C: Money
D: Pancakes

20

Seven years of what is said to result from breaking a mirror?

A: Washing up
B: Grass mowing
C: Walking to work
D: Bad luck

50:50 Go to page 443 · Go to page 467 · ? Answers on page 492

1 ◆ £100

21

Which of these is a motor racing circuit near Kent?

A: Brands Devise
B: Brands Concoct
C: Brands Hatch
D: Brands Plan

22

Which event traditionally involves a special white dress?

A: General Election
B: Wedding
C: Funeral
D: London Marathon

23

What is the name for a sensational article that is exclusive to one newspaper?

A: Swoop
B: Snoop
C: Scoop
D: Shoop-shoop

24

Which cosmetic treatment is sometimes used to describe the renovation of a building?

A: Nose-job
B: Face-lift
C: Tummy-tuck
D: Leg-pull

25

What is the specific name for a building used for housing aircraft?

A: Shed
B: Hangar
C: Garage
D: Kennel

50:50 Go to page 443 Go to page 467 ? Answers on page 492

1 ◆ £100

26

Which trio of names refers to ordinary people?

- A: Fred, Jim and Stanley
- B: Bob, Jack and Charlie
- C: Ron, Len and Franky
- D: Tom, Dick and Harry

27

According to the proverb, what can't you judge 'by its cover'?

- A: A duvet
- B: A book
- C: A record
- D: A cushion

28

Which term describes things done with little enthusiasm?

- A: Quarter-brained
- B: Third-shouldered
- C: Half-hearted
- D: Three-fifths cocked

29

What is traditionally called a 'happy event'?

- A: Birth of a baby
- B: Tax reimbursement
- C: Annual holiday
- D: Lottery win

30

According to the rhyme, which job was Little Bo-Peep rather inept at?

- A: Milkmaid
- B: Cook
- C: Shepherdess
- D: Haymaker

50:50 Go to page 443 · Go to page 467 · ? Answers on page 492

1 ◆ £100

31

Which two initials identify the taps in British sinks, baths and basins?

A: A & E
B: H & C
C: L & R
D: B & W

32

Where was a chamber pot traditionally kept in the bedroom?

A: Inside the wardrobe
B: Under the bed
C: Behind the curtains
D: In the linen basket

33

What are the main things needed to play the game of 'ping-pong'?

A: Bats and ball
B: Pencil and paper
C: Dice and counters
D: Knife and fork

34

Which of these is often served to be eaten with cheese?

A: Wet cracker
B: Water biscuit
C: Dripping crisp
D: Damp rusk

35

Which of these is a square on a standard UK Monopoly board?

A: Hospital
B: Theatre
C: Jail
D: Sport stadium

50:50 Go to page 443 · Go to page 467 · ? Answers on page 492

1 ◆ £100

36

What type of radio programme is 'The Archers'?

A: Froth drama
B: Bubble concert
C: Soap opera
D: Suds festival

37

Which of these tools is used to make a picture puzzle?

A: Jigsaw
B: Fret saw
C: Bow saw
D: See-saw

38

What goes before 'Reverend' and 'Honourable' for two titles of respect?

A: Quick
B: March
C: Left
D: Right

39

Who makes a broadcast to the British nation every Christmas Day?

A: Madonna
B: Richard Branson
C: The Queen
D: Victoria Beckham

40

In the UK, which government agency collects tax paid on income?

A: Deductions Unit
B: Inland Revenue
C: Hector's Debt Office
D: Rank of Taxes

50:50 Go to page 443 · Go to page 467 · ? Answers on page 492

1 ◆ £100

41

Which of these is a card game that uses two standard packs?

- A: Tinasta
- B: Canasta
- C: Potasta
- D: Cupasta

42

If a sportsman comes home sporting a bronze medal, which position did he finish in the race?

- A: First
- B: Second
- C: Third
- D: Last

43

What is an accepted way of getting a ride to your destination?

- A: Raining a horse
- B: Icing a bus
- C: Frosting a car
- D: Hailing a taxi

44

Complete the title of the traditional tale: 'Puss in...'?

- A: Slippers
- B: Stilettos
- C: Boots
- D: Wellies

45

Which of these sets of initials does not identify a pop group?

- A: XTC
- B: ELO
- C: ABC
- D: ITV

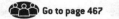

50:50 Go to page 443 Go to page 467 ? Answers on page 492

1 ◆ £100

46

What is one cricket team's batting period at the wicket?

A: Innings
B: Outings
C: Runnings
D: Boutings

47

Which of these is the name of a pencil-and-paper game for two?

A: Hang glider
B: Hang fire
C: Hangman
D: Hangover

48

A lottery jackpot winner would metaphorically 'laugh all the way to the...' where?

A: Tax office
B: Pub
C: Bank
D: Boss

49

Which command is usually shouted at a horse to make it slow down or stop?

A: Thwack
B: Whoa
C: Yesssssss
D: Mush mush

50

Which of these is a type of rodent?

A: Gammonster
B: Baconster
C: Porkster
D: Hamster

50:50 Go to page 443 | Go to page 467 | ? Answers on page 492

51

Who became President of the United States in 2001?

A: Geoff W. Shrub
B: Gordon W. Copse
C: George W. Bush
D: Graham W. Hedgerow

52

Which of these is a type of glove?

A: Gauntlet
B: Stocking
C: Tie
D: Blouse

53

What nickname is given to professional divers?

A: Tadpolemen
B: Newtmen
C: Toadmen
D: Frogmen

54

'Flying saucer' is an informal name for what?

A: CID
B: BBC
C: UFO
D: NUT

55

Which of these creatures is not extinct?

A: Dodo
B: Sabre-toothed tiger
C: Woolly mammoth
D: Horse

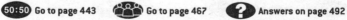

50:50 Go to page 443 Go to page 467 ? Answers on page 492

1 ◆ £100

56

Which of these is not a suit in a standard pack of playing cards?

A: Hearts
B: Spades
C: Clubs
D: Rubies

57

What is the name of a floating marker found in the sea or a river?

A: Gurl
B: Mann
C: Laydee
D: Buoy

58

Which part of the human body could be fastened in a 'bun'?

A: Feet
B: Shoulders
C: Hair
D: Knees

59

Which of these is a slang term for money?

A: Bread
B: Wine
C: Meat
D: Lager

60

What type of structure do beavers build?

A: Dam
B: Blarst
C: Bovver
D: Ratts

50:50 Go to page 443 Go to page 467 ? Answers on page 492

1 ◆ £100

61

What food is traditionally made by bees?

A: Bread
B: Cheese
C: Onions
D: Honey

62

Which of these is a type of musical instrument popular in Scotland?

A: Sackflutes
B: Satchelorgans
C: Bagpipes
D: Caserecorders

63

In terms of dates, what does the abbreviation 'BC' stand for?

A: Before Christmas
B: Before Coins
C: Before Christ
D: Before Chimps

64

Which of these words is a cricketing implement and a flying mammal?

A: Bat
B: Ball
C: Bail
D: Box

65

Mick Jagger is the lead singer with which rock group?

A: The Rolling Stocks
B: The Rolling Hills
C: The Rolling Stones
D: The Rolling Drunks

50:50 Go to page 443 Go to page 467 ? Answers on page 492

1 ◆ £100

66

Which of these is often worn by men at a wedding?

A: Top hat
B: Bottom hat
C: Middle hat
D: Side hat

67

Which term refers to an able and valued assistant, whatever the gender?

A: Left-hand woman
B: Right-hand man
C: Left-foot boy
D: Right-foot girl

68

What word describes an old car and a sausage?

A: Hanger
B: Klanger
C: Banger
D: Slanger

69

Which of these is an American rock band?

A: Limp Bizkit
B: Flaccid Teacake
C: Soft Crispbread
D: Floppy Scone

70

'The Penguin' is an enemy of which comic book hero?

A: Batman
B: Owlman
C: Voleman
D: Thrushman

50:50 Go to page 443 Go to page 467 ? Answers on page 492

1 ◆ £100

71

Which biblical character built an Ark to escape from the great floods?

A: Goliath
B: Pontius Pilate
C: Judas
D: Noah

72

Which of these is the name of a particularly strong wind?

A: Hurricane
B: Deluge
C: Heatwave
D: Shower

73

Who would traditionally live in an igloo?

A: Aztec
B: Eskimo
C: Viking
D: Aborigine

74

The nose of which creature is usually referred to as the 'trunk'?

A: Cat
B: Dog
C: Elephant
D: Squirrel

75

Which of these is a type of card game?

A: Porty
B: Rummy
C: Winey
D: Aley

50:50 Go to page 443 Go to page 467 ? Answers on page 492

76

The chihuahua is a small breed of which animal?

A: Dog
B: Dolphin
C: Deer
D: Damsonfly

77

What is the name of the highest mountain in Scotland?

A: Bob Nevis
B: Bill Nevis
C: Baz Nevis
D: Ben Nevis

78

Which of these words can mean a breed of bird and something used on a building site?

A: Raven
B: Thrush
C: Heron
D: Crane

79

In the Bible, what did Moses famously part?

A: His hair
B: Butting rams
C: Angry motorists
D: The Red Sea

80

Which of these is an island in the Irish Sea?

A: Isle of Woman
B: Isle of Child
C: Isle of Boy
D: Isle of Man

50:50 Go to page 443 | Go to page 467 | ? Answers on page 492

81

What are filled in to produce the statistics used in a survey?

- A: Billionaires
- B: Questionnaires
- C: Legionnaires
- D: March 'Ares

82

Which word can be a unit of speed and something used to fasten shoelaces?

- A: Knot
- B: Hitch
- C: Rod
- D: Tie

83

Which of these animals has a shell?

- A: Snipe
- B: Snail
- C: Snake
- D: Snapper

84

What was the name of the world's first adhesive postage stamp?

- A: Penny Magnolia
- B: Penny Dirty-White
- C: Penny Black
- D: Penny Off-Grey

85

Which of these is a TV programme presented by Rolf Harris?

- A: Animal Supermarket
- B: Animal Hospital
- C: Animal Leisure Centre
- D: Animal University

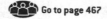

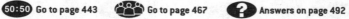

50:50 Go to page 443 | Go to page 467 | ? Answers on page 492

1 ◆ £100

86

Which of these is an island group off the southwest coast of England?

- A: Wallee Isles
- B: Frivvolus Isles
- C: Nuttee Isles
- D: Scilly Isles

87

What type of geographical features are the Himalayas?

- A: Islands
- B: Deserts
- C: Caves
- D: Mountains

88

Which of these is a character in the TV sitcom 'Only Fools and Horses'?

- A: Tel-Boy
- B: Kel-Boy
- C: Del-Boy
- D: Bel-Boy

89

By what name is the golfer Eldrick Woods better known?

- A: Lion
- B: Cougar
- C: Tiger
- D: Hamster

90

Which of these would be most likely to use an 'anvil'?

- A: Blacksmith
- B: Blackjones
- C: Blacktaylor
- D: Blackharris

50:50 Go to page 443 · Go to page 467 · Answers on page 492

1 ◆ £100

91

In the Garden of Eden, which creature tempted Eve?

A: Spider
B: Scorpion
C: Serpent
D: Sheepdog

92

Which of these is a nickname for London?

A: The Huge Pollution
B: The Massive Smog
C: The Enormous Cloud
D: The Big Smoke

93

What would you expect to find in the American town of Niagara Falls?

A: Volcano
B: Desert
C: Waterfall
D: Swamp

94

Which of these was a popular group of the 1970s?

A: Beach Town Rockers
B: Bay City Rollers
C: Cove Village Riders
D: Shore County Runners

95

Which of these is located in the Arctic?

A: North Staff
B: North Pike
C: North Pole
D: North Stick

50:50 Go to page 443 Go to page 467 ? Answers on page 492

1 ◆ £100

96

In the nursery rhyme, who had a farm?

A: Old Mackenzie
B: Old McFadden
C: Old Macdonald
D: Old McHerbert

97

Which of these is an official title of Prince Philip?

A: Duke of Edinburgh
B: Duke of Cardiff
C: Duke of London
D: Duke of Great Yarmouth

98

Who starred in the film thriller 'Hannibal'?

A: Anthony Leapkins
B: Anthony Skipkins
C: Anthony Jumpkins
D: Anthony Hopkins

99

According to the nursery rhyme,
what frightened Little Miss Muffet?

A: Snake
B: Spider
C: Scorpion
D: The Blair Witch

100

Which of these was a race of
mythological warrior women?

A: Niles
B: Danubes
C: Amazons
D: Severns

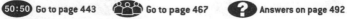

50:50 Go to page 443 Go to page 467 ? Answers on page 492

1 ◆ £100

101

Which TV quiz is hosted by Anne Robinson?

A: The Weakest Link
B: Who Wants To Be A Millionaire?
C: The People Versus
D: 100%

102

Which of these is a book by Charles Dickens?

A: Paul Daniels
B: Ali Bongo
C: Paul Xenon
D: David Copperfield

103

What do Americans often refer to as 'candy'?

A: Tomatoes
B: Burglaries
C: Sweets
D: Houses

104

Someone who is lacking in experience could be said to be 'wet behind the...' what?

A: Knees
B: Ears
C: Curtain
D: Bike sheds

105

Which television show, created by Gerry Anderson, features the Tracy Brothers?

A: Thunderbirds
B: Lightningfish
C: Rainreptiles
D: Snowmammals

50:50 Go to page 443 · Go to page 467 · ? Answers on page 492

106

Which of these is the name of a continent?

A: South Georgia
B: South America
C: South Africa
D: South Park

107

What are you said to have lost if you seem to be going mad?

A: Your marbles
B: Your footballs
C: Your Barbies
D: Your Pokémon cards

108

Which of these was a game show hosted by Ted Rogers?

A: 12-11-10
B: 9-8-7
C: 6-5-4
D: 3-2-1

109

Who married Tom Cruise in 1990?

A: Nadine Calfman
B: Nolene Puppyman
C: Nancy Foalman
D: Nicole Kidman

110

What is the name of the traditional theatre area of New York?

A: Largeway
B: Bigway
C: Broadway
D: Plumpway

50:50 Go to page 443
Go to page 467
? Answers on page 492

1 ◆ £100

111

Which of these would be worn by someone trying to give up smoking?

- A: Eye patch
- B: Nicotine patch
- C: Elbow patch
- D: Cabbage patch

112

What are painted at the side of a British road to indicate waiting restrictions?

- A: Single green spots
- B: Double yellow lines
- C: Triple green stripes
- D: Quadruple blue dots

113

Which of these phrases refers to a very short period of time?

- A: Split second
- B: Split infinitive
- C: Split skirt
- D: Split pea

114

What sound do a horse's hooves make on a hard surface?

- A: Flip-flop
- B: Hip-hop
- C: Clip-clop
- D: Drip-drop

115

Which of these animals is most likely to wear a saddle?

- A: Guinea pig
- B: Horse
- C: Rabbit
- D: Kangaroo

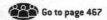

50:50 Go to page 443 Go to page 467 ? Answers on page 492

1 ◆ £100

116

What is the step of a ladder called?

A: Bung
B: Hung
C: Rung
D: Sung

117

Complete the title of the successful 2001 film: 'Bridget Jones's...'?

A: Diary
B: Bathmat
C: Key ring
D: Badger

118

Which of these is a type of accommodation?

A: Floorsit
B: Chairsit
C: Tablesit
D: Bedsit

119

Metaphorically, where is the 'flea' when you are given a sharp rebuke?

A: Up your nose
B: Under your tongue
C: In your ear
D: Between your toes

120

Which of these means to breathe with short, quick breaths?

A: Pant
B: Knicker
C: Y-front
D: Thong

50:50 Go to page 443 Go to page 467 ? Answers on page 492

121

Complete the title of the book by L. M. Montgomery: 'Anne of...'?

- A: Blue Tiles
- B: Green Gables
- C: Yellow Rafters
- D: Pink Porches

122

Which of these is a supermodel?

- A: Kate Grass
- B: Kate Lichen
- C: Kate Moss
- D: Kate Weed

123

Which TV sitcom was set in a holiday camp?

- A: Hi-De-Hi!
- B: Hoo-De-Hoo!
- C: Hum-De-Hum!
- D: Hee-De-Hee!

124

Which of these foods has its own day just before Lent?

- A: Pancake
- B: Iced bun
- C: Danish pastry
- D: Jam doughnut

125

What name is given to the liquid preparation for cleansing sheep of parasites?

- A: Sheep sauce
- B: Sheep dip
- C: Sheep gravy
- D: Sheep fondue

50:50 Go to page 443 · Go to page 467 · ? Answers on page 492

1 ◆ £100

126

Which of these are problems that occur during the early stages of a project?

A: Hairing troubles
B: Nailing troubles
C: Teething troubles
D: Skinning troubles

127

What is the term for the edible internal organs of an animal?

A: Offal
B: Onal
C: Inal
D: Outal

128

Which of these is an exercise?

A: Press stud
B: Press gang
C: Press-up
D: Press cutting

129

Someone who is easy to overcome or influence is a... what?

A: Puttover
B: Puffover
C: Pushover
D: Pullover

130

Which of these might you use to style your hair?

A: Gnoo
B: Mousse
C: Elck
D: Byson

50:50 Go to page 443 Go to page 467 ? Answers on page 492

1 ◆ £100

131

In medieval folklore, who is the king of the fairies?

A: Pokémon
B: Oberon
C: Mastodon
D: Da Doo Ron Ron

132

What name is given to someone who is over interested in other people's business?

A: Nosy pointer
B: Nosy parker
C: Nosy poker
D: Nosy picker

133

Which of these words means to dabble or play in shallow water?

A: Waddle
B: Diddle
C: Paddle
D: Poodle

134

What phrase is used to describe a 'narrow escape'?

A: Close depilatory cream
B: Close wax
C: Close electrolysis
D: Close shave

135

Which of these is an informal term for a noisy celebratory party?

A: Shoulderpoke
B: Elbowshovel
C: Shindig
D: Anklestab

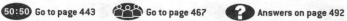

50:50 Go to page 443 Go to page 467 ? Answers on page 492

1 ◆ £100

136

Which TV drama series is set in the fictional village of Skelthwaite?

A: Where the Blood Is
B: Where the Heart Is
C: Where the Brain Is
D: Where the Facial Hair Is

137

According to the proverb, people in glass houses shouldn't throw... what?

A: Stones
B: Custard pies
C: Wobblies
D: Parties

138

Which of these is often administered to children on their birthday?

A: Gumps
B: Flumps
C: Bumps
D: Mumps

139

Tony Blair become leader of which party in 1994?

A: Labour Party
B: Graft Party
C: Toil Party
D: Grind Party

140

Which of these is a TV panel show featuring Loyd Grossman?

A: Up the Chimney
B: Through the Keyhole
C: Out the Window
D: Down the U-bend

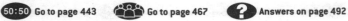

50:50 Go to page 443 Go to page 467 ? Answers on page 492

1 ◆ £100

141

Which type of anaesthetic numbs the whole body and induces a loss of consciousness?

- A: Corporal anaesthetic
- B: Sergeant anaesthetic
- C: Captain anaesthetic
- D: General anaesthetic

142

'Gesundheit' is an expression usually said after someone has... what?

- A: Had a baby
- B: Passed their A levels
- C: Milked a cow
- D: Sneezed

143

Which of these is a hairstyle of long, matted or tightly curled strands?

- A: Horrorkeys
- B: Terrormortises
- C: Frightfasteners
- D: Dreadlocks

144

What was the name of the religious wars of the Middle Ages?

- A: Crusades
- B: Marinades
- C: Lemonades
- D: Serenades

145

Which of these is another term for bad-tempered?

- A: Jumpery
- B: Socky
- C: Vesty
- D: Shirty

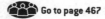

50:50 Go to page 443 Go to page 467 ? Answers on page 492

146

What is the name of the BBC teletext service?

A: Ceefax
B: Ceeshore
C: Ceeslug
D: Ceeweed

147

Which of these would be used to make gravy?

A: Browning
B: Keats
C: Tennyson
D: Wordsworth

148

Who became President of South Africa in 1994?

A: Wellington Mandela
B: Nelson Mandela
C: Churchill Mandela
D: Montgomery Mandela

149

What is the name for the soft, fine feathers of a bird?

A: Left
B: Right
C: Up
D: Down

150

Which of these words describes a thin, weakly person?

A: Grassy
B: Reedy
C: Flowery
D: Weedy

50:50 Go to page 443 Go to page 467 ? Answers on page 492

1 ◆ £100

151

What does a conductor use to keep an orchestra in time?

- A: Baton
- B: Handkerchief
- C: Hairbrush
- D: Underpants

152

Which of these are associated with Wembley Stadium?

- A: Solo Spire
- B: Twin Towers
- C: Triple Turrets
- D: Quadruple Queues

153

In legend, who was employed to rid Hamelin of its rats?

- A: Pied Piper
- B: Pied Pianist
- C: Pied Cellist
- D: Pied Trombonist

154

Which animal name is given to the centre of a target?

- A: Bull
- B: Boar
- C: Beaver
- D: Badger

155

Which of these is a popular type of billiard game?

- A: Pool
- B: Puddle
- C: Pond
- D: Port

50:50 Go to page 443 · Go to page 467 · ? Answers on page 492

1 ◆ £100

156

What does a limbo dancer traditionally dance under?

A: Bed
B: Car
C: Baguette
D: Pole

157

Which of these words is an informal name for an important person?

A: Bigdig
B: Bigjig
C: Bigwig
D: Bigpig

158

Complete the title of the BBC programme: 'Ready Steady...'?

A: Cook
B: Clean
C: Wash
D: Wipe

159

Which of these is a garden plant?

A: Nattering nettle
B: Chatting chickweed
C: Rambling rose
D: Talking tulip

160

Batman is known for wearing which of these items of clothing?

A: Cape
B: Peep-toe sandals
C: Stetson
D: Dungarees

50:50 Go to page 443 Go to page 467 ? Answers on page 492

1 ◆ £100

161

Which of these is a religious song?

- A: Hymn
- B: Hurr
- C: Uss
- D: Themme

162

Which snooker player became a team captain on 'A Question of Sport'?

- A: John Canarie
- B: John Parrott
- C: John Coccatoo
- D: John Budgey

163

Which of these is a weapon used to hurl stones?

- A: Catapult
- B: Dogapult
- C: Batapult
- D: Pigapult

164

An older person is sometimes described as 'long in the...'?

- A: Hair
- B: Tooth
- C: World
- D: Socks

165

What name is given to a group of 144 items?

- A: Foul
- B: Gross
- C: Naff
- D: Vile

166

Which of these is a city in South Wales?

A: Hensea
B: Goosesea
C: Swansea
D: Ducksea

167

Complete this description of someone who looks down on others: 'High and...'?

A: Flighty
B: Blightie
C: Mighty
D: Nightie

168

Which of these is a squiggle drawn absent-mindedly?

A: Doodle
B: Oodle
C: Noodle
D: Poodle

169

Which of these is a musical?

A: My Fair Lady
B: My Ginger Lady
C: My Brunette Lady
D: My Raven Lady

170

Complete the title of the Jerry Lee Lewis hit: 'Great Balls of...'?

A: Cheese
B: Fire
C: Marble
D: Wool

50:50 Go to page 443 Go to page 467 ? Answers on page 492

1 ◆ £100

171

Which of these was a hit for Madonna?

A: American Pie
B: Swiss Roll
C: Danish Pastry
D: French Tart

172

What are you said to do with someone when you inflict a severe defeat on them?

A: Wipe the floor
B: Clean the windows
C: Sweep the path
D: Mow the lawn

173

Which of these words means 'bullied' or 'threatened'?

A: Backblown
B: Browbeaten
C: Bonebashed
D: Bustboxed

174

What is the name for the dome-shaped hut of some North American Indian peoples?

A: Wigwam
B: Digdam
C: Zigzam
D: Bigbam

175

Which of these is a popular TV gardening programme?

A: Ground Level
B: Ground Force
C: Ground Control
D: Ground Almonds

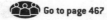

50:50 Go to page 443 Go to page 467 ? Answers on page 492

1 ◆ £100

176

Which famous couple is most associated with the wearing of fig leaves?

- A: Adam and Eve
- B: Tom and Jerry
- C: David and Goliath
- D: Posh and Becks

177

What is the capital of Hungary?

- A: Budaplague
- B: Budapest
- C: Budabother
- D: Budanuisance

178

Which of these is a regular payment from a bank or building society?

- A: Standing joke
- B: Standing order
- C: Standing stone
- D: Standing ovation

179

Which of these is the name of an Irish county?

- A: Chutney
- B: Ketchup
- C: Mayo
- D: Vinaigrette

180

The largest portion of something is said to be which animal's share?

- A: Elephant's
- B: Lion's
- C: Hippo's
- D: Rottweiler's

50:50 Go to page 443 Go to page 467 ? Answers on page 492

50:50

15	£1 MILLION
14	£500,000
13	£250,000
12	£125,000
11	£64,000
10	£32,000
9	£16,000
8	£8,000
7	£4,000
6	£2,000
5	£1,000
4	£500
3	£300
2 ◆	£200
1 ◆	£100

2 ◆ £200

1

Someone who is having a surgical operation is said to be going 'under the...' what?

A: Knife
B: Fork
C: Spoon
D: Plate

2

What are 'hash browns'?

A: Burnt slices of toast
B: Strong walking shoes
C: Fried grated potato
D: Worn corduroy trousers

3

Which name applies to a young unopened edible mushroom?

A: Zip
B: Button
C: Press-stud
D: Toggle

4

Which of these refers to denim trousers?

A: Genes
B: Geans
C: Jeans
D: Jeens

5

Which of these is a district of London known for its eateries, bars and nightclubs?

A: Soho
B: Tally-ho
C: Westward ho!
D: Ho-ho-ho

50:50 Go to page 445 | Go to page 469 | ? Answers on page 492

2 ◆ £200

6

What date in February is Leap Year Day?

A: 28th
B: 29th
C: 30th
D: 31st

7

How does the 'little star' shine, according to the rhyme?

A: Dazzle, dazzle
B: Twinkle, twinkle
C: Sparkle, sparkle
D: Flicker, flicker

8

Which word goes before 'wallop' to mean a load of nonsense?

A: Cods
B: Crabs
C: Clams
D: Cockles

9

Which of these is a dairy product also known as Devonshire cream?

A: Clots cream
B: Clottish cream
C: Clotting cream
D: Clotted cream

10

People who express themselves in a roundabout way are said to 'beat about the...' what?

A: Drum
B: Clock
C: House
D: Bush

50:50 Go to page 445 Go to page 469 ? Answers on page 492

2 ◆ £200

11

Which of these is a bend in the arm at the elbow?

A: Staff | B: Cheat
C: Shank | D: Crook

12

Which of these is the most likely place to find a 'porthole'?

A: Computer | B: Wine bottle
C: Ship | D: Camera

13

Which of these punctuation marks is also a name for a person called Dorothy?

A: Spot | B: Dot
C: Dash | D: Hash

14

Which utensil in a set of fireside irons is also the name of a card game?

A: Brush | B: Poker
C: Tongs | D: Shovel

15

What is the real name of the actor sometimes known as Sly Stallone?

A: Stanley | B: Silas
C: Selwyn | D: Sylvester

50:50 Go to page 445 Go to page 469 ? Answers on page 492

2 ◆ £200

16

Which of these is a piece of furniture?

A: Welsh dresser
B: Irish setter
C: French roll
D: Dutch auction

17

What is the traditional shape of a pizza?

A: Triangular
B: Square
C: Round
D: Octagonal

18

What is the name for a large letter in upper case?

A: Capital
B: Original
C: Print
D: Primary

19

Which of these actions do you associate with a deck chair?

A: Rocking
B: Swivelling
C: Folding
D: Extending

20

Which of these is the Greek goddess of the harvest?

A: Millimetre
B: Centimetre
C: Demeter
D: Metre

50:50 Go to page 445 Go to page 469 ? Answers on page 492

2 ◆ £200

21

If you are said to 'rabbit', what do you do a lot of?

A: Hopping
B: Nibbling
C: Chatting
D: Having children

22

With which type of clothing do you associate the name 'Bermuda'?

A: Shorts
B: Gloves
C: Socks
D: Underpants

23

What is the name for a wrapped biscuit containing a motto with a prediction written on it?

A: Chance cracker
B: Lucky snap
C: Fortune cookie
D: Crystal crisp

24

In which publication are you most likely to find strip cartoons?

A: Mail order catalogue
B: Glossy magazine
C: Children's comic
D: Holiday brochure

25

Which of these words for money is also a nickname for a policeman?

A: Silver
B: Tanner
C: Copper
D: Change

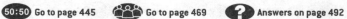

50:50 Go to page 445 · Go to page 469 · ? Answers on page 492

2 ◆ £200

26

According to the proverb, which member of the family shouldn't you teach 'to suck eggs'?

A: Father
B: Mother
C: Grandfather
D: Grandmother

27

What does an enthusiast watch at 'The Dogs'?

A: Stock cars
B: Greyhound racing
C: Speedway
D: Horse racing

28

Complete the simile: 'As happy as...' ?

A: Larry
B: Barry
C: Harry
D: Gary

29

Which suit in a standard pack of playing cards could also refer to a golf set?

A: Hearts
B: Diamonds
C: Clubs
D: Spades

30

Which phrase refers to something that only experiences a short period of popularity?

A: Taste of the day
B: Sweet of the week
C: Flavour of the month
D: Tang of the season

50:50 Go to page 445 · Go to page 469 · ? Answers on page 492

2 ◆ £200

31

Cymbals belong to which section of the orchestra?

A: String
B: Brass
C: Woodwind
D: Percussion

32

What is 'quarter past two' on the twenty-four hour clock?

A: 12:13
B: 14:15
C: 16:17
D: 18:19

33

Which of these people wears a 'tutu' while earning a living?

A: Ballerina
B: Parish priest
C: Bus conductress
D: Pantomime dame

34

Which of these is the name of the largest city in Australia?

A: Stanley
B: Sonny
C: Sydney
D: Sandy

35

What is a main feature of the French 'cancan' dance?

A: Feather fans
B: Juggling
C: High kicks
D: Clogs

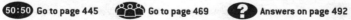

50:50 Go to page 445 · Ask the audience: Go to page 469 · ? Answers on page 492

2 ◆ £200

36

Which of these is a city in Somerset that was called Aquae Sulis by the Romans?

- A: Shower Head
- B: Tap Dance
- C: Bath Spa
- D: Looe Rolls

37

In theology, what is a 'cherub'?

- A: Winged angel
- B: Gemstone
- C: Pumpkin
- D: Fairy godmother

38

What were used to send messages by semaphore code?

- A: Flags
- B: Pigeons
- C: Drums
- D: Smoke signals

39

What does 'RI' stand for when it appears on a school timetable?

- A: Research Information
- B: Registration Inspection
- C: Reading Internet
- D: Religious Instruction

40

What type of tape is called 'Scotch' tape by Americans?

- A: Sticky tape
- B: Tickertape
- C: Steel tape
- D: Red tape

50:50 Go to page 445 · Go to page 469 · ? Answers on page 492

2 ◆ £200

41

Which letter is associated with a road junction and a short-sleeved shirt?

A: A
B: B
C: M
D: T

42

In what kind of weather conditions would a parasol normally be used?

A: Rainy
B: Sunny
C: Foggy
D: Windy

43

Which of these words stays the same in its plural form?

A: Sheep
B: Child
C: Tooth
D: Mouse

44

Which of these expressions means to behave foolishly?

A: Blaze the trail
B: Bite the dust
C: Draw the line
D: Act the goat

45

In which sport is the ball balanced on a tee?

A: Tennis
B: Golf
C: Darts
D: Squash

50:50 Go to page 445 · Go to page 469 · ? Answers on page 492

2 ◆ £200

46

Which of these terms can mean 'six of one; half a dozen of the other'?

- A: Swings and roundabouts
- B: Dodgems and slides
- C: Helters and skelters
- D: Dippers and wheels

47

What do you traditionally tie a knot in, to remind you to do something?

- A: Handkerchief
- B: Tea towel
- C: Bed sheet
- D: Sleeve

48

Which of these is a well-known TV chef?

- A: Alan Titchmarsh
- B: Anna Ford
- C: Ainsley Harriott
- D: Anne Robinson

49

What was the first name of the scientist Einstein?

- A: Allan
- B: Albert
- C: Alexander
- D: Alistair

50

Which of these is another term for the dog known as the Irish setter?

- A: Blue setter
- B: Pink setter
- C: Orange setter
- D: Red setter

50:50 Go to page 445 · Go to page 469 · ? Answers on page 492

2 ◆ £200

51

Which of these words means clear and easily understood?

- A: Lucite
- B: Lucid
- C: Lukewarm
- D: Lucerne

52

Which 'Queen of Scots' was executed by Elizabeth I of England?

- A: Marjorie
- B: Millicent
- C: Maureen
- D: Mary

53

Which of these is a film directed by Alfred Hitchcock?

- A: Loony
- B: Nutter
- C: Weirdo
- D: Psycho

54

In English legend, what object was sought by King Arthur and his knights?

- A: Holy Mail
- B: Holy Pail
- C: Holy Whale
- D: Holy Grail

55

Complete the title of the 1977 film: 'Close Encounters of the...'?

- A: First Kind
- B: Second Kind
- C: Third Kind
- D: Fourth Kind

50:50 Go to page 445 Go to page 469 ? Answers on page 492

2 ◆ £200

56

Which of these is a multiple Olympic medal winner?

- A: Simon Bluetomb
- B: Stuart Whitecrypt
- C: Solomon Blackvault
- D: Steven Redgrave

57

Which soul singer had several hit records with the Miracles?

- A: Foggy Robinson
- B: Misty Robinson
- C: Smokey Robinson
- D: Sugar Ray Robinson

58

'Pretty Vacant' was a hit single for which pioneering punk rock band?

- A: Love Rifles
- B: Nookie Bazookas
- C: Crumpet Muskets
- D: Sex Pistols

59

Where would a 'manatee' usually be found?

- A: In space
- B: Underwater
- C: Up a tree
- D: In mid-air

60

Which of these is a state of the USA?

- A: New Panama
- B: New Guatemala
- C: New Mexico
- D: New El Salvador

50:50 Go to page 445 Go to page 469 ? Answers on page 492

61

Which of these is a famous jazz musician?

A: Dizzy Gillespie
B: Woozy Gillespie
C: Shakey Gillespie
D: Tipsy Gillespie

62

What was the first name of the famous actor Lord Olivier?

A: Ralph
B: Alec
C: John
D: Laurence

63

The daffodil is a national symbol of which country?

A: Turkey
B: Egypt
C: Australia
D: Wales

64

Which of these was a scientific breakthrough pioneered by Francis Crick?

A: BBC
B: RAC
C: DNA
D: ITV

65

What item is often referred to as a 'brolly'?

A: Lampshade
B: Overcoat
C: Umbrella
D: Curtain

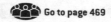

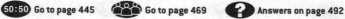

50:50 Go to page 445 Go to page 469 ? Answers on page 492

66

'Johnny B Goode' was a hit single for which singer?

A: Chuck Herb
B: Chuck Fruit
C: Chuck Pulse
D: Chuck Berry

67

Which film won the Best Picture Oscar at the 2001 Oscars?

A: Gladiator
B: Boxer
C: Wrestler
D: Streetfighter

68

Which of these is a David Lean movie starring Alec Guinness?

A: Bridge on the River Thames
B: Bridge on the River Severn
C: Bridge on the River Kwai
D: Bridge on the River Ouse

69

In which part of the world are planes and boats rumoured to have disappeared?

A: Bahamas Square
B: Borneo Circle
C: Barbados Cube
D: Bermuda Triangle

70

Which of these is a past prime minister of Great Britain?

A: Anthony Eden
B: Anthony Gethsemane
C: Anthony Sinai
D: Anthony Tarsus

50:50 Go to page 445 Go to page 469 ? Answers on page 492

2 ◆ £200

71

Which of these countries is in Asia?

A: Chad | B: Ecuador
C: El Salvador | D: Myanmar

72

'Handy' Andy Kane is an expert in which field?

A: Cookery | B: DIY
C: Gardening | D: Animal husbandry

73

Which of these is a Bafta Award-winning programme on Channel 4?

A: So Michael Parkinson | B: So Ian Wright
C: So Des O'Connor | D: So Graham Norton

74

Which of these is a film directed by Richard Attenborough?

A: Gandhi | B: Columbus
C: Perón | D: Livingstone

75

Which part of Europe is particularly associated with vampires and other monsters?

A: Essex | B: Majorca
C: Normandy | D: Transylvania

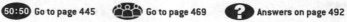

50:50 Go to page 445 Go to page 469 ? Answers on page 492

2 ◆ £200

76

Which of these is a film starring Jodie Foster?

A: The Silence of the Piglets
B: The Silence of the Kittens
C: The Silence of the Puppies
D: The Silence of the Lambs

77

In the TV series 'Flipper', what type of creature was the title character?

A: Shark
B: Squid
C: Killer whale
D: Dolphin

78

Which of these is a film starring Steve McQueen and Paul Newman?

A: The Enormous Furnace
B: The Towering Inferno
C: The Gigantic Blaze
D: The Massive Bonfire

79

Rob Andrew and Kenny Logan have both played for which rugby club?

A: Wasps
B: Ants
C: Beetles
D: Lice

80

What nationality is Sven Goran Eriksson, the coach of England's football team?

A: Australian
B: Turkish
C: Brazilian
D: Swedish

50:50 Go to page 445 · Go to page 469 · ? Answers on page 492

81

Which TV series is hosted by Gary Rhodes?

A: Wondercook
B: Masterchef
C: Toproaster
D: Greatgourmand

82

In medieval times, what traditionally filled a moat?

A: Water
B: Arrows
C: Mead
D: Livestock

83

What surname is shared by the rower Steve and the actress Vanessa?

A: Pinsent
B: Foster
C: Redgrave
D: Cracknell

84

Which of these is a book in the New Testament of the Bible?

A: Exodus
B: Genesis
C: Revelation
D: Deuteronomy

85

The New York Yankees are a famous team in which sport?

A: Ice hockey
B: Baseball
C: Basketball
D: American football

50:50 Go to page 445 Go to page 469 Answers on page 492

86

Which of these is a former world champion boxer?

- A: Sugar Ray Leonard
- B: Honey Ron Larry
- C: Caramel Rick Lonny
- D: Treacle Ralph Lawrence

87

Which of these is a drink made from vodka and tomato juice?

- A: Bloody Maureen
- B: Bloody Millicent
- C: Bloody Mary
- D: Bloody Marion

88

What catches the air to slow the descent of a parachute?

- A: Canopy
- B: Kite
- C: Umbrella
- D: Sunshade

89

Which of these is a best-selling author?

- A: Danielle Brass
- B: Danielle Steel
- C: Danielle Pewter
- D: Danielle Bronze

90

Which of these foods is humorously referred to as 'rabbit food'?

- A: Porridge
- B: Fruit cake
- C: Salad
- D: Lime jelly

50:50 Go to page 445 · Go to page 469 · ? Answers on page 492

2 ◆ £200

91

Which first name is shared by former 'Blue Peter' presenters Noakes and Leslie?

A: Simon | B: Peter
C: John | D: Richard

92

What was the real first name of Dusty Springfield?

A: Mindy | B: Mary
C: Molly | D: Mandy

93

Which of these vegetables is associated with a 'pod'?

A: Cauliflower | B: Carrot
C: Pea | D: Turnip

94

What name is given to the fat exuded by roasting meat?

A: Weeping | B: Dripping
C: Soaking | D: Oozing

95

Which of these is another term for a quilt?

A: Ductule | B: Dungaree
C: Duvet | D: Dura

50:50 Go to page 445 Go to page 469 ? Answers on page 492

2 ◆ £200

96

After decimalisation, what was the lowest coin denomination to be silver-coloured?

A: 1p
B: 2p
C: 5p
D: 10p

97

Which of these would not be described as a court card?

A: Nine of clubs
B: Jack of spades
C: King of hearts
D: Queen of diamonds

98

Complete the phrase: 'As cool as a...'?

A: Curator
B: Cucumber
C: Cushion
D: Cuticle

99

What type of creature is a gannet?

A: Insect
B: Bird
C: Reptile
D: Fish

100

At the start of a standard game of snooker, the red balls are formed into what shape?

A: Triangle
B: Square
C: Hexagon
D: Circle

50:50 Go to page 445 Go to page 469 ? Answers on page 492

2 ◆ £200

101

What name is given to the organisers of entertainment at Butlin's?

- A: Greensocks
- B: Blueshoes
- C: Redcoats
- D: Yellowhats

102

The word 'pub' is a shortened version of which phrase?

- A: Public relations
- B: Public enemy
- C: Public house
- D: Public transport

103

Which of these words can precede 'punishment' and 'gains tax'?

- A: Compact
- B: Corrosive
- C: Cerebral
- D: Capital

104

Which of these is a form of hockey?

- A: Splinty
- B: Stinty
- C: Swinty
- D: Shinty

105

Which of these is most likely to be placed in a slot machine?

- A: Slice of bread
- B: Sheet of paper
- C: Coin
- D: Boiling water

50:50 Go to page 445 · Go to page 469 · Answers on page 492

2 ◆ £200

106

If something is described as 'teeny', it is extremely... what?

A: Small
B: Sharp
C: Large
D: Loud

107

The phrase 'Shall I be mother?' is most associated with which activity?

A: Washing the dishes
B: Sweeping the floor
C: Pouring the tea
D: Cleaning the windows

108

Complete the phrase meaning something that is a pleasure or relief to see: 'A sight for...'?

A: Poor eyes
B: Sore eyes
C: Four eyes
D: More eyes

109

Which of these is an informal term for a helicopter?

A: Popper
B: Shopper
C: Topper
D: Chopper

110

What is the American term for a curriculum vitae?

A: Resuscitator
B: Restraint
C: Resurgent
D: Résumé

50:50 Go to page 445 | Go to page 469 | Answers on page 492

2 ◆ £200

111

Which of these is a station on the Central Line of the London Underground?

A: Marble Bend
B: Marble Curve
C: Marble Arch
D: Marble Semicircle

112

Which of these is a small flat with just one main room?

A: Studio flat
B: Radio flat
C: Audio flat
D: Rodeo flat

113

Which of these is a small enclosure for domestic animals?

A: Stapler
B: Paper
C: Pen
D: Eraser

114

Which of these is a short moral story?

A: Table
B: Fable
C: Cable
D: Sable

115

What is usually dried in a tumble dryer?

A: Laundry
B: Clay
C: Fish
D: Hair

50:50 Go to page 445 Go to page 469 ? Answers on page 492

116

Which of these is a small antelope?

A: Gazebo
B: Gazette
C: Gazpacho
D: Gazelle

117

Which of these is a disease caused by a lack of vitamin C?

A: Plurvy
B: Scurvy
C: Churvy
D: Grurvy

118

The name of which bird can also mean 'frolic'?

A: Puffin
B: Lark
C: Robin
D: Albatross

119

Complete the title of the popular hymn: 'Onward, Christian...'?

A: Soldiers
B: Sailors
C: Pilots
D: Policemen

120

Which animals are fought by a matador?

A: Lions
B: Bulls
C: Rhinos
D: Sharks

50:50 Go to page 445 Go to page 469 ? Answers on page 492

2 ◆ £200

121

What would you be most likely to do with ink?

A: Eat it
B: Drink it
C: Sleep on it
D: Write with it

122

Which of these phrases refers to flattery?

A: Buttering up
B: Cheesing up
C: Margarining up
D: Yoghurting up

123

Which of these is a childish name for the stomach?

A: Dummy
B: Gummy
C: Tummy
D: Yummy

124

Which of these is most likely to be 'pitched'?

A: Curtain
B: Gun
C: Lamp
D: Tent

125

What is the name given to a thin slice of bacon?

A: Giddier
B: Hastier
C: Rasher
D: Wilder

50:50 Go to page 445 Go to page 469 ? Answers on page 492

2 ◆ £200

126

Which word means 'make fun of' and 'eat greedily'?

A: Chaff
B: Mock
C: Scoff
D: Tease

127

Which shape refers to a person's close group of friends or colleagues?

A: Triangle
B: Circle
C: Square
D: Hexagon

128

What is another name for almond paste?

A: Marzitin
B: Marzican
C: Marzipot
D: Marzipan

129

What did Britain's polytechnics become?

A: Barracks
B: Hospitals
C: Prisons
D: Universities

130

What is the name of the game in which messages are passed quietly from person to person?

A: French hearsay
B: Greek tittle-tattle
C: Albanian rumours
D: Chinese whispers

50:50 Go to page 445 Go to page 469 ? Answers on page 492

2 ◆ £200

131

Which of these is most likely to be 'French polished'?

A: Furniture
B: Cricket ball
C: Fingernails
D: Windows

132

Complete the name of the famous crime partnership: Bonnie and...?

A: Hardy
B: Clyde
C: Jerry
D: Cher

133

Which word best describes someone who is old-fashioned and badly dressed?

A: Frothy
B: Frilly
C: Fruity
D: Frumpy

134

Which surname links the Welsh singers Tom and Aled?

A: Evans
B: Jones
C: Rhys
D: Williams

135

What is the name for a ride on someone's back and shoulders?

A: Bunnyback
B: Kittyback
C: Piggyback
D: Froggyback

50:50 Go to page 445 Go to page 469 ? Answers on page 492

136

Where on the body would a tiara be worn?

- A: Feet
- B: Head
- C: Wrist
- D: Neck

137

Which of these are often fed to dogs?

- A: Dog biscuits
- B: Dog cakes
- C: Dog puddings
- D: Dog meringues

138

Which phrase means 'not wearing clothes' and 'no plans for the weekend'?

- A: Nothing daunted
- B: Nothing doing
- C: Nothing on
- D: Nothing to it

139

Which fairground ride consists of spinning cars on a rotating track?

- A: Tangoers
- B: Foxtrotters
- C: Marchers
- D: Waltzers

140

Who was the lead singer with the band Queen?

- A: Freddie Pluto
- B: Freddie Saturn
- C: Freddie Mercury
- D: Freddie Jupiter

50:50 Go to page 445 Go to page 469 ? Answers on page 492

2 ◆ £200

141

Complete the title of the Roald Dahl book: 'James and the...'?

A: Colossal Apple
B: Giant Peach
C: Huge Strawberry
D: Enormous Grape

142

What are you said to do when annoyed about doing or saying something you regret?

A: Pinch yourself
B: Kiss yourself
C: Kick yourself
D: Tickle yourself

143

'Ding dong' is a sound associated with what?

A: Bell
B: Cow
C: Vending machine
D: Plug hole

144

What is the usual name for an ink pot which sits in a hole in a desk?

A: Inkflask
B: Inkjar
C: Inkvase
D: Inkwell

145

What is the vital piece of sporting equipment for a surfer?

A: Ball
B: Board
C: Bat
D: Basket

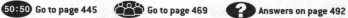

50:50 Go to page 445 Go to page 469 ? Answers on page 492

2 ◆ £200

146

What kind of wave is another name for a good idea?

A: Brainwave
B: Mexican wave
C: Electrical wave
D: Permanent wave

147

Complete the title of the pantomime: 'Jack and the...'?

A: Beanstalk
B: Boots
C: Beauty
D: Beast

148

What is the name for a front leg of a four-legged animal?

A: Wonleg
B: Tooleg
C: Threleg
D: Foreleg

149

In Britain, who is correctly addressed as 'Your Majesty'?

A: Prime Minister
B: Archbishop of Canterbury
C: French ambassador
D: Sovereign

150

With which kind of transport
is a chauffeur most associated?

A: Aeroplane
B: Car
C: Ship
D: Train

50:50 Go to page 445 Go to page 469 ? Answers on page 492

2 ◆ £200

151

'Ammo' is the traditional abbreviation for which word?

- A: Ammonia
- B: Ammunition
- C: Amethyst
- D: America

152

In a school, who used to be made to wear a conical paper hat?

- A: Head girl
- B: Dunce
- C: Dinner lady
- D: Youngest teacher

153

Which of these is a word meaning 'vanish'?

- A: Disappear
- B: Disappoint
- C: Disapprobation
- D: Disapprove

154

What is the tradename for the recorded light music played in public places?

- A: Mazit
- B: Muzak
- C: Luzit
- D: Smuzic

155

Which of these is a famous Las Vegas hotel?

- A: Buckingham Palace
- B: Caesars Palace
- C: Lambeth Palace
- D: Fulham Palace

50:50 Go to page 445 · Go to page 469 · ? Answers on page 492

156

Which of these is a small pointed beard?

A: Horsee
B: Goatee
C: Sheepee
D: Bullee

157

What kind of cabin is most associated with the pioneers of the American West?

A: Straw
B: Brick
C: Log
D: Concrete

158

Who would be most likely to suffer from 'morning sickness'?

A: Newborn baby
B: Middle-aged man
C: Pregnant woman
D: Teenage boy

159

In films, who is the person who replaces the actor for any dangerous scenes?

A: Dangerman
B: Riskman
C: Dareman
D: Stuntman

160

The football club Real Madrid is based in which country?

A: France
B: Spain
C: Italy
D: Germany

50:50 Go to page 445 Go to page 469 ? Answers on page 492

2 ◆ £200

161

When describing trees, what is the opposite of 'deciduous'?

A: Everbrown
B: Evergreen
C: Everyellow
D: Everblue

162

If you were 'angling', which of these might you be trying to catch?

A: Salmon
B: Ladybird
C: Peacock
D: Giraffe

163

According to the Bible, which creature swallowed Jonah?

A: Gorilla
B: Fish
C: Koala
D: Hippopotamus

164

Which of these is an informal name for a chat?

A: Chinshake
B: Chintremor
C: Chinshiver
D: Chinwag

165

Which of these was an early form of radio?

A: Crystal ball
B: Crystal gazer
C: Crystal palace
D: Crystal set

50:50 Go to page 445 Go to page 469 ? Answers on page 492

2 ◆ £200

166

Plimsolls are what type of clothing?

A: Shoes

B: Trousers

C: Gloves

D: Underpants

167

Which kind of hat is most associated with Charlie Chaplin?

A: Beret

B: Cap

C: Bowler hat

D: Tam-o'-shanter

168

Which animal makes a braying sound?

A: Monkey

B: Lion

C: Donkey

D: Wolf

169

Which word can mean 'an idiot' and 'a dessert'?

A: Fool

B: Ass

C: Twit

D: Berk

170

Which expression refers to a spirit thought to watch over and protect a person?

A: Independent demon

B: Guardian angel

C: Observer devil

D: Telegraph saint

50:50 Go to page 445 · Go to page 469 · ? Answers on page 492

2 ◆ £200

171

Which Trevor is particularly associated with 'ITV News at Ten'?

- A: McAndrew
- B: McArthur
- C: McDonald
- D: McGregor

172

Which of these was a hit for Abba?

- A: S.O.S.
- B: P.T.O.
- C: V.I.P.
- D: H.G.V.

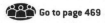

50:50 Go to page 445 Go to page 469 Answers on page 492

50:50

15		£1 MILLION
14		£500,000
13		£250,000
12		£125,000
11		£64,000
10		£32,000
9		£16,000
8		£8,000
7		£4,000
6		£2,000
5		£1,000
4		£500
3	◆	£300
2	◆	£200
1	◆	£100

3 ◆ £300

1

Which of these games depends on dice throws?

- A: Beggar-my-neighbour
- B: Draughts
- C: Snakes and Ladders
- D: Bingo

2

What is the purpose of a matrimonial ceremony?

- A: Marriage
- B: Christening
- C: Funeral
- D: Communion

3

Which of these is a long-running TV panel game?

- A: Call My Bluff
- B: Shout My Cliff
- C: Challenge My Rock
- D: Ring My Bank

4

Someone who buys something at an exorbitant price is said to pay... how?

- A: Through the nose
- B: Above the hand
- C: Over the head
- D: Beyond the reach

5

What is the name for the whiskers that grow in front of a man's ears down the side of his face?

- A: Sideboards
- B: Cupboards
- C: Dressers
- D: Cabinets

50:50 Go to page 447 · Go to page 471 · ? Answers on page 493

3 ◆ £300

6

Which of these is a playground toy?

A: Hopping cord
B: Skipping rope
C: Jumping cable
D: Bouncing twine

7

What colour is a traditional meadow buttercup?

A: White
B: Pink
C: Blue
D: Yellow

8

In the UK, which abbreviation refers to a senior citizen?

A: APO
B: OAP
C: POA
D: OPA

9

Which type of transport is moored in a berth?

A: Ship
B: Train
C: Aircraft
D: Bus

10

In a contest, which word means that all sides have achieved exactly the same score?

A: Collar
B: Cuff
C: Lapel
D: Tie

50:50 Go to page 447 · Go to page 471 · ? Answers on page 493

11

Which of these words refers to an odd number?

- A: Duet
- B: Couplet
- C: Hat-trick
- D: Brace

12

If something is easy to do, with no problems, it is described as 'plain...' what?

- A: Talking
- B: Sailing
- C: Making
- D: Singing

13

What are played on a concert harp?

- A: Keys
- B: Strings
- C: Valves
- D: Chimes

14

Which of these birds is flightless?

- A: Partridge
- B: Roadrunner
- C: Pheasant
- D: Penguin

15

A person with nowhere to turn is said to be 'up' which kind of waterway?

- A: The stream
- B: The creek
- C: The channel
- D: The brook

50:50 Go to page 447 Go to page 471 ? Answers on page 493

3 ◆ £300

16

Which German city gives its name to a type of perfumed liquid?

A: Bonn
B: Cologne
C: Bremen
D: Berlin

17

Which phrase describes an older woman who dresses in styles more suitable for younger people?

A: Herring dressed as sprat
B: Hen dressed as chicken
C: Mutton dressed as lamb
D: Beef dressed as veal

18

What is the reverse recitation of numbers that precedes a rocket launch?

A: Countback
B: Countdown
C: Countout
D: Countover

19

How many people are mentioned in the rhyme that begins 'Tinker, tailor…'?

A: 5
B: 6
C: 7
D: 8

20

Which country borders Canada to the North and South?

A: USA
B: Denmark
C: Iceland
D: Mexico

50:50 Go to page 447
Go to page 471
? Answers on page 493

3 ◆ £300

21

Hans Christian Andersen wrote a story about which 'ugly' creature?

A: Bug
B: Dachshund
C: Pug
D: Duckling

22

Which description is often used if something is very easy to achieve?

A: Slice of bread
B: Round of toast
C: Piece of cake
D: Finger of shortbread

23

Someone who perspires a lot does what?

A: Scratches
B: Sniffs
C: Scuffs
D: Sweats

24

Which of these means 'a play on words'?

A: Pan
B: Pen
C: Pin
D: Pun

25

Which animal is traditionally pulled out of the magician's hat?

A: Rabbit
B: Rat
C: Piglet
D: Cat

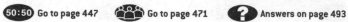

50:50 Go to page 447 Go to page 471 ? Answers on page 493

26

What colour are the ten bottles that are standing on the wall, in the counting-down song?

A: Clear
B: Green
C: Brown
D: Blue

27

A person uttering a load of rubbish is said to be talking... what?

A: Pigrinse
B: Boarscrub
C: Hogwash
D: Piglethosedown

28

Which of these means a botched job?

A: Horse's mouth
B: Rabbit's foot
C: Bull's eye
D: Pig's ear

29

Who would you consult for treatment of 'corns'?

A: Dentist
B: Farmer
C: Comedy writer
D: Chiropodist

30

Which unenthusiastic person spoils the fun for others?

A: Saturated duvet
B: Soaked pillow
C: Sopping sheet
D: Wet blanket

50:50 Go to page 447 Go to page 471 ? Answers on page 493

3 ◆ £300

31

Little Weed is a friend of which children's TV characters?

A: The Flowerpot Men
B: The Chimneypot Fellas
C: The Yoghurtpot Boys
D: The Chamberpot Lads

32

'The Met' is a nickname for which British establishment?

A: London Underground
B: National Phone Network
C: Birmingham Bus Service
D: Metropolitan Police

33

Which of these people work for the CID?

A: Coffee tasters
B: Turf accountants
C: Flower arrangers
D: Police detectives

34

A peninsula is a geographical feature that is almost entirely surrounded by... what?

A: Prairie
B: Woodland
C: Desert
D: Water

35

What does the letter 'Y' stand for in the abbreviation YMCA?

A: Youth
B: Yacht
C: Yorkshire
D: Young

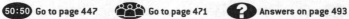

50:50 Go to page 447 Go to page 471 ? Answers on page 493

3 ◆ £300

36

Which piece of crockery is fashioned into the shape of a stout man wearing a tricorn hat?

A: Robby bowl
B: Toby jug
C: Booby cup
D: Moby pot

37

Which term means to be in an advantageous position?

A: Standing high
B: Hopping mad
C: Sitting pretty
D: Spitting blood

38

What is the nickname of Norman Watts in the TV soap 'Coronation Street'?

A: Loopy
B: Curly
C: Baldy
D: Wringlets

39

Which word means to dip a biscuit into a hot drink to soften it?

A: Junk
B: Gunk
C: Sunk
D: Dunk

40

Which people enjoy jumping from great heights, whilst attached to an elasticated rope?

A: Bungee jumpers
B: Bengee droppers
C: Bingee springers
D: Bee Gee bouncers

50:50 Go to page 447 · Go to page 471 · Answers on page 493

3 ◆ £300

41

What is the popular term for a mid-morning break for a cup of tea or coffee?

- A: Nineses
- B: Tenses
- C: Elevenses
- D: Middayses

42

What is the name of the sleep that many animals enjoy during the winter months?

- A: Gestation
- B: Hibernation
- C: Immolation
- D: Lactation

43

On which day does the USA celebrate its independence?

- A: October 31st
- B: July 4th
- C: February 14th
- D: December 25th

44

Which of these is a type of flowering plant?

- A: Laura of the Valley
- B: Lindsay of the Valley
- C: Lily of the Valley
- D: Louise of the Valley

45

The word 'bovine' refers to which type of animal?

- A: Dog
- B: Cat
- C: Cow
- D: Horse

50:50 Go to page 447 Go to page 471 ? Answers on page 493

3 ◆ £300

46

What was the first name of the US president known as 'JFK'?

A: Jeremy
B: Joel
C: Jonah
D: John

47

What would a Native American traditionally do with a 'moccasin'?

A: Eat it
B: Shoot it
C: Wear it
D: Climb it

48

The word 'monsoon' is traditionally associated with what?

A: Heavy rainfall
B: Heavy taxes
C: Heavy food
D: Heavy metal

49

Where does the Pope live?

A: Kremlin
B: Vatican
C: Chequers
D: White House

50

Which of these was an Oscar-winning film starring Mel Gibson?

A: Braveheart
B: Weakheart
C: Softheart
D: Monkeyheart

50:50 Go to page 447 Go to page 471 ? Answers on page 493

3 ◆ £300

51

In which sea is the island of Sicily?

A: North
B: Red
C: Mediterranean
D: South China

52

In relation to the legal profession, what do the letters 'QC' stand for?

A: Queen's Curtains
B: Queen's Corgis
C: Queen's Counsel
D: Queen's Castle

53

Who was Fred Astaire's regular dance partner on the silver screen?

A: Ginger Rogers
B: Curly Rogers
C: Blondie Rogers
D: Red Rogers

54

Which of these is a state in Australia?

A: Kingsland
B: Princeland
C: Dukeland
D: Queensland

55

The Royal Observatory is located in which area of London?

A: Bluewich
B: Greenwich
C: Redwich
D: Blackwich

50:50 Go to page 447 Go to page 471 ? Answers on page 493

3 ◆ £300

56

What is another name for the 'daddy-long-legs'?

A: Digger fly
B: Crane fly
C: Pulley fly
D: Bulldozer fly

57

Which of these is a rude noise made with the lips and tongue?

A: Strawberry
B: Raspberry
C: Elderberry
D: Damsonberry

58

Which weapon was named after a US frontiersman who fought at the Alamo?

A: Bolan sword
B: Stardust pistol
C: Holder rifle
D: Bowie knife

59

Who was the host of 'Opportunity Knocks' on TV?

A: Howie Blue
B: Harry Grey
C: Hughie Green
D: Harvey Black

60

On which island was the TV detective series 'Bergerac' set?

A: Madagascar
B: Jersey
C: Cuba
D: Crete

50:50 Go to page 447 Go to page 471 ? Answers on page 493

61

Which TV presenter first found fame on 'That Was The Week That Was'?

A: David Snow
B: David Chill
C: David Ice
D: David Frost

62

What was the first name of the infamous conspirator Mr Fawkes?

A: Graham
B: Gerry
C: Guy
D: Gordon

63

Which of these is a pain of the lower back?

A: Lumbago
B: Migraine
C: Conjunctivitis
D: Tennis elbow

64

Auburn hair is approximately which colour?

A: Black
B: White
C: Blue
D: Red

65

The word 'moggy' is used to describe which animal?

A: Sheep
B: Cow
C: Cat
D: Badger

50:50 Go to page 447 Go to page 471 ? Answers on page 493

3 ◆ £300

66

On which type of TV show would you usually see Kevin Woodford?

A: Sport
B: Cookery
C: Political
D: Sitcom

67

What name do Americans often give to a dinner jacket?

A: Tuxedo
B: Mackintosh
C: Cardigan
D: Poncho

68

With which branch of the arts is Luciano Pavarotti particularly associated?

A: Ballet
B: Cinema
C: Sculpture
D: Opera

69

In the film 'Babe', what type of animal was the title character?

A: Pig
B: Cow
C: Dog
D: Goose

70

Which fictional character is the star of the film 'Thunderball'?

A: James Bond
B: Indiana Jones
C: Hannibal Lecter
D: Brett Maverick

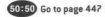

50:50 Go to page 447 Go to page 471 ? Answers on page 493

3 ◆ £300

71

Lawrence Dallaglio is a former England captain in which sport?

A: Snooker
B: Rhythmic gymnastics
C: Ice dancing
D: Rugby union

72

Which of these is a film starring Robert De Niro?

A: Engine Driver
B: Bus Driver
C: Lady Driver
D: Taxi Driver

73

On which part of the body are 'sideburns' grown?

A: Arms
B: Feet
C: Knees
D: Face

74

In which London building is Traitor's Gate?

A: Houses of Parliament
B: Tower of London
C: National Gallery
D: Mermaid Theatre

75

In the Old Testament book of Exodus, Moses led the Israelites from which country?

A: Turkey
B: Greece
C: Italy
D: Egypt

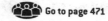

50:50 Go to page 447 Go to page 471 ? Answers on page 493

3 ◆ £300

76

Which of these couples features in the Old Testament of the Bible?

A: George and Mildred
B: Samson and Delilah
C: Pat and Frank
D: Posh and Becks

77

In which sport could you be given 'out' by the third umpire?

A: Football
B: Rugby
C: Cricket
D: Snooker

78

What did Sir Walter Raleigh allegedly throw over a puddle to stop Elizabeth I getting her feet wet?

A: Doublet
B: Cloak
C: Kilt
D: Battering ram

79

Which of these is the name of a famous magical nanny?

A: Mandy Baggins
B: Molly Cummins
C: Mary Poppins
D: Becky Higgins

80

Suggs was the lead singer of which group?

A: Insanity
B: Nonsensical
C: Madness
D: Dementia

50:50 Go to page 447 Go to page 471 ? Answers on page 493

3 ◆ £300

81

Which of these is a breed of spaniel?

A: Clocker
B: Cocker
C: Crocker
D: Chocker

82

How many sides does a pentagon have?

A: Four
B: Five
C: Six
D: Seven

83

What name is traditionally given to a woman's collection of things in preparation for her marriage?

A: Top drawer
B: Second drawer
C: Third drawer
D: Bottom drawer

84

Which of these is a game consisting of throwing a ring of rubber over an upright peg?

A: Quotas
B: Quolls
C: Quoits
D: Quoths

85

In 1947, the first of the Dead Sea Scrolls were found in a cave near which sea?

A: Red Sea
B: Mediterranean Sea
C: Baltic Sea
D: Dead Sea

50:50 Go to page 447 Go to page 471 ? Answers on page 493

3 ◆ £300

86

Which liquid might be described as 'corked'?

A: Lemonade
B: Wine
C: Bitter
D: Milk

87

What term is used to define the surname a woman used before she was married?

A: Damsel name
B: Wench name
C: Maiden name
D: Spinster name

88

With which time of year is a robin particularly associated?

A: Christmas
B: Easter
C: Midsummer Day
D: Bonfire Night

89

In the series of films starring Sylvester Stallone, 'Rocky' is a down-and-out what?

A: Boxer
B: Lawyer
C: Actor
D: Police officer

90

Which of these conditions is particularly associated with the cartoon character Mr Magoo?

A: Hiccups
B: Flatulence
C: Big feet
D: Short-sightedness

50:50 Go to page 447 Go to page 471 ? Answers on page 493

3 ◆ £300

91

What name is given to the cylindrical sweet which often has a resort's name running through it?

A: Rock
B: Stone
C: Granite
D: Marble

92

On a road map, which letter denotes a motorway?

A: M
B: F
C: S
D: X

93

Which of these words can precede 'lightning' and 'metal'?

A: Pillow
B: Mattress
C: Sheet
D: Quilt

94

The term 'somnambulist' refers to someone who does what in their sleep?

A: Walks
B: Snores
C: Dribbles
D: Laughs

95

Which of these is another term for a non-alcoholic drink?

A: Spongy drink
B: Squishy drink
C: Soggy drink
D: Soft drink

50:50 Go to page 447 Go to page 471 ? Answers on page 493

3 ◆ £300

96

'Tagliatelle' is a type of what?

- A: Disco dance
- B: Paint
- C: Fabric
- D: Pasta

97

Which of these is a holiday with travel and accommodation included in the price?

- A: Package holiday
- B: Parcel holiday
- C: Present holiday
- D: Pouch holiday

98

On which day of the week is Mother's Day traditionally celebrated?

- A: Friday
- B: Saturday
- C: Sunday
- D: Monday

99

Which of these is a powdered spice?

- A: Pappardelle
- B: Papaya
- C: Papillote
- D: Paprika

100

What name is given to the division of a road for use by cyclists?

- A: Cycle street
- B: Cycle lane
- C: Cycle avenue
- D: Cycle cul-de-sac

50:50 Go to page 447 Go to page 471 ? Answers on page 493

3 ◆ £300

101

Which of these is a comedy by Keith Waterhouse and Willis Hall?

A: Billy Liar
B: Billy Fibber
C: Billy Storyteller
D: Billy Fabricator

102

What name is given to a French motorway?

A: Autobahn
B: Freeway
C: Interstate
D: Autoroute

103

'Bunny' is a child's name for which creature?

A: Cow
B: Pig
C: Rabbit
D: Frog

104

What, on a beach, may be referred to as 'shingle'?

A: Deck chairs
B: Seaweed
C: Pebbles
D: Ice-cream vans

105

Which of these is another term for the forefinger?

A: Index
B: Appendix
C: Glossary
D: Bibliography

50:50 Go to page 447 Go to page 471 ? Answers on page 493

3 ◆ £300

106

How many days are there in a leap year?

A: 364 B: 365
C: 366 D: 368

107

Which of these is a type of large prawn usually fried in breadcrumbs?

A: Scampi B: Grampi
C: Trampi D: Champi

108

What type of creature is a starling?

A: Bird B: Fish
C: Insect D: Reptile

109

Which of these is an illegal musical recording?

A: Bootleg B: Shoeshin
C: Pumpcalf D: Broguefoot

110

Complete the name of the 1980s band: Spandau...?

A: Ballet B: Sculpture
C: Opera D: Pantomime

50:50 Go to page 447 Go to page 471 Answers on page 493

3 ◆ £300

111

What provides the artificial light for a photograph to be taken at night?

- A: Flash
- B: Spark
- C: Twinkle
- D: Gleam

112

Which of these is a short prayer of thanks said before a meal?

- A: Grace
- B: Poise
- C: Elegance
- D: Statuesqueness

113

What is the name for a necklace worn tightly round the throat?

- A: Choker
- B: Garrotter
- C: Throttler
- D: Strangler

114

Which condition means that a writer has run out of inspiration?

- A: Author's obstruction
- B: Novelist's stoppage
- C: Poet's inconvenience
- D: Writer's block

115

Which of these phrases means "Hurry up!"?

- A: Get your skis on
- B: Get your trainers on
- C: Get your skates on
- D: Get your flippers on

50:50 Go to page 447 Go to page 471 ? Answers on page 493

3 ◆ £300

116

In which game do players identify a murderer, a weapon and the scene of crime?

A: Cluedo
B: Trivial Pursuit
C: Monopoly
D: Pictionary

117

What is the popular name for a Boeing 747 airliner?

A: July jet
B: Jungle jet
C: Junior jet
D: Jumbo jet

118

What is the name for a self-contained part of a house where an elderly relative lives?

A: Grandad annex
B: Granny flat
C: Uncle apartment
D: Auntie suite

119

Which of these is a type of Italian black coffee?

A: Depresso
B: Compresso
C: Espresso
D: Suppresso

120

Which liquid is most commonly used for pickling?

A: Apple juice
B: Milk
C: Petrol
D: Vinegar

50:50 Go to page 447 Go to page 471 ? Answers on page 493

3 ◆ £300

121

Who is most likely to be known as a 'trolley dolly'?

A: Air stewardess
B: Pharmacist
C: TV producer
D: Refuse collector

122

Which word often describes a hero who does not get the praise he deserves?

A: Unflung
B: Unhung
C: Unrung
D: Unsung

123

Which parts of the body have 'lashes'?

A: Ears
B: Eyes
C: Kidneys
D: Lips

124

What is another name for twelve o'clock midday?

A: Boon
B: Moon
C: Noon
D: Soon

125

Which fruit is pressed to make a popular cooking oil?

A: Avocado
B: Apricot
C: Olive
D: Guava

50:50 Go to page 447 · Go to page 471 · ? Answers on page 493

3 ◆ £300

126

If someone is described as a 'brunette', it refers to the colour of what?

A: Eyes
B: Hair
C: Teeth
D: Feet

127

Which of these was an award-winning BBC series?

A: Looking at Dinosaurs
B: Walking With Dinosaurs
C: Living Like Dinosaurs
D: Running From Dinosaurs

128

What kind of 'suit' refers to complete nakedness?

A: Birthday suit
B: Spacesuit
C: Dinner suit
D: Three-piece suit

129

Which of these sports uses goalposts?

A: Cricket
B: Tennis
C: Golf
D: Football

130

What is the exciting end to an episode of a serial, which leaves the audience in suspense?

A: Boulderhanger
B: Cliffhanger
C: Craghanger
D: Rockhanger

50:50 Go to page 447 · Go to page 471 · ? Answers on page 493

131

Which creature is sometimes known as a 'chook'?

- A: Chicken
- B: Tiger
- C: Sloth
- D: Giraffe

132

If steak is 'rare', what colour should it be in the middle?

- A: Black
- B: Green
- C: Red
- D: Yellow

133

What is the American name for the underground rail system?

- A: Sublime
- B: Subtitle
- C: Suburb
- D: Subway

134

Which of these phrases is used to describe an excessively shy person?

- A: Dwindling chrysanthemum
- B: Evaporating fuchsia
- C: Retreating primrose
- D: Shrinking violet

135

What is the name of the cake made from oats and syrup?

- A: Flapjack
- B: Rapjohn
- C: Snapjoe
- D: Tapjim

50:50 Go to page 447 · Ask the audience: Go to page 471 · ? Answers on page 493

3 ◆ £300

136

Which fruit's name is given to an unwelcome third party?

A: Raspberry
B: Strawberry
C: Gooseberry
D: Bilberry

137

Which of these is a popular pastime?

A: Traindotting
B: Trainspotting
C: Trainstriping
D: Trainchopping

138

What type of footballer is positioned near the sidelines of the pitch?

A: Dinger
B: Singer
C: Ringer
D: Winger

139

What name is given to an object of value passed through a family for generations?

A: Heirboom
B: Heirdoom
C: Heirloom
D: Heirzoom

140

Which of these people is most likely to work in a salon?

A: Butcher
B: Hairdresser
C: Policeman
D: Teacher

50:50 Go to page 447 Go to page 471 ? Answers on page 493

3 ◆ £300

141

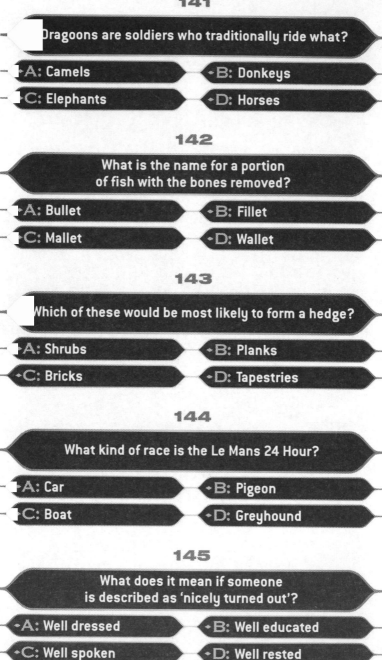

Dragoons are soldiers who traditionally ride what?

A: Camels
B: Donkeys
C: Elephants
D: Horses

142

What is the name for a portion of fish with the bones removed?

A: Bullet
B: Fillet
C: Mallet
D: Wallet

143

Which of these would be most likely to form a hedge?

A: Shrubs
B: Planks
C: Bricks
D: Tapestries

144

What kind of race is the Le Mans 24 Hour?

A: Car
B: Pigeon
C: Boat
D: Greyhound

145

What does it mean if someone is described as 'nicely turned out'?

A: Well dressed
B: Well educated
C: Well spoken
D: Well rested

50:50 Go to page 447 · Go to page 471 · ? Answers on page 493

3 ◆ £300

146

On which part of the body are 'flip-flops' traditionally worn?

A: Hands
B: Feet
C: Knees
D: Eyes

147

What kind of dog is a Jack Russell?

A: Corgi
B: Labrador
C: Spaniel
D: Terrier

148

Which of these is a brightly coloured diving bird?

A: Earlfisher
B: Dukefisher
C: Princefisher
D: Kingfisher

149

Mouth-to-mouth resuscitation is also known by what name?

A: Kiss of life
B: Kiss of knife
C: Kiss of fife
D: Kiss of wife

150

In which building would you be most likely to see a pulpit?

A: Barn
B: Church
C: Hospital
D: Restaurant

50:50 Go to page 447 Go to page 471 ? Answers on page 493

3 ◆ £300

151

Which of these phrases means 'very amusing'?

A: Head-turning
B: Toe-curling
C: Rib-tickling
D: Back-breaking

152

A drought is a shortage of what?

A: Air
B: Food
C: Light
D: Water

153

What is papier-mâché made from?

A: Rags
B: Paper
C: Glass
D: Aluminium

154

Which of these has presented 'Newsnight' and 'Tomorrow's World' on television?

A: Peter Sun
B: Peter Rain
C: Peter Hail
D: Peter Snow

155

Contact lenses help you to do what more easily?

A: Breathe
B: Hear
C: See
D: Sit down

50:50 Go to page 447 Go to page 471 ? Answers on page 493

3 ◆ £300

156

What is the meaning of the phrase 'bone idle'?

A: Very old
B: Very lazy
C: Very hungry
D: Very tired

157

In 1991, Leningrad changed its name back to what?

A: St Paulsburg
B: St Patricksburg
C: St Petersburg
D: St Philipsburg

158

Which of these is a kind of joke intended to make the victim look foolish?

A: Sceptical
B: Optical
C: Practical
D: Statistical

159

What kind of stones are put down for people to walk on?

A: Caving stones
B: Paving stones
C: Raving stones
D: Saving stones

160

Which of these words follows 'tiddly' to make a popular game?

A: Winks
B: Works
C: Wakes
D: Walks

50:50 Go to page 447 · Go to page 471 · ? Answers on page 493

3 ◆ £300

161

What kind of creature is a minnow?

- A: Bird
- B: Insect
- C: Fish
- D: Mammal

162

A curly lock of hair is sometimes known as a... what?

- A: Ringlet
- B: Looplet
- C: Disclet
- D: Bandlet

163

Which of these is an area of London?

- A: Monkey and Pub
- B: Elephant and Castle
- C: Badger and Hospital
- D: Warthog and Church

164

Which of these is a term for a cigarette stub?

- A: Andd
- B: Butt
- C: Iff
- D: Orr

50:50 Go to page 447 Go to page 471 ? Answers on page 493

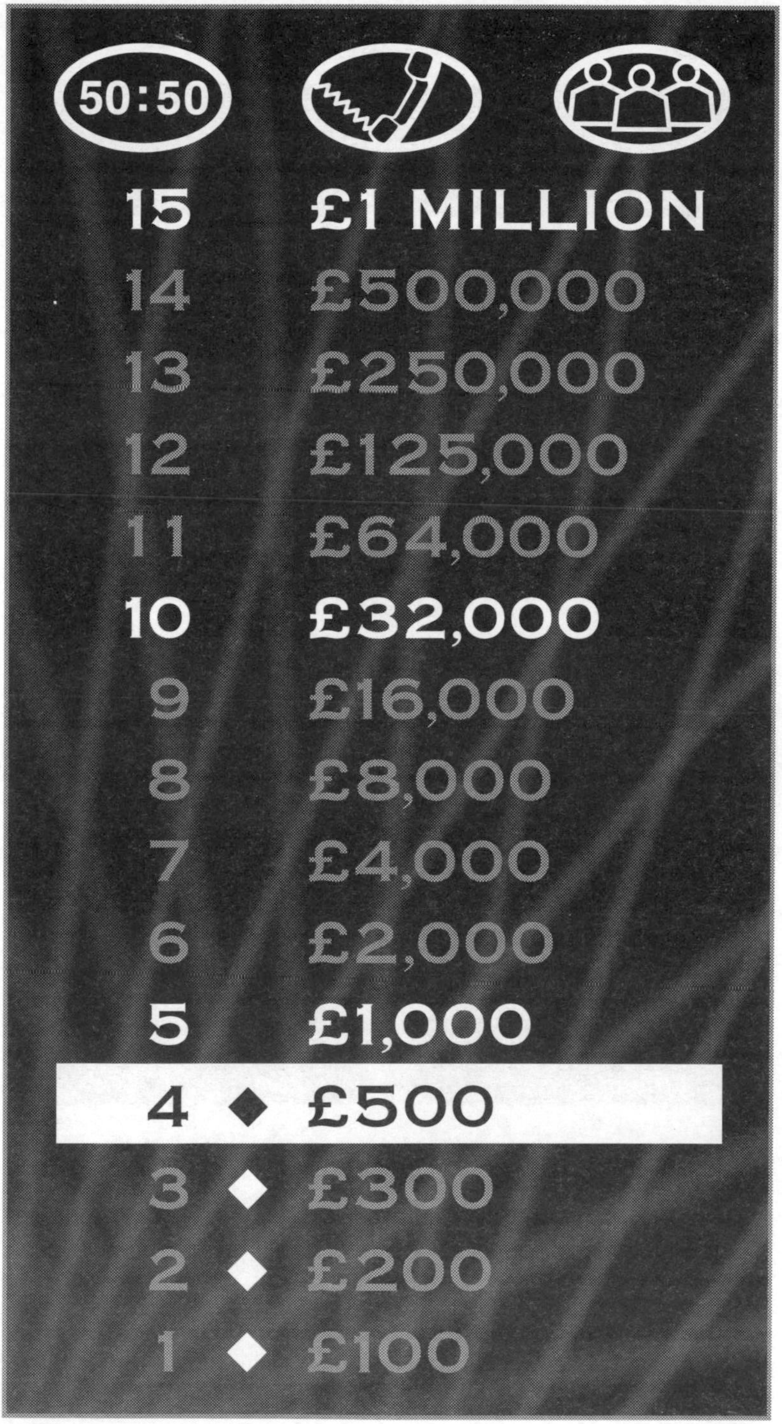
50:50
15 £1 MILLION
14 £500,000
13 £250,000
12 £125,000
11 £64,000
10 £32,000
9 £16,000
8 £8,000
7 £4,000
6 £2,000
5 £1,000
4 ◆ £500
3 ◆ £300
2 ◆ £200
1 ◆ £100

4 ◆ £500

1

A traditional Devon cream tea is cream and jam spread on... what?

- A: Scones
- B: Bread
- C: Teacakes
- D: Toast

2

Which of these athletes won a medal at the 1972 Olympic Games?

- A: Denise Lewis
- B: Mary Peters
- C: Sally Gunnell
- D: Katherine Merry

3

What 'lane' was a hit for the Beatles?

- A: Penny Lane
- B: Pound Lane
- C: Copper Lane
- D: Guinea Lane

4

Which of these is a method of obtaining gold?

- A: Grilling
- B: Kettling
- C: Potting
- D: Panning

5

In the folk tale, who had to deal with 40 thieves?

- A: Sinbad
- B: Ali Baba
- C: Jafar
- D: Mowgli

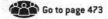

50:50 Go to page 449 Go to page 473 ? Answers on page 494

4 ◆ £500

6

Which of these precedes the word 'Circus' to form a famous London location?

- A: Piccadilly
- B: Haymarket
- C: Whitehall
- D: Maida Vale

7

Which word goes before 'bread', 'toast' and 'stick' for three things to eat?

- A: Buttered
- B: Brown
- C: British
- D: French

8

What are the respiratory organs of fish?

- A: Fins
- B: Scales
- C: Gills
- D: Fingers

9

Which two articles are associated with billiards?

- A: Cue and ball
- B: Puck and stick
- C: Jack and wood
- D: Racquet and shuttle

10

Which of these is a title of a Bond movie?

- A: Silverhair
- B: Goldfinger
- C: Diamondtooth
- D: Rubycheek

50:50 Go to page 449 · Go to page 473 · ? Answers on page 494

11

Complete the title of the Thomas Hardy novel: 'The Mayor of...'?

- A: Casterbridge
- B: Cambridge
- C: Chesterbridge
- D: Calderbridge

12

Which of these condiments is also the nickname for an old and experienced sailor?

- A: Mustard
- B: Salt
- C: Pepper
- D: Vinegar

13

What is the nickname of Gravelly Hill interchange, where the A38 and A5127 meet the M6?

- A: Linguini Crossroads
- B: Lasagne Intersection
- C: Tagliatelle Link
- D: Spaghetti Junction

14

Which Spice Girl has the surname Chisholm?

- A: Baby
- B: Scary
- C: Sporty
- D: Posh

15

'Rouge' is the French word for which colour?

- A: Blue
- B: Red
- C: Yellow
- D: Green

50:50 Go to page 449 · Go to page 473 · ? Answers on page 494

4 ◆ £500

16

Complete the American phrase: 'A dime a...'?

A: Gross
B: Century
C: Dozen
D: Score

17

How would you play an ocarina?

A: Blow it
B: Pluck it
C: Strike it
D: Scratch it

18

Which of these is a county in the Republic of Ireland?

A: Ringpull
B: Cork
C: Widget
D: Marble

19

What do Americans call a designated area for leaving motor transport?

A: Parking Lot
B: Automotive Park
C: Motor Grid
D: Vehicle Station

20

What type of weapon was a blunderbuss, used in the 16th to 18th centuries?

A: Sword
B: Wooden cosh
C: Gun
D: Cannon

50:50 Go to page 449 · Go to page 473 · ? Answers on page 494

4 ◆ £500

21

Which of these is another term for a peanut?

A: Zebra nut
B: Monkey nut
C: Caterpillar nut
D: Donkey nut

22

According to Lewis Carroll, which character did Alice follow down the rabbit hole to get to Wonderland?

A: Curious Rabbit
B: King Rabbit
C: Cheshire Rabbit
D: White Rabbit

23

Which sport is associated with Royal Ascot?

A: Three-day eventing
B: Golf
C: Horse racing
D: Tennis

24

What is a men's basic haircut, especially in the Armed Forces?

A: Short front and top
B: Short top and back
C: Short back and sides
D: Short sides and front

25

What is a common name for a photograph of a face, especially one taken for police records?

A: Cupshot
B: Tumblershot
C: Beakershot
D: Mugshot

50:50 Go to page 449 Go to page 473 ? Answers on page 494

4 ◆ £500

26

Which of these is a term for a very tall building?

A: Cloudtoucher
B: Starviewer
C: Skyscraper
D: Godfinder

27

The word 'lava' is most associated with which household appliance?

A: Toaster
B: Kettle
C: Lamp
D: Percolator

28

Which of these men was an enemy of Robin Hood?

A: Clive of Camborne
B: Guy of Gisborne
C: Oliver of Osborne
D: Simon of Swinborne

29

What name is given to a person who lacks pigment in skin and hair?

A: Albino
B: Merino
C: Domino
D: Casino

30

Which of these does not involve speaking?

A: Dibble
B: Gabble
C: Jabber
D: Yatter

50:50 Go to page 449 Go to page 473 ? Answers on page 494

4 ◆ £500

31

What is the name of the flat low-lying drained areas of eastern England?

A: Dens
B: Fens
C: Pens
D: Zens

32

'Mock turtle' is a type of... what?

A: Soup
B: Tropical beetle
C: Paste jewellery
D: Flowering shrub

33

Which artist is well known for cutting off his ear?

A: Picasso
B: Goya
C: Raphael
D: Van Gogh

34

Which of these is applied with a palette knife?

A: Greasepaint
B: Oil paint
C: Emulsion paint
D: Gloss paint

35

If a job is described as 'sedentary', what does it literally involve?

A: Running an office
B: Driving a car
C: Delivering mail
D: Sitting down

50:50 Go to page 449 Go to page 473 ? Answers on page 494

36

What is the name for a person who carries out menial jobs for others?

A: Dogsbody
B: Dog's dinner
C: Dog's tooth
D: Dog's hind leg

37

Which of these was a top ten single for Prince in 1984?

A: Pink Cloud
B: Purple Rain
C: Blue Thunder
D: Green Snow

38

The Starship Enterprise is a feature of which TV show?

A: The Time Tunnel
B: Land of the Giants
C: Lost in Space
D: Star Trek

39

What is metaphorically 'popped' in a proposal of marriage?

A: Your clogs
B: The question
C: The weasel
D: Champagne cork

40

Which of these was an important soldier in World War II?

A: Horatio Nelson
B: Field Marshal Montgomery
C: Duke of Wellington
D: Francis Drake

50:50 Go to page 449
Go to page 473
? Answers on page 494

4 ◆ £500

41

Which of these is a film starring Kevin Costner?

- A: LBJ
- B: FDR
- C: GWB
- D: JFK

42

Who played Don Corleone in the 1973 film 'The Godfather'?

- A: Frank Sinatra
- B: Marlon Brando
- C: Gregory Peck
- D: George C. Scott

43

Which of these is a film set during the Vietnam War?

- A: Apocalypse Now
- B: Apocalypse Then
- C: Apocalypse Later
- D: Apocalypse Never

44

If someone is 'vexed', what emotion are they experiencing?

- A: Anger
- B: Happiness
- C: Fear
- D: Elation

45

Which fictional character travels in the TARDIS?

- A: Avon
- B: Arnold Rimmer
- C: Ford Prefect
- D: Doctor Who

50:50 Go to page 449 Go to page 473 ? Answers on page 494

4 ◆ £500

46

Which of these is a type of bird?

- A: Nightbottle
- B: Nightcan
- C: Nightjar
- D: Nighttin

47

Vera Duckworth is a character in which TV soap?

- A: Emmerdale
- B: EastEnders
- C: Coronation Street
- D: Brookside

48

Which of these books details the hunt for a great white whale?

- A: Heart of Darkness
- B: Lord Jim
- C: The Call of the Wild
- D: Moby Dick

49

Who played Mark Antony alongside Elizabeth Taylor in the 1963 film 'Cleopatra'?

- A: Richard Harris
- B: Roger Moore
- C: Richard Burton
- D: Albert Finney

50

Which of these men was involved in the Gunfight at the OK Corral?

- A: Doc Holliday
- B: Billy the Kid
- C: General Custer
- D: Roy Rogers

50:50 Go to page 449 · Go to page 473 · ? Answers on page 494

4 ◆ £500

51

In 'The Wrong Trousers', what type of animal is Gromit?

A: Sheep
B: Penguin
C: Dog
D: Pig

52

Which of these is a novel by Daniel Defoe?

A: Moll Flanders
B: Moll Foggia
C: Moll Frankfurt
D: Moll Florence

53

The TV series 'All Creatures Great and Small' primarily looked at the lives of whom?

A: Firemen
B: Vets
C: Nurses
D: Teachers

54

Which of these is the name of an Oscar-winning film of the 1990s?

A: New York Hush Hush
B: Chicago Under Wraps
C: Boston Secret
D: L.A. Confidential

55

The Bronx is an area of which major city?

A: New York
B: London
C: Paris
D: Moscow

50:50 Go to page 449 Go to page 473 ? Answers on page 494

4 ◆ £500

56

Which of these is a character in 'The Wizard of Oz'?

- A: The Steel Woodsman
- B: The Tin Woodsman
- C: The Nickel Woodsman
- D: The Copper Woodsman

57

Camp David is the country retreat of which public figure?

- A: Sultan of Brunei
- B: US President
- C: Pope
- D: Prince Charles

58

Which animal shares its name with a droopy moustache?

- A: Elephant
- B: Gnu
- C: Rhinoceros
- D: Walrus

59

Albania is a country on which continent?

- A: Asia
- B: Europe
- C: Africa
- D: South America

60

What type of transportation is a schooner?

- A: Bicycle
- B: Boat
- C: Glider
- D: Hovercraft

50:50 Go to page 449 · Go to page 473 · ? Answers on page 494

4 ◆ £500

61

Which of these is a game show presented by Jerry Springer?

A: Avarice
B: Greed
C: Lust
D: Sloth

62

Who starred in the 1977 film 'Smokey and the Bandit'?

A: Robert De Niro
B: Burt Reynolds
C: Ben Kingsley
D: Laurence Olivier

63

Julia Roberts won an Oscar for her role in which 2000 film?

A: Erin Brockovich
B: Gladiator
C: Crouching Tiger, Hidden Dragon
D: Chocolat

64

Which pop group's first UK hit was 'I Am I Feel' in 1996?

A: Patricia's Playroom
B: Alisha's Attic
C: Sasha's Snug
D: Letitia's Lobby

65

The name 'Peggy' is derived from which other name?

A: Julia
B: Anne
C: Margaret
D: Joan

50:50 Go to page 449 Go to page 473 ? Answers on page 494

4 ◆ £500

66

Which mollusc shares its name with a secretive person?

A: Oyster
B: Snail
C: Squid
D: Clam

67

Lord Voldemort is the arch-enemy of which fictional schoolboy?

A: Billy Bunter
B: Tucker Jenkins
C: Harry Potter
D: Tom Brown

68

Which of these is another term for a private investigator?

A: Private nose
B: Private ear
C: Private eye
D: Private mouth

69

What was the streetcar named in the title of the Tennessee Williams play?

A: Lust
B: Attraction
C: Want
D: Desire

70

Which of these pop groups is most associated with the city of Liverpool?

A: The Beatles
B: Fleetwood Mac
C: The Rolling Stones
D: The Who

50:50 Go to page 449 · Go to page 473 · ? Answers on page 494

4 ◆ £500

71

England play Scotland in rugby union for which trophy?

A: Ryder Cup
B: Solheim Cup
C: America's Cup
D: Calcutta Cup

72

What is 'a wee dram' to a Scotsman?

A: Few pennies
B: Temper tantrum
C: Tot of whisky
D: Sporran

73

Which of these is an album by Michael Jackson?

A: Horrible
B: Naughty
C: Bad
D: Disobedient

74

The US city Dallas is located in which state?

A: Arizona
B: California
C: Colorado
D: Texas

75

Which of these was a member of TV's 'The Goodies'?

A: John Cleese
B: Bill Oddie
C: Peter Sellers
D: Marty Feldman

50:50 Go to page 449 Go to page 473 ? Answers on page 494

4 ◆ £500

76

Which British actress appeared in the Oscar-winning film 'Traffic'?

A: Liz Hurley
B: Catherine Zeta-Jones
C: Lysette Anthony
D: Michelle Collins

77

Billie Jean King was a major name in which sport during the 1960s and 1970s?

A: Athletics
B: Tennis
C: Golf
D: Cricket

78

In which London square is the Christmas tree an annual gift from the people of Norway?

A: Soho Square
B: Belgrave Square
C: Trafalgar Square
D: Sloane Square

79

Which of these 'lock' words is the name of part of a horse?

A: Fetlock
B: Sherlock
C: Hemlock
D: Padlock

80

What is the main concern of the organization BUPA?

A: Health
B: Motoring
C: Building
D: Animals

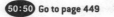

50:50 Go to page 449 Go to page 473 ? Answers on page 494

4 ◆ £500

81

Traditionally, which of these drinks is colourless?

A: Vodka
B: Grenadine
C: Kir
D: Cassis

82

In which of these sports do the players use a bat?

A: Billiards
B: Archery
C: Badminton
D: Baseball

83

In total, how many US states begin with the letter K?

A: One
B: Two
C: Three
D: Four

84

What does the letter 'H' stand for in the abbreviation HGV?

A: Haulage
B: Hidden
C: Hydraulic
D: Heavy

85

Which word describes miles, yards, feet and inches?

A: Imperial
B: Imperfect
C: Impractical
D: Impossible

50:50 Go to page 449 Go to page 473 ? Answers on page 494

4 ◆ £500

86

What does a lexicographer specifically compile?

A: Telephone directories
B: Crosswords
C: Dictionaries
D: Quiz books

87

What was the title of the Bangles' first UK chart hit?

A: Manic Monday
B: Touched Tuesday
C: Weird Wednesday
D: Frantic Friday

88

Which of these is the title of a Shakespeare play?

A: The Tornado
B: The Storm
C: The Tempest
D: The Cyclone

89

Which deadly sin shares its name with an animal?

A: Anger
B: Gluttony
C: Lust
D: Sloth

90

With which day of the week is the Observer newspaper associated?

A: Monday
B: Wednesday
C: Friday
D: Sunday

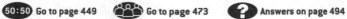

50:50 Go to page 449 · Go to page 473 · ? Answers on page 494

91

What is the Japanese name for Japan?

A: Cippon
B: Nippon
C: Sippon
D: Yippon

92

Which word can mean both ‘a gift’ and ‘in attendance’?

A: Donation
B: Bonus
C: Token
D: Present

93

What is the name for a group of thirteen witches?

A: Cove
B: Coven
C: Cover
D: Covey

94

Which of these was a medieval form of punishment?

A: Billory
B: Tillory
C: Pillory
D: Hillory

95

In the TV series ‘On The Buses’, who was the bane of Inspector Blake’s life?

A: Butler
B: Butcher
C: Baker
D: Banker

50:50 Go to page 449 Go to page 473 ? Answers on page 494

96

Which word is used to refer to a heavy and inescapable responsibility?

A: Grindstone
B: Millstone
C: Tombstone
D: Limestone

97

In what kind of restaurant is a banana fritter most likely to be served?

A: Chinese
B: French
C: Greek
D: Mexican

98

In which part of the human body is the palate?

A: Foot
B: Ear
C: Mouth
D: Knee

99

What is traditionally put in a 'quiver'?

A: Arrow
B: Egg
C: Ice
D: Oar

100

Who won an Oscar for his role in 'Reversal of Fortune'?

A: Jeremy Beadle
B: Jeremy Spake
C: Jeremy Paxman
D: Jeremy Irons

50:50 Go to page 449 Go to page 473 ? Answers on page 494

4 ◆ £500

101

Which items of clothing are most associated with the term 'denier'?

A: Hats
B: Boots
C: Tights
D: Gloves

102

On television, Barry Norman is best known as a critic of what?

A: Food
B: Film
C: Fashion
D: Football

103

In which of these 2001 summer blockbusters did David Duchovny star?

A: Evolution
B: The Mummy Returns
C: Shrek
D: Tomb Raider

104

According to the traditional saying, oysters should not be eaten unless there is a what in the month?

A: E
B: J
C: R
D: U

105

Which of these words refers to a small exclusive group of friends?

A: Antique
B: Clique
C: Oblique
D: Unique

50:50 Go to page 449 Go to page 473 ? Answers on page 494

106

Pad thai is a dish from which country?

A: Sri Lanka
B: Thailand
C: Indonesia
D: Malaysia

107

Brandy butter is a traditional accompaniment to which dessert?

A: Spotted dick
B: Baked Alaska
C: Apple crumble
D: Christmas pudding

108

Which of these is a creation of Enid Blyton?

A: Pingu
B: Postman Pat
C: Noddy
D: Paddington

109

What was the name of the 'Rat' who was introduced to attract viewers to TV-AM in the 1980s?

A: Richard
B: Roland
C: Robin
D: Russell

110

Complete the title of the science fiction TV series: 'Star Trek: Deep Space...'?

A: Three
B: Five
C: Seven
D: Nine

50:50 Go to page 449 Go to page 473 ? Answers on page 494

4 ◆ £500

111

Which book contains records of a survey of England begun in 1086?

A: Moonsday
B: Domesday
C: Boomsday
D: Lunesday

112

In ancient times, a toga was a garment worn by citizens of which city?

A: Giza
B: Babylon
C: Rome
D: Delhi

113

The name for which type of dog comes from the Latin for 'earth'?

A: Poodle
B: Terrier
C: Spaniel
D: Setter

114

Which first name is shared by TV presenter Chegwin and Boyzone member Duffy?

A: Kevin
B: Kieran
C: Keith
D: Kelvin

115

The leek is a traditional symbol of which country?

A: Wales
B: Scotland
C: England
D: Northern Ireland

50:50 Go to page 449 Go to page 473 ? Answers on page 494

4 ◆ £500

116

Which of these instruments has an extending spike at its base to support it?

A: Clarinet
B: Clavichord
C: Cornet
D: Cello

117

The company Moss Bros is most associated with the hiring out of what?

A: Cars
B: Staff
C: Dress suits
D: Power tools

118

Which of these is particularly associated with a collection of nursery rhymes?

A: Mother Cat
B: Mother Rat
C: Mother Pig
D: Mother Goose

119

What type of building is the Old Bailey in London?

A: Children's hospital
B: Royal observatory
C: Youth theatre
D: Criminal court

120

With which type of people is the phrase 'Shiver my timbers' most associated?

A: Teachers
B: Sailors
C: Miners
D: Vicars

50:50 Go to page 449 Go to page 473 ? Answers on page 494

4 ◆ £500

121

What is the surname of the actor with the first name Keanu?

- A: Pitt
- B: Cruise
- C: Reeves
- D: Depp

122

In which European country is the city of Verona?

- A: Spain
- B: France
- C: Austria
- D: Italy

123

Which of these terms means to cook by long, slow simmering?

- A: Grill
- B: Stew
- C: Deep-fry
- D: Scramble

124

In hairdressing, 'perm' is a shortenedversion of which phrase?

- A: Permission wave
- B: Permutation wave
- C: Permafrost wave
- D: Permanent wave

125

Which of these is an informal term for a roll of fat around someone's midriff?

- A: Spare change
- B: Spare rib
- C: Spare room
- D: Spare tyre

50:50 Go to page 449 Go to page 473 ? Answers on page 494

4 ◆ £500

126

In which country is the city of Avignon?

A: France
B: Italy
C: Austria
D: Switzerland

127

Complete the title of the Gershwin opera: 'Porgy and...'?

A: Bertha
B: Bonny
C: Biddy
D: Bess

128

A 'laptop' is a small what?

A: Bed
B: Computer
C: Dog
D: Egg

129

In which part of the UK is the town of Kilmarnock?

A: Scotland
B: Wales
C: Northern Ireland
D: England

130

What is the ninth month of the year?

A: July
B: August
C: September
D: October

50:50 Go to page 449 Go to page 473 ? Answers on page 494

4 ◆ £500

131

Which word goes before 'knot' and 'Smith' to make well known phrases?

A: Sister
B: Uncle
C: Daddy
D: Granny

132

'Aggro' is the shortened form of which word?

A: Agglomeration
B: Aggradation
C: Aggregation
D: Aggravation

133

Which of these phrases refers to a race in which the competitors finish at exactly the same time?

A: Dead glow
B: Dead heat
C: Dead sweat
D: Dead warmth

134

Someone who has a narrow escape is said to get away by the skin of... what?

A: His feet
B: His hair
C: His teeth
D: His chest

135

Which of these words means 'accident'?

A: Misfit
B: Mishap
C: Mismatch
D: Misspent

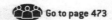

50:50 Go to page 449 Go to page 473 ? Answers on page 494

136

What is the female equivalent of a marquess?

A: Marchalin
B: Marchioness
C: Marquisa
D: Marquette

137

Which meal is associated with a public celebration of a successful harvest?

A: Breakfast
B: Lunch
C: Tea
D: Supper

138

What is the capital of Sweden?

A: Gothenburg
B: Helsingborg
C: Stockholm
D: Uppsala

139

The Quakers are also known as the Society of...?

A: Brothers
B: Chapels
C: Friends
D: Light

140

Which of these is an unattainable or fanciful hope?

A: Pipe band
B: Pipe cleaner
C: Pipe dream
D: Pipeline

50:50 Go to page 449 Go to page 473 ? Answers on page 494

4 ◆ £500

141

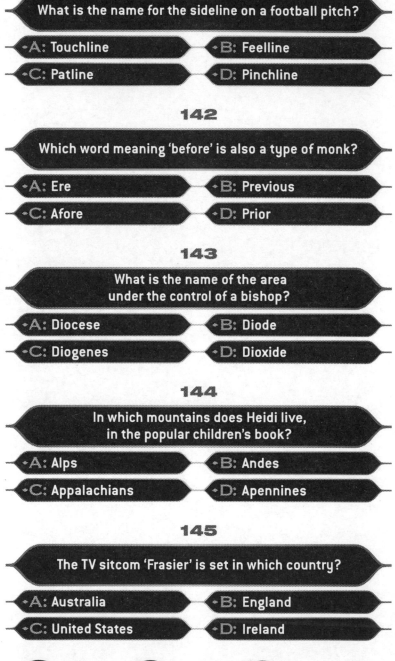

What is the name for the sideline on a football pitch?

A: Touchline
B: Feelline
C: Patline
D: Pinchline

142

Which word meaning 'before' is also a type of monk?

A: Ere
B: Previous
C: Afore
D: Prior

143

What is the name of the area under the control of a bishop?

A: Diocese
B: Diode
C: Diogenes
D: Dioxide

144

In which mountains does Heidi live, in the popular children's book?

A: Alps
B: Andes
C: Appalachians
D: Apennines

145

The TV sitcom 'Frasier' is set in which country?

A: Australia
B: England
C: United States
D: Ireland

50:50 Go to page 449
Go to page 473
? Answers on page 494

4 ◆ £500

146

What is the word 'o'clock' an abbreviation for?

A: On the clock
B: Off the clock
C: Of the clock
D: Over the clock

147

Which of these was a number one hit for Right Said Fred?

A: Profoundly Potty
B: Deeply Dippy
C: Beautifully Batty
D: Greatly Goofy

148

What kind of geographical feature is the Tiber in Italy?

A: Lake
B: River
C: Mountain
D: Island

149

Which of these is a skin inflammation caused by hot weather?

A: Bristly heat
B: Prickly heat
C: Spiny heat
D: Thorny heat

150

What is the name for a group of eggs laid together?

A: Clutch
B: Grasp
C: Snatch
D: Hold

50:50 Go to page 449 Go to page 473 ? Answers on page 494

4 ◆ £500

151

Which of these athletics events is classed as a 'field event'?

A: 400 metres
B: Pole vault
C: Steeplechase
D: 100 metres

152

What is the second bill, often printed in red, telling you the account remains unpaid?

A: Remainder
B: Remember
C: Remander
D: Reminder

153

Which legendary character secretly watched Lady Godiva when he should have turned a blind eye?

A: Doubting Thomas
B: Puffing Billy
C: Jumping Jack
D: Peeping Tom

154

What is the meaning of the word 'veracity'?

A: Beauty
B: Truth
C: Hope
D: Charity

155

Which of these people are most likely to be doing a 'stretch'?

A: Sleepwalker
B: Water skier
C: Politician
D: Prisoner

50:50 Go to page 449 Go to page 473 ? Answers on page 494

4 ◆ £500

156

Which part of a church is used as the Communion table?

- A: Altar
- B: Nave
- C: Transept
- D: Crypt

50:50 Go to page 449 Go to page 473 Answers on page 494

15 £1 MILLION
14 £500,000
13 £250,000
12 £125,000
11 £64,000
10 £32,000
9 £16,000
8 £8,000
7 £4,000
6 £2,000
5 ◆ £1,000
4 ◇ £500
3 ◇ £300
2 ◇ £200
1 ◇ £100

5 ◆ £1,000

1

Which of these is the male of the red deer?

- A: Stag
- B: Hog
- C: Pig
- D: Dog

2

'School' is a collective term for which animals?

- A: Porpoises
- B: Hippos
- C: Penguins
- D: Frogs

3

What is the name of a group of strikers who try to stop others going into work during a dispute?

- A: Packet row
- B: Peck it rule
- C: Picket line
- D: Pocket file

4

A 'fractured tibia' is which type of injury?

- A: Broken bone
- B: Pulled muscle
- C: Torn ligament
- D: Dislocated finger

5

Which of these is a system for receiving television programmes?

- A: Cable
- B: Cord
- C: Rope
- D: Wire

50:50 Go to page 451 · Go to page 475 · ? Answers on page 494

5 ◆ £1,000

6

Who was the lead vocalist with Culture Club?

A: Kid Billy
B: Young Jimmy
C: Boy George
D: Beau Belle

7

Which of these US cities is on the coast?

A: Memphis
B: Houston
C: Miami
D: Salt Lake City

8

What type of room is a 'parlour'?

A: Bathroom
B: Hall
C: Living room
D: Kitchen

9

What was a traditional form of transport pulled by humans?

A: Tandem
B: Rickshaw
C: Canal barge
D: Cable car

10

NASA is an American agency concerned with what?

A: Food
B: Immigration
C: Agriculture
D: Space

50:50 Go to page 451 | Go to page 475 | ? Answers on page 494

5 ◆ £1,000

11

What is the surgical instrument with a scissor-like action used for holding and extracting?

A: Scalpel
B: Suture
C: Syringe
D: Forceps

12

Which word describes a volcano which is neither extinct nor erupting?

A: Rampant
B: Dormant
C: Gallant
D: Extant

13

Which of these is a piece of equipment used in printing?

A: Press
B: Nudge
C: Push
D: Shove

14

Where is the metaphorical 'slap' of reprimand?

A: On the thigh
B: On the head
C: On the back
D: On the wrist

15

Which dance shares its name with the Spanish word meaning 'sauce'?

A: Tango
B: Salsa
C: Rumba
D: Conga

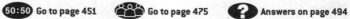

50:50 Go to page 451 · Go to page 475 · ? Answers on page 494

5 ◆ £1,000

16

If you were travelling in a gondola under the Bridge of Sighs, where would you be?

A: Rotterdam
B: Amsterdam
C: Venice
D: Birmingham

17

Which British city has the STD telephone code 020 followed by a 7 or 8?

A: Liverpool
B: London
C: Edinburgh
D: Newcastle

18

Complete the famous quote when England won the World Cup in 1966: 'They think it's all over...'?

A: It is now!
B: They're right!
C: Three cheers!
D: Hip, hip hooray!

19

Which of these punctuation marks most resemble a ditto sign?

A: Exclamation marks
B: Asterisks
C: Brackets
D: Apostrophes

20

Acupunture involves which specific type of equipment?

A: Needles
B: Ice bags
C: Suction pads
D: Weights

50:50 Go to page 451 Go to page 475 ? Answers on page 494

5 ◆ £1,000

21

An 'arc' is a section of which of these mathematical shapes?

A: Circle
B: Polygon
C: Triangle
D: Parallelogram

22

Which word follows 'wedded' to make a popular phrase referring to a happy marriage?

A: Bliss
B: Delight
C: Joy
D: Rapture

23

Limerick, after which the humorous verse was named, is a county in which country?

A: Scotland
B: USA
C: Iceland
D: Republic of Ireland

24

What accurately describes any place inside the Arctic and Antarctic Circles?

A: Temperate
B: Equatorial
C: Tropical
D: Polar

25

Which department deals with the preparation and dispensing of drugs in a hospital?

A: X-ray
B: Outpatients
C: Physiotherapy
D: Pharmacy

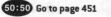

50:50 Go to page 451 Go to page 475 ? Answers on page 494

5 ◆ £1,000

26

A beginner uses 'nursery slopes' in which sport?

A: Skiing
B: Crown green bowling
C: Golf
D: Curling

27

Which material is made from a 'fleece'?

A: Cotton
B: Wool
C: Linen
D: Silk

28

If you bought a catalogue of exhibits whilst visiting the Louvre Museum, how would you pay?

A: Swiss francs
B: Spanish pesetas
C: Italian lira
D: French francs

29

In which game is 501 the traditional starting point?

A: Tiddlywinks
B: Bingo
C: Darts
D: Monopoly

30

What does an American put into the car when he fills up with 'gas'?

A: Air
B: Petrol
C: Water
D: Oil

50:50 Go to page 451 Go to page 475 ? Answers on page 494

5 ◆ £1,000

31

What is the name of Tony Blair's wife?

A: Charity
B: Cheryl
C: Cherie
D: Cherry

32

Which of these TV soaps is shown on Channel 5?

A: Hollyoaks
B: Emmerdale
C: Doctors
D: Family Affairs

33

What is the modern word for a person who yearns to be someone else, especially a rich celebrity?

A: Cannabe
B: Shallnabe
C: Wannabe
D: Didnabe

34

'Colonel' Tom Parker was the manager of which famous singer?

A: Elvis Presley
B: Jimi Hendrix
C: Jim Morrison
D: Janis Joplin

35

Which of these is a film starring Keanu Reeves?

A: The Matrix
B: Alien Resurrection
C: Space Cowboys
D: The Mummy

50:50 Go to page 451 | Go to page 475 | ? Answers on page 494

5 ◆ £1,000

36

Who is the star of the film 'Gone in 60 Seconds'?

A: Nicolas Cage
B: Nicolas Trap
C: Nicolas Cell
D: Nicolas Chokey

37

In the 'Tom and Jerry' cartoons, what type of creature is Jerry?

A: Dog
B: Canary
C: Mouse
D: Cat

38

In which of the services would a 'rating' serve?

A: Air Force
B: Army
C: Navy
D: Police force

39

Which of these historical figures ruled the Roman Empire in the first century AD?

A: Genghis Khan
B: Nero
C: Attila the Hun
D: Hannibal

40

On which part of the body is a 'boater' traditionally worn?

A: Head
B: Knee
C: Elbow
D: Hand

50:50 Go to page 451 Go to page 475 ? Answers on page 494

5 ◆ £1,000

41

What type of word is 'stormy'?

- A: Noun
- B: Adjective
- C: Verb
- D: Pronoun

42

Which of these terms is actually a key on a computer keyboard?

- A: Space capsule
- B: Space bar
- C: Space shot
- D: Space shuttle

43

'You Sexy Thing' was a hit record by which group?

- A: Hot Toddy
- B: Cocoa
- C: Eggnog
- D: Hot Chocolate

44

Which moronic TV character is played by Steve Coogan?

- A: Alan Partridge
- B: Adam Goose
- C: Aidan Gannet
- D: Adrian Peacock

45

Steve Ovett is an Olympic gold medallist in which sport?

- A: Rowing
- B: Athletics
- C: Tennis
- D: Shooting

50:50 Go to page 451 Go to page 475 ? Answers on page 494

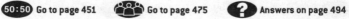

5 ◆ £1,000

46

Which of these is a type of cocktail made from vodka, orange juice and Galliano?

A: Henry Wallbanger
B: Harry Wallbanger
C: Harvey Wallbanger
D: Hughie Wallbanger

47

Angus Deayton hosts which TV panel show?

A: They Think It's All Over
B: Have I Got News For You
C: A Question of TV
D: If I Ruled the World

48

In which TV series did Raymond Burr play a wheelchair-bound detective?

A: Metalside
B: Tinside
C: Ironside
D: Steelside

49

Ellis Island was the centre of immigration for people wishing to enter which country?

A: Switzerland
B: United States
C: Russia
D: Austria

50

Which of these items of clothing would usually be worn around the neck?

A: Briefs
B: Strides
C: Trilby
D: Cravat

50:50 Go to page 451 Go to page 475 ? Answers on page 494

5 ◆ £1,000

51

What name is given to an ordinary woman who acts as though she were aristocratic?

- A: Lady Dirt
- B: Lady Grime
- C: Lady Muck
- D: Lady Mess

52

Which pop star is known for his friendship with a chimpanzee named Bubbles?

- A: Stevie Wonder
- B: Ray Charles
- C: Michael Jackson
- D: Smokey Robinson

53

Which of these is an album by the Bee Gees?

- A: Friday Night Madness
- B: Saturday Night Fever
- C: Sunday Night Lunacy
- D: Monday Night Insanity

54

If you are suffering from 'alopecia', what are you losing?

- A: Memory
- B: Weight
- C: Hair
- D: Teeth

55

Which of these is a book written by J. R. R. Tolkien?

- A: The Hobbit
- B: The Railway Children
- C: Swallows and Amazons
- D: The BFG

50:50 Go to page 451 Go to page 475 ? Answers on page 494

5 ◆ £1,000

56

The Tyrol is a mountainous region in which of these countries?

A: Austria
B: Nepal
C: USA
D: New Zealand

57

Which of these was a contestant on the second UK series of 'Big Brother'?

A: Suds
B: Bubble
C: Soap
D: Car

58

Which of these is an Oscar-winning film starring Dustin Hoffman?

A: The Freshman
B: The Sophomore
C: The Graduate
D: The Post-Grad

59

What type of film is 'The Good, the Bad and the Ugly', starring Clint Eastwood?

A: Musical
B: Western
C: Science fiction
D: Film noir

60

Which of these words best describes an 'avaricious' person?

A: Greedy
B: Studious
C: Pleasant
D: Timid

50:50 Go to page 451 Go to page 475 ? Answers on page 494

5 ◆ £1,000

61

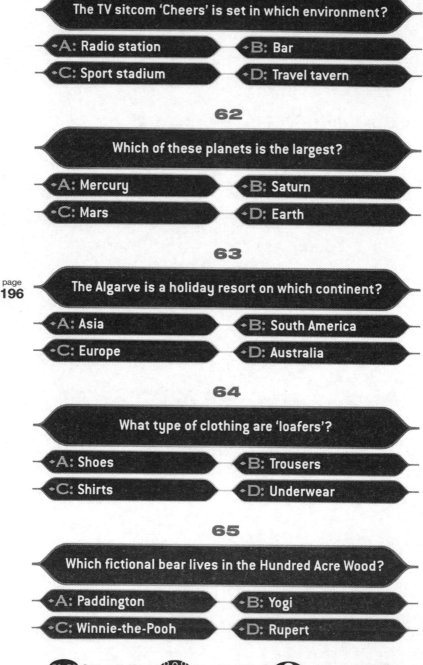

The TV sitcom 'Cheers' is set in which environment?

- A: Radio station
- B: Bar
- C: Sport stadium
- D: Travel tavern

62

Which of these planets is the largest?

- A: Mercury
- B: Saturn
- C: Mars
- D: Earth

63

The Algarve is a holiday resort on which continent?

- A: Asia
- B: South America
- C: Europe
- D: Australia

64

What type of clothing are 'loafers'?

- A: Shoes
- B: Trousers
- C: Shirts
- D: Underwear

65

Which fictional bear lives in the Hundred Acre Wood?

- A: Paddington
- B: Yogi
- C: Winnie-the-Pooh
- D: Rupert

50:50 Go to page 451 Go to page 475 ? Answers on page 494

5 ◆ £1,000

66

Gavin Hastings and his brother Scott represented Scotland in which sport?

A: Football
B: Tennis
C: Snooker
D: Rugby union

67

Which Wild West figure did Paul Newman portray in a 1969 film?

A: Pecos Bill
B: Wyatt Earp
C: Doc Holliday
D: Butch Cassidy

68

Which of these is the title of an Arnold Schwarzenegger film?

A: False Facts
B: True Lies
C: Fake Truths
D: Real Fiction

69

Who delivered the controversial 'Rivers of Blood' speech in 1968?

A: Margaret Thatcher
B: Jeffrey Archer
C: Enoch Powell
D: David Mellor

70

Which of these is a 2001 film starring Ben Affleck?

A: Rorke's Drift
B: River Plate
C: Tet Offensive
D: Pearl Harbor

50:50 Go to page 451 Go to page 475 ? Answers on page 494

5 ◆ £1,000

71

What is the name of the central character in the animated TV series 'Futurama'?

A: Boil
B: Bake
C: Fry
D: Flambé

72

Which of these conflicts occurred during the 1950s?

A: Korean War
B: American Civil War
C: Napoleonic War
D: Boer War

73

In the Bible, Goliath belonged to which tribe?

A: Brutes
B: Ignoramuses
C: Luddites
D: Philistines

74

Which of these animals makes a 'trumpeting' sound?

A: Whale
B: Crocodile
C: Tarantula
D: Elephant

75

Which financial institutions manage money?

A: Bends
B: Banks
C: Beds
D: Borders

50:50 Go to page 451 Go to page 475 ? Answers on page 494

5 ◆ £1,000

76

Jack and Annie Walker were the original couple to run which 'Coronation Street' pub?

- A: The Ramblers Rest
- B: The Rovers Return
- C: The Rangers Retreat
- D: The Riders Refuge

77

Who played 007 seven times on film between 1973 and 1985?

- A: Demi Moore
- B: Roger Moore
- C: Dudley Moore
- D: Mary Tyler Moore

78

Which of these islands follows the word 'New' to give the name of a US state?

- A: Madagascar
- B: Corsica
- C: Majorca
- D: Jersey

79

On which continent are the cities of Montevideo and Caracas?

- A: Africa
- B: Asia
- C: Europe
- D: South America

80

Which of these words means 'negligent'?

- A: Tireless
- B: Fearless
- C: Careless
- D: Hairless

50:50 Go to page 451 Go to page 475 ? Answers on page 494

5 ◆ £1,000

81

In 'Top Gun', what was the profession of Tom Cruise's character?

A: Cowboy
B: Hitman
C: Pilot
D: Stuntman

82

Sudan is the largest country on which continent?

A: Asia
B: South America
C: Europe
D: Africa

83

Which of these is the name of an old Spanish coin?

A: Singloon
B: Doubloon
C: Triploon
D: Quadroon

84

What kind of animal is a 'bronco'?

A: Goat
B: Horse
C: Dog
D: Monkey

85

In which part of the world is Guatemala?

A: Southeast Asia
B: Central America
C: Northern Europe
D: Central Asia

50:50 Go to page 451 Go to page 475 ? Answers on page 494

5 ◆ £1,000

86

What was the name of the bush kangaroo in the 1960s Australian series?

A: Hoppy
B: Jumpy
C: Leapy
D: Skippy

87

'Compliments of the season' is another way of saying what?

A: Good morning
B: Merry Christmas
C: Bless you
D: Excuse me

88

Which of these birds do not feature in the song 'The Twelve Days of Christmas'?

A: Geese
B: Swans
C: Hens
D: Pheasants

89

What is the name of the structure with equipment for drilling an oil well?

A: Oil farm
B: Oil plant
C: Oil rig
D: Oil shop

90

Which musical of the 1970s has now become a cult show, involving audience participation?

A: The Rocky Mountain Show
B: The Rocky Horror Show
C: The Rocky Balboa Show
D: The Rocky Roller Show

50:50 Go to page 451 · Go to page 475 · ? Answers on page 494

91

What is the name for a protective cover for a CD or record?

A: Mitten
B: Hood
C: Galosh
D: Sleeve

92

Which author is most associated with the game of 'Poohsticks'?

A: C. S. Lewis
B: A. A. Milne
C: J. K. Rowling
D: E. B. White

93

Which of these is a traditional main ingredient of paella?

A: Rice
B: Spaghetti
C: Ciabatta
D: Bulghur wheat

94

What is a 'plum duff'?

A: Card game
B: Suet pudding
C: Butterfly
D: Golfing term

95

Which of these hosted a TV chat show on three evenings a week for seven years?

A: Jimmy Young
B: Ken Bruce
C: Terry Wogan
D: Steve Wright

50:50 Go to page 451 Go to page 475 ? Answers on page 494

5 ◆ £1,000

96

Complete the title of a number one single for Madonna: 'Into the…'?

A: Tube | B: Groove
C: Room | D: Tomb

97

Which of these is not one of the first names of the Three Tenors?

A: Luciano | B: Placido
C: Julio | D: José

98

Which creatures are most associated with the 'dawn chorus'?

A: Insects | B: Birds
C: Crustaceans | D: Fish

99

Calamari is another term for which seafood?

A: Crab | B: Shrimp
C: Lobster | D: Squid

100

Which name is shared by the legendary figures Turpin and Whittington?

A: Alf | B: Dick
C: Fred | D: Will

50:50 Go to page 451 Go to page 475 ? Answers on page 494

5 ◆ £1,000

101

In which country is the city of Bangkok?

A: Vietnam
B: Indonesia
C: Malaysia
D: Thailand

102

What name is given to the series of monologues by Alan Bennett?

A: Talking Heads
B: Listening Heads
C: Nodding Heads
D: Shaking Heads

103

For which task is a 'snuffer' most likely to be used?

A: Dusting plants
B: Making beds
C: Extinguishing candles
D: Cracking eggs

104

Which of these is an amateur steeplechase for horses used in hunting?

A: Line-to-line
B: Dot-to-dot
C: Point-to-point
D: Mark-to-mark

105

Maurice Micklewhite is the real name of which actor?

A: Clint Eastwood
B: Michael Caine
C: Harrison Ford
D: Mel Gibson

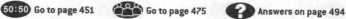

50:50 Go to page 451 Go to page 475 ? Answers on page 494

5 ◆ £1,000

106

Which of these is a novel by John Grisham?

A: The Pelican Brief
B: The Pigeon Brief
C: The Penguin Brief
D: The Partridge Brief

107

Which group had hit singles with 'Real Gone Kid' and 'Fergus Sings The Blues'?

A: Deacon Green
B: Deacon Red
C: Deacon Yellow
D: Deacon Blue

108

The talon is another term for which part of a bird?

A: Beak
B: Tail feather
C: Claw
D: Wing

109

In which country was the jeep first developed?

A: Japan
B: United States
C: France
D: Australia

110

Which of these is a regular character in 'Coronation Street'?

A: Steve McDonald
B: Steve Ovett
C: Steve Cram
D: Steve Buscemi

50:50 Go to page 451 · Go to page 475 · ? Answers on page 494

5 ◆ £1,000

111

The peseta is the unit of currency in which country?

A: Italy
B: Greece
C: Austria
D: Spain

112

What is the informal term for large-scale processing of numerical data on computer?

A: Number munching
B: Number lunching
C: Number bunching
D: Number crunching

113

Which TV soap is set in a hotel?

A: Hollyoaks
B: Emmerdale
C: Brookside
D: Crossroads

114

Which professional wears a cassock in his job?

A: Physiotherapist
B: Pilot
C: Policeman
D: Priest

115

Melvyn Bragg is most associated with which TV show?

A: The East End Show
B: The North Pole Show
C: The South Bank Show
D: The West Life Show

50:50 Go to page 451 Go to page 475 ? Answers on page 494

5 ◆ £1,000

116

Which type of bean is particularly associated with the dish chilli con carne?

A: Broad
B: Runner
C: Kidney
D: Mung

117

By what name was Spice Girl Mel B also known?

A: Scary Spice
B: Spooky Spice
C: Strange Spice
D: Startling Spice

118

'Tabby' is a variety of which type of creature?

A: Cat
B: Budgerigar
C: Fish
D: Mouse

119

Which Jane was created by the author Charlotte Brontë?

A: Jayne Mansfield
B: Jane Fonda
C: Jane Eyre
D: Jane Tennison

120

With which of these groups is Roy Wood most associated?

A: Worloch
B: Wizzard
C: Whitch
D: Warewoolf

50:50 Go to page 451 Go to page 475 ? Answers on page 494

5 ◆ £1,000

121

What is the 'Gay Gordons'?

A: Open top car
B: Gin cocktail
C: Cheesecake
D: Old-time dance

122

Which of these is one of the teenagers who works with the cartoon character Scooby-Doo?

A: Delia
B: Dilys
C: Daphne
D: Delores

123

On television, how many comprised 'The Likely Lads'?

A: Two
B: Three
C: Four
D: Six

124

In which US sitcom did Danny DeVito play Louie De Palma?

A: Train
B: Taxi
C: Tram
D: Tube

125

In bed, which part of the body is usually supported by a pillow?

A: Foot
B: Head
C: Hip
D: Knee

50:50 Go to page 451 · Go to page 475 · ? Answers on page 494

5 ◆ £1,000

126

Which of these words describes someone who is naive and idealistic?

- A: Moony-eyed
- B: Sunny-eyed
- C: Starry-eyed
- D: Planetty-eyed

127

What is the name for a life-size dummy used to display clothes?

- A: Sequin
- B: Harlequin
- C: Mannequin
- D: Palanquin

128

Which of these is the name of a Hollywood star?

- A: Doris Dawn
- B: Doris Morning
- C: Doris Day
- D: Doris Night

129

'Foliage' is a mass of what?

- A: Flies
- B: Leaves
- C: Snowflakes
- D: Words

130

Which of these people would be most interested in mummies and pyramids?

- A: Sociologist
- B: Egyptologist
- C: Pharmacologist
- D: Ornithologist

50:50 Go to page 451   Go to page 475   ? Answers on page 494

5 ◆ £1,000

131

Complete this exclamation of surprise: 'Stone the...'?

A: Crows
B: Jays
C: Magpies
D: Ravens

132

Which of these words refers to studying for a degree?

A: Reading
B: Rolling
C: Rotating
D: Rocking

133

A hacker is someone who illegally breaks into what?

A: Banks
B: Computers
C: Post offices
D: Prisons

134

Which word goes before 'mantis' to make the name of an insect?

A: Singing
B: Praying
C: Reading
D: Sleeping

135

What kind of rebellion is particularly associated with Fletcher Christian and the Bounty?

A: Strike
B: Mutiny
C: Riot
D: Uprising

50:50 Go to page 451 Go to page 475 ? Answers on page 494

5 ◆ £1,000

136

Which of these does a repertory company do?

A: Sell food
B: Make electrical goods
C: Perform plays
D: Look after animals

137

In total, how many degrees are there in a circle?

A: 90
B: 180
C: 270
D: 360

138

In which county is Sherwood Forest?

A: Surrey
B: Northumberland
C: Shropshire
D: Nottinghamshire

139

In the 'Arabian Nights', what was the occupation of Sinbad?

A: Baker
B: Ratcatcher
C: Sailor
D: Tailor

140

What kind of bet backs a horse to win or be placed?

A: Each-side
B: Each-way
C: Each-end
D: Each-head

50:50 Go to page 451 Go to page 475 ? Answers on page 494

5 ◆ £1,000

141

Which organ of the body is also the word for a supplementary section at the end of a book?

A: Pancreas
B: Appendix
C: Liver
D: Spleen

142

What is the measure of capacity for oil?

A: Box
B: Barrel
C: Bottle
D: Basket

143

Which word means both a foolish person and coagulated blood?

A: Nerd
B: Clot
C: Twit
D: Ass

144

What is the airport code for London's Heathrow airport?

A: HRL
B: LHA
C: LHR
D: HRA

145

Which of these words means 'scorch'?

A: Binge
B: Hinge
C: Singe
D: Whinge

50:50 Go to page 451 Go to page 475 ? Answers on page 494

5 ◆ £1,000

146

What colour is the ball at the top of a Belisha beacon?

A: Blue
B: Green
C: Orange
D: Violet

147

Which European language is spoken in Sicily?

A: Dutch
B: Spanish
C: Greek
D: Italian

148

Complete the title of the George Orwell novel: 'Animal...'?

A: Circus
B: Farm
C: Hospital
D: Street

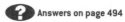

50:50 Go to page 451 Go to page 475 ? Answers on page 494

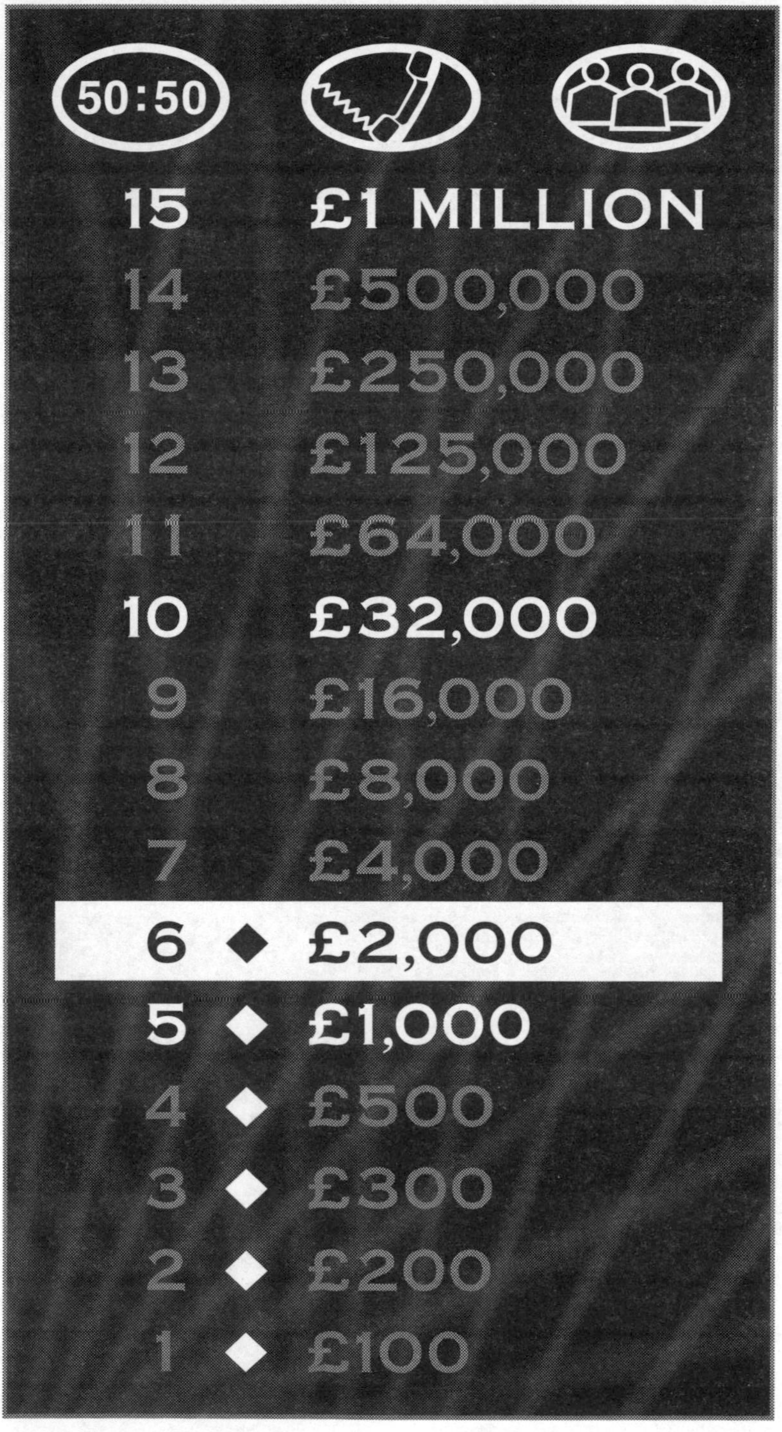
50:50
15 £1 MILLION
14 £500,000
13 £250,000
12 £125,000
11 £64,000
10 £32,000
9 £16,000
8 £8,000
7 £4,000
6 ◆ £2,000
5 ◆ £1,000
4 ◆ £500
3 ◆ £300
2 ◆ £200
1 ◆ £100

6 ◆ £2,000

1

With which type of music is Garth Brooks most closely associated?

- A: Country and western
- B: Heavy metal
- C: Chamber
- D: Sea shanties

2

Which of these is a book by Dashiell Hammett?

- A: The Cretan Hawk
- B: The Sardinian Osprey
- C: The Maltese Falcon
- D: The Sicilian Eagle

3

Andy Summers, Stewart Copeland and Sting formed which rock group?

- A: CID
- B: The Force
- C: Law and Order
- D: Police

4

'Tarragon' is a type of what?

- A: Soldier
- B: Sparkling white wine
- C: French bread
- D: Herb

5

Which of these is a device used with a computer?

- A: Scanner
- B: Spanner
- C: Strimmer
- D: Strainer

50:50 Go to page 453 · Go to page 477 · ? Answers on page 495

6 ◆ £2,000

6

What is the female equivalent of a count?

A: Countrix
B: Countette
C: Countess
D: Countana

7

What describes the spectacles in the saying that makes everything seem much better than it really is?

A: Rose-tinted
B: Green-coloured
C: Red-hued
D: Blue-shaded

8

In which game can England win 'The Ashes'?

A: Tennis
B: Rugby union
C: Football
D: Cricket

9

The name of which English county is associated with a traditional stew called a 'hot pot'?

A: Yorkshire
B: Lancashire
C: Derbyshire
D: Lincolnshire

10

A complete set of what is traditionally stored in a canteen?

A: Pans
B: Bottles
C: Cutlery
D: Crockery

50:50 Go to page 453 Go to page 477 ? Answers on page 495

6 ◆ £2,000

11

Vatican City is an enclave within which European capital?

A: Madrid | B: Rome
C: Geneva | D: Athens

12

Which of these adjectives correctly describes William the Conqueror?

A: Alsatian | B: Norman
C: Breton | D: Parisian

13

In the traditional nursery rhyme, who found Lucy Locket's lost pocket?

A: Kitty Fisher | B: Mistress Mary
C: Polly Flinders | D: Elsie Marley

14

Zebedee featured in the children's TV programme 'The Magic...' what?

A: Carpet | B: Roundabout
C: Lamp | D: Garden

15

What is the basic currency of Japan?

A: Ying | B: Yang
C: Yen | D: Yon

50:50 Go to page 453 Go to page 477 ? Answers on page 495

6 ◆ £2,000

16

With which period of American history do you associate bootleggers and speakeasies?

A: Gold rush
B: Civil War
C: Prohibition
D: Settlement of the West

17

What does the word 'masonry' refer to?

A: Stonework
B: Metalwork
C: Woodwork
D: Paintwork

18

Meaning a writing desk, which of these is the correct spelling?

A: Burow
B: Bewrau
C: Bureau
D: Bewroh

19

What was the name of the Labour Party leader succeeded by Neil Kinnock?

A: Michael Foot
B: Maurice Furlong
C: Malcolm Inch
D: Mitchell Yard

20

'Memo' is the abbreviation used for which word?

A: Memorandum
B: Memorabilia
C: Memorial
D: Memento

50:50 Go to page 453 · Go to page 477 · ? Answers on page 495

6 ◆ £2,000

21

What do termites resemble?

A: Large wasps
B: Large ants
C: Large moths
D: Large centipedes

22

Which of these places in the UK has 'on-Trent' in its official name?

A: Newcastle
B: Stoke
C: Henley
D: Stockton

23

In the garden, what would be destroyed by a fungicide?

A: Greenfly
B: Caterpillars
C: Mould
D: Weeds

24

Which of these birds is also the name of a group of islands in the Atlantic?

A: Pelicans
B: Turkeys
C: Puffins
D: Canaries

25

If Princess Margaret had become a reigning British Queen, which number Margaret would she have been?

A: I
B: II
C: III
D: IV

50:50 Go to page 453 Go to page 477 ? Answers on page 495

6 ◆ £2,000

26

What are you doing if you're 'tripping the light fantastic'?

- A: Parachute jumping
- B: Tightrope walking
- C: Ballroom dancing
- D: Travelling the world

27

In imperial money, what was the specific name for twenty-one shillings?

- A: Guinea
- B: Groat
- C: Sovereign
- D: Crown

28

Which of these names do you associate with Tomb Raider?

- A: Tara Loft
- B: Lara Croft
- C: Cara Soft
- D: Sara Toft

29

The Riviera is a popular holiday region stretching between which two countries?

- A: Portugal and Spain
- B: Spain and France
- C: France and Italy
- D: Italy and Greece

30

Which of these words refers to peas, beans and lentils?

- A: Pulse vegetables
- B: Heart greens
- C: Beat seeds
- D: Throb pods

50:50 Go to page 453 Go to page 477 ? Answers on page 495

6 ◆ £2,000

31

What is 'The Lancet'?

- A: Medical journal
- B: Annual almanack
- C: Daily horoscope
- D: Builder's bible

32

Which music of the 1980s was rap with an electronic backing?

- A: Tip-top
- B: Hip-hop
- C: Bip-bop
- D: Flip-flop

33

What colour is the rising sun on the national flag of Japan?

- A: Orange
- B: Yellow
- C: Purple
- D: Red

34

Which American frontier town was a lawless place on the Santa Fe Trail?

- A: Evasion City
- B: Dodge City
- C: Sidestep City
- D: Bob 'n' Weave City

35

Which of these is the home country of Volvo cars and the pop group Abba?

- A: Sweden
- B: Poland
- C: Belgium
- D: Netherlands

50:50 Go to page 453 Go to page 477 ? Answers on page 495

6 ◆ £2,000

36

Who is normally referred to as a 'Maître d''?

A: Barman
B: Bellboy
C: Cellarman
D: Head waiter

37

What is the military command for leaving the parade?

A: Fall over
B: Fall back
C: Fall apart
D: Fall out

38

In 1998, the death penalty was finally abolished for which act of betrayal in the UK?

A: High pressure
B: High tension
C: High spirits
D: High treason

39

Which two colours normally make up a monochrome photograph?

A: Blue and green
B: Black and white
C: Red and yellow
D: Brown and cream

40

What is officially counted in the UK's ten-yearly 'census'?

A: Population
B: Unsolved crimes
C: Tax owed
D: Dartmoor ponies

50:50 Go to page 453 Go to page 477 ? Answers on page 495

6 ◆ £2,000

41

Stormin' Norman Schwarzkopf was a major figure in which conflict?

- A: Gulf War
- B: Korean War
- C: Boer War
- D: World War I

42

Penny was the first person to leave which house in 2001?

- A: Big Brother House
- B: House of Lords
- C: House of Pain
- D: Noel's House Party

43

Saskatchewan is a province of which country?

- A: New Zealand
- B: Canada
- C: Australia
- D: South Africa

44

Who became leader of the Labour Party in 1992?

- A: James Callaghan
- B: John Smith
- C: Ramsay MacDonald
- D: Tony Blair

45

Which of these is a bone of the human body?

- A: Humerus
- B: Hillairyus
- C: Larfible
- D: Comikkal

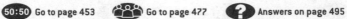

50:50 Go to page 453 Go to page 477 ? Answers on page 495

6 ◆ £2,000

46

Which former US president has a wife called Nancy?

A: Gerald Ford
B: Franklin D. Roosevelt
C: Richard Nixon
D: Ronald Reagan

47

In the Bible, who famously ventured into the lions' den?

A: Esau
B: Joseph
C: Daniel
D: Saul

48

di Amin was the leader of which country in the 1970s?

A: Cambodia
B: Uganda
C: Chile
D: Haiti

49

What do Americans often refer to as 'sneakers'?

A: Socks
B: Gloves
C: Shorts
D: Trainers

50

Which people interrupt public speakers with aggressive or abusive comments?

: Hackers
B: Hecklers
C: Hucksters
D: Honkers

50:50 Go to page 453 · Go to page 477 · ? Answers on page 495

6 ◆ £2,000

51

What is 'nitroglycerin'?

A: Soap
B: Explosive
C: Vitamin supplement
D: Toothpaste

52

Charlie Higson and Paul Whitehouse featured in which TV show?

A: The Fast Show
B: That Was The Week That Was
C: The Goodies
D: Not the Nine O'Clock News

53

Which TV sitcom was set on Craggy Island?

A: Father Ted
B: Home to Roost
C: Man About the House
D: Desmond's

54

In which of these sports would a tiebreak be played if the scores reached 6-6?

A: Snooker
B: Tennis
C: Football
D: Cricket

55

Buenos Aires is the capital city of which country?

A: Mexico
B: Venezuela
C: Chile
D: Argentina

50:50 Go to page 453 Go to page 477 ? Answers on page 495

6 ◆ £2,000

56

Acapulco is a resort in which country?

- A: Mexico
- B: South Africa
- C: Thailand
- D: Australia

57

Which of these is an Oscar-winning film starring Bette Davis?

- A: All About Eartha
- B: All About Eve
- C: All About Elizabeth
- D: All About Elspeth

58

Which of these is an Oscar-winning movie of the 1970s?

- A: The French Connection
- B: The Irish Connection
- C: The Swedish Connection
- D: The German Connection

59

What was the first name of Mr Hemingway, author of 'The Old Man and the Sea'?

- A: Elmore
- B: Ernest
- C: Edison
- D: Ellroy

60

If someone is rendered dull-witted by a series of blows, they are said to be...?

- A: Punch-drunk
- B: Blow-wrecked
- C: Smack-hammered
- D: Fist-tipsy

50:50 Go to page 453 Go to page 477 ? Answers on page 495

6 ◆ £2,000

61

What does the letter 'S' stand for in the abbreviation VHS?

- A: Standard
- B: Synchronisation
- C: Syndication
- D: System

62

In Greek mythology, what type of creature was the three-headed Cerberus?

- A: Snake
- B: Lion
- C: Dog
- D: Bull

63

Which of these is a stage musical based on a book by Charles Dickens?

- A: Les Misérables
- B: Oliver!
- C: My Fair Lady
- D: The Beautiful Game

64

Who played Pop Larkin in the TV show 'The Darling Buds of May'?

- A: John Thaw
- B: Leo McKern
- C: David Jason
- D: Nigel Hawthorne

65

Which of these was a popular pop group of the 1960s?

- A: Harry's Hermits
- B: Helga's Hermits
- C: Herman's Hermits
- D: Hilda's Hermits

50:50 Go to page 453 Go to page 477 ? Answers on page 495

6 ◆ £2,000

66

'Altostratus' is an example of what?

A: Rain
B: Thunder
C: Lightning
D: Cloud

67

Which football manager is known for his close association with faith healer Eileen Drewery?

A: Glenn Hoddle
B: Alex Ferguson
C: Sven Goran Eriksson
D: Ron Atkinson

68

Malmö is a fortified city in which European country?

A: Sweden
B: Spain
C: Bulgaria
D: Estonia

69

Which of these was prime minister of Canada in the 1970s?

A: Gerald Ford
B: Jim Callaghan
C: Pierre Trudeau
D: Bob Hawke

70

What type of monster does Buffy slay in the title of the popular TV show?

A: Vampires
B: Mummies
C: Ghouls
D: Werewolves

50:50 Go to page 453 Go to page 477 ? Answers on page 495

6 ◆ £2,000

71

With which branch of the arts is Francis Ford Coppola most commonly associated?

- A: Film
- B: Ballet
- C: Architecture
- D: Fashion

72

Giuseppe is the first name of which composer?

- A: Mozart
- B: Beethoven
- C: Verdi
- D: Berlioz

73

Which of these was an Olympic champion in 1980?

- A: Linford Christie
- B: Robin Cousins
- C: Lynn Davies
- D: David Hemery

74

Ilie Nastase was a star of which sport in the 1970s?

- A: Golf
- B: Boxing
- C: Tennis
- D: Cricket

75

Which of these played cricket for England in the 1980s?

- A: Arnold Piglet
- B: Allan Lamb
- C: Arthur Calf
- D: Ainsley Foal

50:50 Go to page 453 Go to page 477 ? Answers on page 495

6 ◆ £2,000

76

Aviemore is a holiday resort in which country?

A: Wales
B: Northern Ireland
C: Scotland
D: England

77

In which country is the port of Dunkirk?

A: France
B: Spain
C: Netherlands
D: Belgium

78

Which of these is a social gathering of people to play cards?

A: Bridge Trip
B: Whist Drive
C: Snap Ride
D: Happy Family Journey

79

Anthony Rowley features in which children's rhyme?

A: Ding Dong Bell
B: Oh Soldier, Soldier
C: The House That Jack Built
D: A Frog He Would A-wooing Go

80

Which of these is a semi-sweet biscuit?

A: Progestive
B: Congestive
C: Digestive
D: Ingestive

50:50 Go to page 453 Go to page 477 ? Answers on page 495

6 ◆ £2,000

81

Which phrase was coined from Thomas, who hired out horses to customers who had to take the nearest one?

A: Robson's fancy
B: Dobson's selection
C: Jobson's pick
D: Hobson's choice

82

What is the word for severe measures taken to combat illegal or undesirable behaviour?

A: Comedown
B: Climbdown
C: Crackdown
D: Countdown

83

What type of disaster shook Beckindale in 1993 in the TV soap 'Emmerdale'?

A: River flood
B: Gas explosion
C: Air crash
D: Farm fire

84

Which domestic animals are affected by the viral disease BSE?

A: Pigs
B: Goats
C: Horses
D: Cattle

85

Which of these names identifies a common butterfly that feeds on brassicas?

A: Turnip Blue
B: Lettuce Green
C: Carrot Red
D: Cabbage White

50:50 Go to page 453 Go to page 477 Answers on page 495

6 ◆ £2,000

86

What type of food is 'mangetout'?

A: Biscuit
B: Pea
C: Sweet
D: Breakfast cereal

87

Which of these words is used to make up the word 'modem'?

A: Modelling
B: Moderate
C: Modern
D: Modulator

88

In 'The Muppet Show', what kind of animal was Fozzie?

A: Bear
B: Dog
C: Frog
D: Pig

89

Which of these is a tourist attraction in Rome?

A: Swiss Stairs
B: Spanish Steps
C: Lebanese Ladder
D: English Elevator

90

Who wrote 'The Hitchhiker's Guide to the Galaxy'?

A: Douglas Adams
B: Terry Pratchett
C: Neil Gaiman
D: Doug Naylor

50:50 Go to page 453 Go to page 477 ? Answers on page 495

6 ◆ £2,000

91

Which of these rivers is sacred to the Hindus?

- A: Amazon
- B: Ganges
- C: Mississippi
- D: Nile

92

Which country invaded Tibet in 1950?

- A: China
- B: India
- C: Russia
- D: Nepal

93

What is the first name of the wife of novelist Jeffrey Archer?

- A: Davina
- B: Alexandra
- C: Mary
- D: Rachel

94

Which of these words refers to the stars?

- A: Astral
- B: Lunar
- C: Solar
- D: Terrestrial

95

Snow and sugar snap are varieties of which vegetable?

- A: Onion
- B: Sprout
- C: Pea
- D: Artichoke

50:50 Go to page 453 Go to page 477 ? Answers on page 495

6 ◆ £2,000

96

Which TV sitcom was written by Victoria Wood?

A: Dinnerladies
B: Taxi Drivers
C: Traffic Wardens
D: Weather Forecasters

97

What was the first name of the poet Chaucer?

A: James
B: Geoffrey
C: John
D: Jeremy

98

Located in Kent, what is the name of the largest shopping centre in Europe?

A: Whitewater
B: Bluewater
C: Redwater
D: Blackwater

99

Which of these is a type of wading bird?

A: Spoonbill
B: Slicebill
C: Scoopbill
D: Shovelbill

100

Romania is bordered by which sea?

A: Adriatic
B: Black
C: Red
D: Dead

50:50 Go to page 453 · Go to page 477 · ? Answers on page 495

6 ◆ £2,000

101

What was the first name of Mr. Ventura, the pet detective played on screen by Jim Carrey?

A: Ace
B: King
C: Queen
D: Jack

102

Which part of the body is affected by a 'stye'?

A: Gums
B: Eye
C: Ear
D: Nose

103

Who plays Pauline Fowler in 'EastEnders'?

A: Wendy Richard
B: Pam St Clement
C: Barbara Windsor
D: Tamzin Outhwaite

104

Which of these are smooth racing-car tyres?

A: Slimeys
B: Slicks
C: Slanders
D: Slims

105

What was the real name of Judy Garland?

A: Marion Morrison
B: Frances Gumm
C: Doris von Kappelhoff
D: Norma Jean Baker

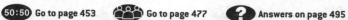

50:50 Go to page 453 · Go to page 477 · ? Answers on page 495

6 ◆ £2,000

106

Who had hit singles with 'Walking Away' and '7 Days' in 2000?

- A: Colin Daniel
- B: Casper Dylan
- C: Craig David
- D: Clive Derek

107

What was the title of Margaret Mitchell's only novel?

- A: Breakfast at Tiffany's
- B: A Streetcar Named Desire
- C: How Green Was My Valley
- D: Gone With The Wind

108

In Roman numerals, which of these represent the number 2000?

- A: VV
- B: MM
- C: CC
- D: LL

109

Which of these names is a 'Beale' not a 'Fowler' in the TV soap 'EastEnders'?

- A: Arthur
- B: Mark
- C: Ian
- D: Martin

110

According to the A series, which of these sheets of paper is the largest?

- A: A2
- B: A3
- C: A4
- D: A5

50:50 Go to page 453 | Go to page 477 | ? Answers on page 495

111

What is the term for gold or silver before it is made into coins?

- A: Mullion
- B: Pillion
- C: Scallion
- D: Bullion

112

Which of these New Zealand cities is the name of a Womble?

- A: Christchurch
- B: Auckland
- C: Wellington
- D: Hamilton

113

What is the particular interest of an 'epicure'?

- A: Poetry
- B: Art
- C: Food
- D: Music

114

Who had a UK hit with 'When the Going Gets Tough, the Tough Get Going'?

- A: Billy River
- B: Billy Sea
- C: Billy Ocean
- D: Billy Stream

115

Which of these phrases means 'to make money'?

- A: Hoe in
- B: Rake in
- C: Scythe in
- D: Spade in

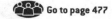

50:50 Go to page 453 Go to page 477 ? Answers on page 495

6 ◆ £2,000

116

What is the name for the background pattern or picture on a computer screen?

- A: Carpet
- B: Linoleum
- C: Emulsion
- D: Wallpaper

117

The islands of the Antilles lie closest to which sea?

- A: Black
- B: Caribbean
- C: Red
- D: Mediterranean

118

The Great Barrier Reef is in which sea?

- A: Coral Sea
- B: Sponge Sea
- C: Loofah Sea
- D: Shell Sea

119

Serrano ham is a speciality of which country?

- A: France
- B: Denmark
- C: Spain
- D: Italy

120

Which three letters were used as an abbreviation for East Germany?

- A: DDT
- B: DDR
- C: ADT
- D: EAR

50:50 Go to page 453 | Go to page 477 | ? Answers on page 495

6 ◆ £2,000

121

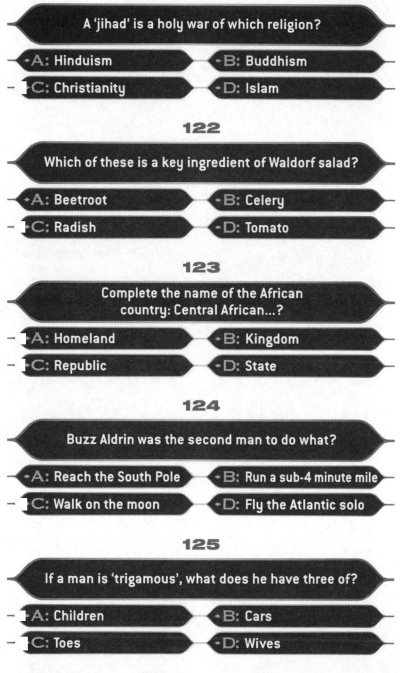

A 'jihad' is a holy war of which religion?

- A: Hinduism
- B: Buddhism
- C: Christianity
- D: Islam

122

Which of these is a key ingredient of Waldorf salad?

- A: Beetroot
- B: Celery
- C: Radish
- D: Tomato

123

Complete the name of the African country: Central African...?

- A: Homeland
- B: Kingdom
- C: Republic
- D: State

124

Buzz Aldrin was the second man to do what?

- A: Reach the South Pole
- B: Run a sub-4 minute mile
- C: Walk on the moon
- D: Fly the Atlantic solo

125

If a man is 'trigamous', what does he have three of?

- A: Children
- B: Cars
- C: Toes
- D: Wives

50:50 Go to page 453 Go to page 477 ? Answers on page 495

6 ◆ £2,000

126

What is the main subject of Rolling Stone magazine?

A: Food
B: Sport
C: Gardening
D: Music

127

Which of these is an artificial gemstone?

A: Thamesstone
B: Rhinestone
C: Nilestone
D: Danubestone

128

What nationality was the explorer David Livingstone?

A: English
B: Irish
C: Scottish
D: Welsh

129

Which of these is a yellow flower?

A: Goatslip
B: Sheepslip
C: Cowslip
D: Horseslip

130

Who plays the leading role
in the 2001 film 'Tomb Raider'?

A: Elizabeth Hurley
B: Angelina Jolie
C: Catherine Zeta-Jones
D: Renée Zellweger

50:50 Go to page 453 Go to page 477 ? Answers on page 495

6 ◆ £2,000

131

The model Jerry Hall comes from which state?

A: California
B: Alaska
C: Florida
D: Texas

132

Which television soap is associated with sponsorship by Cadbury?

A: Brookside
B: Coronation Street
C: EastEnders
D: Hollyoaks

133

Laver bread is a dish associated with which part of the British Isles?

A: England
B: Scotland
C: Ireland
D: Wales

134

Perrier mineral water comes from which country?

A: France
B: Belgium
C: Switzerland
D: Spain

135

Which of these is a regular character in the TV series 'Red Dwarf'?

A: Dog
B: Duck
C: Cat
D: Mouse

50:50 Go to page 453 Go to page 477 ? Answers on page 495

6 ◆ £2,000

136

What is written in the space labelled 'DOB' on an official form?

A: Maiden name
B: Birth date
C: National Insurance number
D: Marital status

137

Who took the fares and gave passengers tickets, before buses became a one-man operation?

A: Puncher
B: Conductor
C: Collector
D: Checker

138

Which book follows Genesis in the Old Testament of the Bible?

A: Ecclesiastes
B: Deuteronomy
C: Exodus
D: Judges

139

Which comedian won TV's 'Celebrity Big Brother' while raising money for 2001's Comic Relief?

A: Lee Evans
B: Jack Dee
C: Lee Hurst
D: Jack Docherty

140

Which capital city would you visit to see the Colosseum, the 1st century AD amphitheatre?

A: Lisbon
B: Athens
C: Paris
D: Rome

50:50 Go to page 453 Go to page 477 ? Answers on page 495

50:50

15		£1 MILLION
14		£500,000
13		£250,000
12		£125,000
11		£64,000
10		£32,000
9		£16,000
8		£8,000
7	◆	£4,000
6	◆	£2,000
5	◆	£1,000
4	◆	£500
3	◆	£300
2	◆	£200
1	◆	£100

7 ◆ £4,000

1

Angela Rippon famously appeared with which comedy double act?

- A: Abbott and Costello
- B: Martin and Lewis
- C: Morecambe and Wise
- D: Little and Large

2

Which of these is a name often given to a cured herring?

- A: Lardy
- B: Bloater
- C: Wobbly
- D: Tubster

3

Animals that have tadpoles as larvae belong to which group in the animal kingdom?

- A: Reptiles
- B: Amphibians
- C: Fish
- D: Rodents

4

Which Doctor partnered Mr Hyde in the story by R. L. Stevenson?

- A: Dr Jekyll
- B: Dr Strangelove
- C: Dr No
- D: Dr Who

5

Which of these is a Greek wine?

- A: Rotunda
- B: Retina
- C: Retsina
- D: Riviera

50:50 Go to page 455 · Go to page 478 · ? Answers on page 495

7 ◆ £4,000

6

Which TV quizmaster is known for saying 'I've started so I'll finish'?

A: Patrick Fitzpatrick
B: Donald McDonald
C: Neil O'Neill
D: Magnus Magnusson

7

What is the customary clothing worn by a nun?

A: Habitat
B: Habituation
C: Habit
D: Habitude

8

Which actor starred opposite Kate Winslet in the film 'Titanic'?

A: Matt Damon
B: Leonardo DiCaprio
C: Jude Law
D: Brad Pitt

9

What is the setting for the TV series 'Holby City'?

A: Railway station
B: Hospital
C: Post Office
D: Football Club

10

Vienna is the capital of which country?

A: Germany
B: Luxembourg
C: Austria
D: Hungary

50:50 Go to page 455 | Go to page 478 | Answers on page 495

7 ◆ £4,000

11

Sid James, Kenneth Williams and Hattie Jacques appeared in which series of films?

A: Carry On
B: Bond
C: Road To
D: Jaws

12

What was Patsy and Edina's favourite tipple in 'Absolutely Fabulous'?

A: White rum
B: Margaux wine
C: Gin & It
D: Bollinger

13

Which British military service featured in the sitcom 'Dad's Army'?

A: Territorial Army
B: Home Guard
C: Desert Rats
D: SAS

14

How did American Indians refer to the white man in the nineteenth century?

A: Lightskin
B: Pinkcheek
C: Paleface
D: Blueeye

15

Who puts the ball into play in a game of baseball?

A: Pitcher
B: Creamer
C: Jugger
D: Pourer

50:50 Go to page 455 Go to page 478 ? Answers on page 495

7 ◆ £4,000

16

Which financial term refers to the dollar in the US and the franc in Switzerland?

A: Basic currency
B: Net gain
C: Capital asset
D: Simple interest

17

What type of seating does a psychiatrist traditionally have for the patients in the consulting room?

A: Sofa
B: Settee
C: Couch
D: Chesterfield

18

Which musical term means 'return to the beginning'?

A: Piano
B: Crescendo
C: Staccato
D: Da capo

19

Madonna sings 'Papa Don't...' what, in the title of her number one hit?

A: Shout
B: Drive
C: Preach
D: Cry

20

Which of these was an English Quaker whose father had a US state named after him?

A: William Penn
B: Joseph Ark
C: Charles Kent
D: Philip de Mont

50:50 Go to page 455 Go to page 478 ? Answers on page 495

7 ◆ £4,000

21

Complete the title of the Oasis album: 'What's The Story...'?

A: Hunky Dory
B: Bremner Rory
C: Backbench Tory
D: Morning Glory

22

Which specific person controls the sale when bidding is involved?

A: Marketeer
B: Buccaneer
C: Auctioneer
D: Pamphleteer

23

Which of these acronyms refers to a type of savings scheme introduced by the Conservatives in 1991?

A: BESSIE
B: LOUISA
C: CASSIE
D: TESSA

24

What is a talisman?

A: Tasmanian devil
B: Lucky mascot
C: Pendant jewel
D: Species of monkey

25

What are runs in cricket, taken when the batsman has not touched the ball?

A: Byebyes
B: Goodbyes
C: Byes
D: By-the-byes

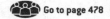

50:50 Go to page 455 · Go to page 478 · ? Answers on page 495

7 ◆ £4,000

26

Which of these was a Conservative prime minister of the 1970s?

A: John Major
B: Winston Churchill
C: Anthony Eden
D: Ted Heath

27

What is the word used in the theatre for an actor who overacts?

A: Bacon
B: Gammon
C: Rasher
D: Ham

28

Which TV soap featured a major character called Bobby Grant?

A: Coronation Street
B: Crossroads
C: Brookside
D: Emmerdale

29

What is the specific name for a stage production or film that is a total flop?

A: Goose
B: Ostrich
C: Turkey
D: Dodo

30

What is traditionally kissed in Ireland to endow the person with 'the gift of the gab'?

A: Blarney Stone
B: Blarney Judge
C: Blarney Policeman
D: Blarney Leprechaun

50:50 Go to page 455 Go to page 478 ? Answers on page 495

31

Which of these words can be added to 'knight' and 'neighbour' to make two new words?

A: Cowl
B: Veil
C: Shawl
D: Hood

32

What is a program code that replicates itself to cause damage, when deviously loaded into a computer?

A: Bacterium
B: T-cell
C: Databug
D: Virus

33

What was the title of Reeves and Mortimer's bizarre panel game?

A: Shooting Sticks
B: Shooting Stars
C: Shooting Rapids
D: Shooting Goals

34

What is a 'euphonium'?

A: Allergic reaction
B: Metallic element
C: Musical instrument
D: Flower

35

Which two related names do you associated with the band Oasis?

A: Pat and Gregory
B: Mark and Luke
C: Noel and Liam
D: Martin and Gary

50:50 Go to page 455 Go to page 478 ? Answers on page 495

7 ◆ £4,000

36

Who publishes the Highway Code on behalf of the UK government?

A: Department of Transport
B: AA
C: Metropolitan Police
D: RAC

37

Which American city was nicknamed Motown?

A: Chicago
B: Houston
C: Dallas
D: Detroit

38

What is a name for a regular walk taken to maintain good health?

A: Institutional
B: Constitutional
C: Destitutional
D: Restitutional

39

Which fruits are picked while 'brambling'?

A: Redcurrants
B: Blackberries
C: Greengages
D: Yellow tomatoes

40

Tony Benn is most associated with which political party?

A: Labour
B: Conservative
C: Liberal Democrat
D: Monster Raving Loony

50:50 Go to page 455 · Go to page 478 · ? Answers on page 495

7 ◆ £4,000

41

Which piece of riding tack is usually placed on the horse's head?

- A: Girth
- B: Stirrup
- C: Bridle
- D: Pommel

42

Which lord mysteriously disappeared in 1974 and is still wanted by the police?

- A: Lord Lichfield
- B: Lord Lucan
- C: Lord Linley
- D: Lord Leyton

43

What is the name of Margaret Thatcher's son, who got lost in the Sahara?

- A: Mike
- B: Maurice
- C: Mark
- D: Malcolm

44

Which of these is a horror film of the 1980s produced by Steven Spielberg?

- A: Phantom
- B: Ghoul
- C: Poltergeist
- D: Spectre

45

Which of these islands is in the Mediterranean?

- A: Corsica
- B: Madagascar
- C: Bermuda
- D: Jersey

50:50 Go to page 455 · Go to page 478 · ? Answers on page 495

7 ◆ £4,000

46

Which of these is an example of Britain's 'fauna'?

A: Orchid
B: Concrete
C: Hedgehog
D: Baobab

47

Which of these was devised by Einstein?

A: Pasteurisation
B: Heart transplants
C: Theory of relativity
D: Antibiotics

48

Who played the title role in the TV sitcom 'The Black Adder'?

A: John Cleese
B: Hugh Laurie
C: Rowan Atkinson
D: Mel Smith

49

Which of these is a TV comedy sketch show?

A: Smack the Kitten
B: Smack the Pony
C: Smack the Puppy
D: Smack the Foal

50

Miss Ellie was a matriarchal figure in which TV soap opera?

A: EastEnders
B: Dallas
C: Coronation Street
D: Dynasty

50:50 Go to page 455 · Go to page 478 · ? Answers on page 495

7 ◆ £4,000

51

James Cracknell is an Olympic gold medallist in which sport?

A: Shooting
B: Athletics
C: Rowing
D: Tennis

52

Which of these is a famous Australian outlaw?

A: Dick Turpin
B: Clyde Barrow
C: Ronnie Biggs
D: Ned Kelly

53

The River Plate is a major waterway on which continent?

A: South America
B: Africa
C: Europe
D: Asia

54

Which US city is known as 'the motor-city'?

A: Chicago
B: Detroit
C: New York
D: Washington

55

Complete the title of the Joan Crawford movie: 'Whatever Happened to Baby...'?

A: Joan
B: Jean
C: Jane
D: June

50:50 Go to page 455 Go to page 478 ? Answers on page 495

7 ◆ £4,000

56

Which of these is the title of a book by John Steinbeck?

A: East of Eden
B: West of Gethsemane
C: North of Sinai
D: South of Ararat

57

What type of animal was the mythological basilisk?

A: Lion
B: Reptile
C: Fish
D: Spider

58

Which of these is a book by Norman Mailer?

A: Silas Marner
B: The Naked and the Dead
C: Little Dorrit
D: Brideshead Revisited

59

What is the title of the 1978 film starring Richard Harris and Richard Burton?

A: The Wild Swans
B: The Wild Geese
C: The Wild Thrushes
D: The Wild Sparrows

60

In Greek mythology, Hades ruled which land?

A: Heaven
B: Sky
C: Sea
D: Hell

50:50 Go to page 455
Go to page 478
? Answers on page 495

7 ◆ £4,000

61

Who played Arkwright in 'Open All Hours'?

A: Ronnie Corbett
B: Richard O'Sullivan
C: Ronnie Barker
D: Geoffrey Palmer

62

What nationality is the fictional sleuth Hercule Poirot?

A: Belgian
B: American
C: Australian
D: Italian

63

Who was the manager of the England football team at the time of the 1990 World Cup?

A: Alf Ramsey
B: Bobby Robson
C: Kevin Keegan
D: Terry Venables

64

Which 1980s TV series starred Bruce Willis and Cybill Shepherd?

A: Sunburning
B: Moonshining
C: Sunlighting
D: Moonlighting

65

Which of these is an album by the Beatles?

A: Shotgun
B: Revolver
C: Pistol
D: Uzi

50:50 Go to page 455 Go to page 478 ? Answers on page 495

7 ◆ £4,000

66

Brian Jones was a member of which rock group?

A: The Beatles
B: The Rolling Stones
C: The Who
D: The Faces

67

What type of animal is the Australian kookaburra?

A: Kangaroo
B: Bear
C: Wild dog
D: Bird

68

Which of these is a former England cricket captain?

A: Ray Wilkins
B: Billy Wright
C: Mike Gatting
D: Bryan Robson

69

Which of these is the name of an esteemed British sculptor?

A: Henry Moore
B: Patrick Moore
C: Roger Moore
D: Bobby Moore

70

What is the first name of the singer Carreras?

A: Placido
B: Willard
C: Luciano
D: José

50:50 Go to page 455 Go to page 478 Answers on page 495

7 ◆ £4,000

71

Sean Kerly is an Olympic gold medallist in which sport?

- A: Rowing
- B: Athletics
- C: Hockey
- D: Tennis

72

Which actor starred in the 1984 film 'Footloose'?

- A: Karl Gammon
- B: Keith Bellies
- C: Karel Chop
- D: Kevin Bacon

73

In which year did Alfred Hitchcock die?

- A: 1960
- B: 1970
- C: 1980
- D: 1990

74

How much do the articles in a 'nickel-and-dime store' allegedly cost?

- A: 1 cent and 5 cents
- B: 5 cents and 10 cents
- C: 10 cents and 25 cents
- D: 25 cents and 1 dollar

75

What is the literal translation of the French word 'château'?

- A: Castle
- B: Church
- C: Cattery
- D: Palace

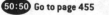

50:50 Go to page 455 | Go to page 478 | ? Answers on page 495

7 ◆ £4,000

76

Which of these words means a ramshackle dwelling place?

A: Huddle
B: Coddle
C: Hovel
D: Coven

77

If you were officially appointed to 'sit on the bench' what would your profession be?

A: Park-keeper
B: Judge
C: Weightlifter
D: Carpenter

78

With which form of transport is the DVLA associated?

A: Aviation
B: Sailing
C: Railways
D: Motoring

79

Americans hollow out pumpkins to make lanterns on which specific day?

A: New Year's Day
B: Independence Day
C: Christmas Day
D: Halloween

80

Which modern phrase refers to twenty-four hours of mishaps?

A: Bad hair day
B: Bitten fingernail day
C: Shut eye day
D: Dirty neck day

50:50 Go to page 455 · Go to page 478 · ? Answers on page 495

7 ◆ £4,000

81

What did children's character Noddy have on his blue hat?

A: Feather
B: Pompom
C: Dickie bow
D: Bell

82

What is the occupation of a seamstress?

A: Cooking
B: Ironing
C: Sewing
D: Lacemaking

83

Which of these was not one of the Monkees?

A: Peter Tork
B: David Cassidy
C: Mike Nesmith
D: Mickey Dolenz

84

Which popular quiz show features the 'Walk of Shame'?

A: Wheel of Fortune
B: Catchphrase
C: Blankety Blank
D: The Weakest Link

85

Which of these is a nonstick surface for pans?

A: Lycra
B: Perspex
C: Teflon
D: Velcro

50:50 Go to page 455 Go to page 478 ? Answers on page 495

7 ◆ £4,000

86

Which word links a type of paint and a delicate porcelain?

- A: Eggcup
- B: Egghead
- C: Eggshell
- D: Eggwhite

87

What would you be most likely to do with 'taffeta'?

- A: Eat it
- B: Drink it
- C: Hit it
- D: Wear it

88

What type of weapon is a 'flintlock'?

- A: Spear
- B: Club
- C: Gun
- D: Sword

89

Proverbially, which fish is used to catch a mackerel?

- A: Trout
- B: Carp
- C: Sprat
- D: Perch

90

A person with a wide range of interests is said to have what sort of tastes?

- A: Catholic
- B: Protestant
- C: Methodist
- D: Orthodox

50:50 Go to page 455 · Go to page 478 · Answers on page 495

7 ◆ £4,000

91

If you are making a sampler, what are you most likely to be doing?

A: Cooking
B: Painting
C: Fishing
D: Sewing

92

What is the technical name for a lie detector?

A: Polygon
B: Polymer
C: Polygraph
D: Polycarbonate

93

Which branch of science is concerned with matter and energy?

A: Biology
B: Chemistry
C: Physics
D: Mathematics

94

In which year did writer Agatha Christie die?

A: 1956
B: 1966
C: 1976
D: 1986

95

Crofter is a term for the owner or tenant of a small what?

A: Farm
B: Shop
C: Boat
D: Computer

50:50 Go to page 455 · Go to page 478 · ? Answers on page 495

7 ◆ £4,000

96

With which country is the archaeologist Howard Carter particularly associated?

A: Greece
B: Turkey
C: Italy
D: Egypt

97

Which of these is particularly associated with weddings at Gretna Green?

A: Bench
B: Anvil
C: Oven
D: Bucket

98

What is the oldest university in England?

A: Oxford
B: Cambridge
C: Bristol
D: York

99

Which of these is approximately 100 miles long?

A: Zambezi
B: Nile
C: Seine
D: Suez Canal

100

Which of these is a rank in the army?

A: Public
B: Private
C: Priory
D: Predicant

50:50 Go to page 455 Go to page 478 Answers on page 495

7 ◆ £4,000

101

Which actor starred in the film comedy 'When Harry Met Sally'?

A: Steve Martin
B: Charlie Sheen
C: Ted Danson
D: Billy Crystal

102

Which of these is a term for a bank cashier?

A: Lecturer
B: Reader
C: Speaker
D: Teller

103

Which Greek god shares his name with the US space programme for landing astronauts on the moon?

A: Zeus
B: Apollo
C: Hermes
D: Eros

104

What did Victoria famously say when at the age of 12 she was told she was heir to the throne?

A: I am not amused
B: Let them eat cake
C: I will be good
D: God save the queen

105

Which of these is a former 'Big Breakfast' presenter?

A: Donna Air
B: Donna Sky
C: Donna Wind
D: Donna Breeze

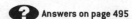

50:50 Go to page 455 · Go to page 478 · ? Answers on page 495

7 ◆ £4,000

106

Which of these phrases means 'the other way round'?

A: Habeas corpus
B: Vice versa
C: Etcetera
D: Verbatim

107

In the TV series 'Sesame Street', who is Bert's best friend?

A: Ernie
B: Eddie
C: Eric
D: Ellis

108

Which of these is a German dish?

A: Paella
B: Zabaglione
C: Bratwurst
D: Bouillabaisse

109

Which of these is the technical term for the disease commonly known as lockjaw?

A: Botulism
B: Trismus
C: Hydrophobia
D: Gingivitis

110

Who are you said to raise if you make a noisy disturbance?

A: Adam
B: Eve
C: Cain
D: Abel

50:50 Go to page 455 Go to page 478 ? Answers on page 495

7 ◆ £4,000

111

Which of these was a type of ammunition fired from a cannon?

- A: Appleshot
- B: Grapeshot
- C: Pearshot
- D: Cherryshot

112

According to the Bible, on what were the Ten Commandments written?

- A: Parchment
- B: Slate
- C: Papyrus
- D: Stone

113

Which of these is an early version of an invention?

- A: Protocol
- B: Proton
- C: Prototype
- D: Protostar

114

What is the usual flavour of the spirit raki?

- A: Lemon
- B: Aniseed
- C: Plum
- D: Coffee

115

Which of these is a type of lifting mechanism?

- A: Block and truckle
- B: Block and tackle
- C: Block and trickle
- D: Block and tickle

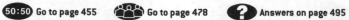

50:50 Go to page 455 · Go to page 478 · ? Answers on page 495

7 ◆ £4,000

116

Which Marx brother shares a name with a fashionable London club?

A: Chico
B: Groucho
C: Harpo
D: Zeppo

117

Which word refers to a rose which bears dense clusters of flowers?

A: Florin
B: Florida
C: Floribunda
D: Florid

118

Which treaty was agreed by European Community members in 1991?

A: Leiden Treaty
B: Maastricht Treaty
C: Rotterdam Treaty
D: Utrecht Treaty

119

The Henley Regatta takes place on which river?

A: Avon
B: Clyde
C: Severn
D: Thames

120

Who had a 1964 hit with 'Walk On By'?

A: Dionne Worcester
B: Dionne Warwick
C: Dionne Workington
D: Dionne Wimbledon

50:50 Go to page 455 Go to page 478 ? Answers on page 495

121

Which of these is a fielding position in cricket?

A: Bully
B: Fully
C: Gully
D: Tully

122

Which of these is a nine-sided figure?

A: Nanagon
B: Nenagon
C: Ninagon
D: Nonagon

123

What is the specific name for ceremonial robes worn by priests?

A: Vestiges
B: Vestas
C: Vestments
D: Vests

124

The Middle Eastern dish falafel is usually made from which pulse?

A: Red lentil
B: Chickpea
C: Mung bean
D: Aduki bean

125

In which kind of transport would you find an altimeter?

A: Aeroplane
B: Car
C: Train
D: Yacht

50:50 Go to page 455 · Go to page 478 · ? Answers on page 495

7 ◆ £4,000

126

Which of these is a diamond pattern often seen on socks?

A: Argyle
B: Kinross
C: Nairn
D: Roxburgh

127

Which of these is a dance in which a person may take another dancer's partner?

A: Excuse-me
B: Pardon-me
C: Help-me
D: Goodness-me

128

The term 'complexion' refers to which part of a person's body?

A: Hair
B: Skin
C: Teeth
D: Eyes

129

Which of these words means 'agree'?

A: Conceal
B: Concede
C: Concur
D: Conclude

130

What is the British name for what Americans call a 'checkroom'?

A: Bank vault
B: Attic
C: Outpatients
D: Left-luggage office

50:50 Go to page 455 Go to page 478 ? Answers on page 495

7 ◆ £4,000

131

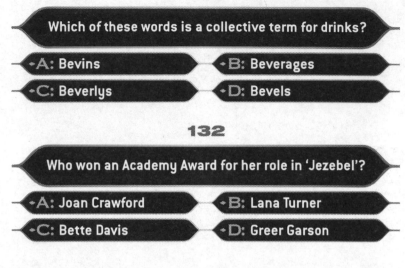

Which of these words is a collective term for drinks?

A: Bevins
B: Beverages
C: Beverlys
D: Bevels

132

Who won an Academy Award for her role in 'Jezebel'?

A: Joan Crawford
B: Lana Turner
C: Bette Davis
D: Greer Garson

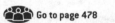

50:50 Go to page 455 Go to page 478 ? Answers on page 495

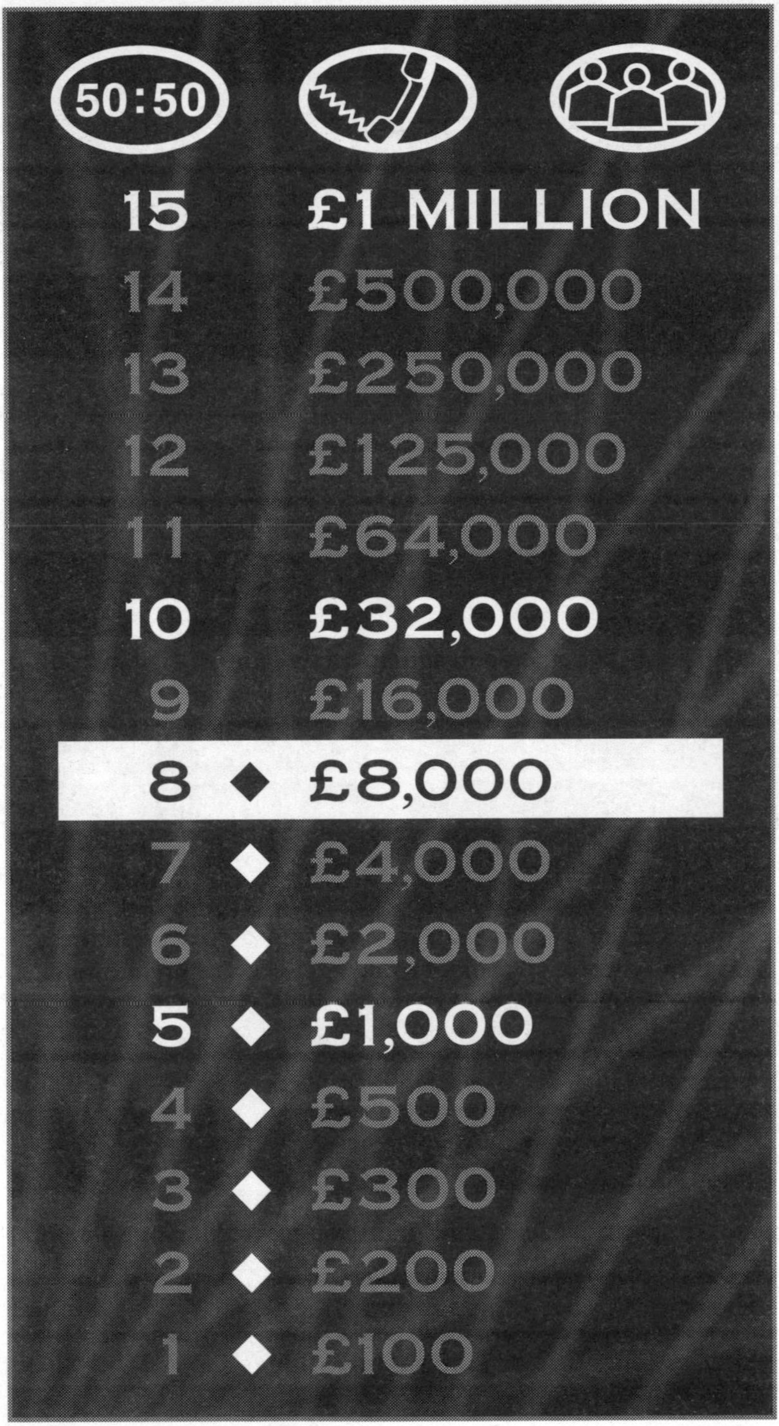
50:50
15 £1 MILLION
14 £500,000
13 £250,000
12 £125,000
11 £64,000
10 £32,000
9 £16,000
8 ◆ £8,000
7 ◆ £4,000
6 ◆ £2,000
5 ◆ £1,000
4 ◆ £500
3 ◆ £300
2 ◆ £200
1 ◆ £100

8 ◆ £8,000

1

Which country stretches for about 2,650 miles down the Pacific coast of South America?

A: Argentina
B: Chile
C: Peru
D: Brazil

2

Ian Hislop is particularly associated with which magazine?

A: Cricketer Monthly
B: Private Eye
C: The Lancet
D: British Medical Journal

3

Which of these is a dessert made from sponge, brandy, chocolate and mascarpone?

A: Eve's pudding
B: Tiramisu
C: Pavlova
D: Zabaglione

4

Which film is the sequel to 'Saturday Night Fever'?

A: Fame
B: Staying Alive
C: Get Shorty
D: Rocky

5

'I Wish It Could Be Christmas Every Day' was a hit single for which band in 1973?

A: Slade
B: The Shadows
C: The Pogues
D: Wizzard

50:50 Go to page 456 Go to page 480 ? Answers on page 496

6

Which surname links war poet Siegfried and hairdresser Vidal?

A: Owen
B: Sassoon
C: Grenfell
D: Sorley

7

What was the full first name of the actress famously known as Nell Gwyn?

A: Elizabeth
B: Eileen
C: Eleanor
D: Elsie

8

David Icke was once a TV presenter in which field?

A: Politics
B: Sport
C: Classical music
D: Science

9

Which of these is a book by W. Somerset Maugham?

A: Of Equine Bondage
B: Of Canine Bondage
C: Of Human Bondage
D: Of Bovine Bondage

10

Which of these is a famous symphony by the composer Dvořák?

A: From the New World
B: From the Old World
C: From the Third World
D: From the Sea World

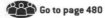

50:50 Go to page 456 Go to page 480 ? Answers on page 496

8 ◆ £8,000

11

In which year was Margaret Thatcher born?

A: 1915
B: 1925
C: 1935
D: 1945

12

The intestines of the body are part of which process in humans?

A: Respiration
B: Reproduction
C: Digestion
D: Perception

13

Which of these birds build their nests in holes in the banks of rivers and streams?

A: Woodpeckers
B: Kingfishers
C: Herons
D: Swifts

14

How many years are there in a 'septennium'?

A: Five
B: Seven
C: Nine
D: Eleven

15

What is a 'stickleback'?

A: Fish
B: Cactus
C: Poisonous plant
D: Toad

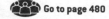

50:50 Go to page 456 Go to page 480 ? Answers on page 496

8 ◆ £8,000

16

What is stored for sale in an American 'lumberyard'?

- A: Paint
- B: Bricks
- C: Stone
- D: Timber

17

Who are the regular concert-goers that attend the annual Henry Wood series at the Royal Albert Hall?

- A: Promenaders
- B: Ramblers
- C: Strollers
- D: Walkers

18

Which of these 'easy' words is a noun?

- A: Easily
- B: Easier
- C: Easiness
- D: Easiest

19

How is the first person plural referred to, when a monarch uses it to speak about him or herself?

- A: The Regal Ours
- B: The Sovereign Us
- C: The Majestic Our
- D: The Royal We

20

Where does a military person wear an 'épaulette'?

- A: On the cap
- B: On the shoulder
- C: On the breast pocket
- D: On the cuff

50:50 Go to page 456 Go to page 480 ? Answers on page 496

21

Big Ben is part of which famous London landmark?

- A: Buckingham Palace
- B: Palace of Westminster
- C: Kensington Palace
- D: Lambeth Palace

22

Which insects are found in apiaries?

- A: Ants
- B: Bees
- C: Grasshoppers
- D: Mosquitoes

23

What were the names of the Martin Clunes and Neil Morrissey characters in 'Men Behaving Badly'?

- A: Gus and Teddy
- B: Gary and Tony
- C: Guy and Terry
- D: Greg and Toby

24

Which of these counties has no mutual border with Somerset?

- A: Wiltshire
- B: Dorset
- C: Devon
- D: West Sussex

25

Which of these is the title of a Noël Coward play?

- A: Hay Fever
- B: Hives
- C: Double Jointed
- D: Itching

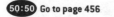

50:50 Go to page 456 · Go to page 480 · ? Answers on page 496

8 ◆ £8,000

26

Hawkeye Pierce and B.J. Hunnicut were characters in which popular TV series?

A: M*A*S*H
B: Happy Days
C: Mork and Mindy
D: The Honeymooners

27

Which of the original Spice Girls famously wore the Union Jack dress?

A: Posh Spice
B: Sporty Spice
C: Baby Spice
D: Ginger Spice

28

The 'hit parade' is an old-fashioned term for what?

A: Army drill
B: Suspect identification
C: Top cricketers
D: Pop charts

29

Which of these princes would call the Queen 'Grandma'?

A: Prince Edward
B: Prince Philip
C: Prince Michael
D: Prince Harry

30

What was the surname of Charles, the Scot who invented rubberised, waterproof cloth made into coats?

A: Sou'wester
B: Macintosh
C: Oilskin
D: Duffel

50:50 Go to page 456 | Go to page 480 | ? Answers on page 496

8 ◆ £8,000

31

Which sport is used to identify a letter in the phonetic alphabet?

A: Bowls
B: Golf
C: Hockey
D: Polo

32

What was the first name of the British prime minister Gladstone?

A: Walter
B: William
C: Wendell
D: Warwick

33

Brothers David and Jonathan Dimbleby are media presenters associated with which subject?

A: Sport
B: Gardening
C: Current affairs
D: Weather forecasting

34

What is 'Nine Men's Morris'?

A: Traditional dance
B: Board game
C: People carrier
D: Auction bidding

35

God spoke from a burning bush to which Old Testament character?

A: Abraham
B: Moses
C: Samuel
D: Jethro

50:50 Go to page 456 Go to page 480 ? Answers on page 496

8 ◆ £8,000

36

Who played Marty McFly in a series of successful films?

A: Harrison Ford
B: Mark Hamill
C: Steve Guttenberg
D: Michael J. Fox

37

'It's Not Unusual' was a UK number one hit single for which singer in 1965?

A: Perry Como
B: Tom Jones
C: Frankie Vaughan
D: Georgie Fame

38

Which of these is a name for someone who comes from Yorkshire?

A: Scouser
B: Geordie
C: Cockney
D: Tyke

39

Which TV presenter was the wife of Desmond Wilcox?

A: Carol Vorderman
B: Esther Rantzen
C: Vanessa Feltz
D: Gloria Hunniford

40

Who plays the slobbish Jim Royle in 'The Royle Family'?

A: Ricky Tomlinson
B: Bill Owen
C: Geoffrey Hughes
D: Tim Healy

50:50 Go to page 456 Go to page 480 ? Answers on page 496

8 ◆ £8,000

41

Which Kent town is part of Ann Widdecombe's constituency?

A: Sevenoaks
B: Maidstone
C: Tunbridge Wells
D: Margate

42

What is a 'periwinkle'?

A: Wig
B: Plant
C: Waterfall
D: Top hat

43

The Slater family, including Mo, Charlie and Zoe, are a feature of which TV soap opera?

A: EastEnders
B: Coronation Street
C: Emmerdale
D: Brookside

44

Which piece of music is used to herald the arrival of the US president?

A: Liberty Bell
B: Hail to the Chief
C: America the Beautiful
D: Land of Hope and Glory

45

Which of these is a magazine that specialises in photographs of celebrities relaxing at home?

A: Hiya!
B: Hey There!
C: Howdy!
D: Hello!

50:50 Go to page 456 Go to page 480 ? Answers on page 496

8 ◆ £8,000

46

Captain Jean-Luc Picard is a character in which cult TV show?

- A: Star Trek: The Next Generation
- B: Blake's 7
- C: Doctor Who
- D: Stargate SG-1

47

Which comedian is known for his association with the 'Badger Parade'?

- A: Harry Hill
- B: Mickey Mountain
- C: Peter Peak
- D: Irvine Incline

48

Who is the host of the TV panel show 'Never Mind the Buzzcocks'?

- A: Nick Hancock
- B: Mark Lamarr
- C: Jonathan Ross
- D: Jack Dee

49

'The Wailers' were the backing group of which reggae singer?

- A: Desmond Dekker
- B: Bob Marley
- C: Jimmy Cliff
- D: Boris Gardner

50

Robbie Fowler captained which football team in 2001?

- A: Liverpool
- B: Manchester United
- C: Arsenal
- D: Tottenham Hotspur

50:50 Go to page 456 Go to page 480 ? Answers on page 496

8 ◆ £8,000

51

The country of Togo forms part of which continent?

A: Africa
B: South America
C: Asia
D: Australia

52

Which football team won the FA Cup, Worthington Cup and UEFA Cup in 2001?

A: Manchester United
B: Liverpool
C: Chelsea
D: Sunderland

53

Jack Sugden, played by Clive Hornby, is a major character in which TV soap?

A: Emmerdale
B: EastEnders
C: Brookside
D: Coronation Street

54

Sheffield is a city in which county?

A: South Yorkshire
B: Lancashire
C: Cheshire
D: Durham

55

Which of these is a well-known play by Eugene O'Neill?

A: The Gasman Cometh
B: The Fishman Cometh
C: The Henman Cometh
D: The Iceman Cometh

50:50 Go to page 456 Go to page 480 ? Answers on page 496

8 ◆ £8,000

56

'Saturday Night's Alright For Fighting' was a UK top ten single for whom in 1973?

A: David Bowie
B: Elton John
C: Peter Frampton
D: David Essex

57

Kingston upon Hull is located at the junction of the Hull river, and which other?

A: Humber
B: Ouse
C: Severn
D: Thames

58

What is the name of the lead singer of the rock band Motorhead?

A: Bono
B: Fish
C: Lemmy
D: The Edge

59

Dictionary Corner is a feature of which TV show?

A: Countdown
B: Fifteen to One
C: 100%
D: Watercolour Challenge

60

Which of these is a play by Arthur Miller?

A: Death of a Milkman
B: Death of a Postman
C: Death of a Salesman
D: Death of a Foreman

50:50 Go to page 456 Go to page 480 ? Answers on page 496

8 ◆ £8,000

61

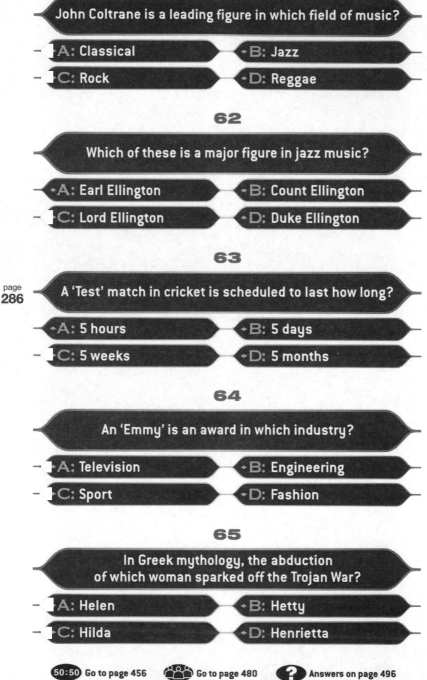

John Coltrane is a leading figure in which field of music?

A: Classical
B: Jazz
C: Rock
D: Reggae

62

Which of these is a major figure in jazz music?

A: Earl Ellington
B: Count Ellington
C: Lord Ellington
D: Duke Ellington

63

A 'Test' match in cricket is scheduled to last how long?

A: 5 hours
B: 5 days
C: 5 weeks
D: 5 months

64

An 'Emmy' is an award in which industry?

A: Television
B: Engineering
C: Sport
D: Fashion

65

In Greek mythology, the abduction of which woman sparked off the Trojan War?

A: Helen
B: Hetty
C: Hilda
D: Henrietta

50:50 Go to page 456 Go to page 480 ? Answers on page 496

66

Who is the arch-enemy of the fictional hero Flash Gordon?

A: Lex Luthor
B: The Mekon
C: Ming the Merciless
D: Professor Moriarty

67

Phil 'The Power' Taylor is a world champion in which sport?

A: Snooker
B: Darts
C: Bowling
D: Pool

68

Which of these is a brandy made from apples?

A: Absinthe
B: Calvados
C: Advocaat
D: Madeira

69

What does the word 'blithe' mean?

A: Downbeat
B: Happy
C: Preachy
D: Talented

70

In Roman mythology, the god Janus was depicted with two... what?

A: Tails
B: Antlers
C: Faces
D: Wings

50:50 Go to page 456 Go to page 480 ? Answers on page 496

8 ◆ £8,000

71

Which dog found the stolen World Cup in 1966, when England became champions?

- A: Chutney
- B: Saucy
- C: Pickles
- D: Pepper

72

What is the correct English spelling for this word?

- A: Humourous
- B: Humourus
- C: Humoros
- D: Humorous

73

Which of these 'electric' words is not a noun?

- A: Electrician
- B: Electron
- C: Electrode
- D: Electrify

74

Which London street of offices is sometimes used to mean the British Government?

- A: Whitehall
- B: Piccadilly
- C: Pall Mall
- D: Embankment

75

Who starred in 'The Stud', a film based on the book written by her sister?

- A: Julie Andrews
- B: Joan Collins
- C: Linda Evans
- D: Shirley MacLaine

50:50 Go to page 456 Go to page 480 ? Answers on page 496

8 ◆ £8,000

76

The four heads sculpted out of the rock at Mount Rushmore in South Dakota are of whom?

- A: Cavalry soldiers
- B: Indian chiefs
- C: US presidents
- D: Pilgrim fathers

77

What type of food is a 'rollmop'?

- A: Jam sponge
- B: Pickled fish
- C: Smoked sausage
- D: Blue cheese

78

Adrian Edmondson and Rik Mayall starred as two no-hopers, Eddie and Richie, in which TV sitcom?

- A: Derrière
- B: Behind
- C: Bottom
- D: Butt

79

What is a 'kittiwake'?

- A: Nocturnal moth
- B: Seabird
- C: Wild cat
- D: Meadow flower

80

In Britain, what is a slang name for a donkey?

- A: Minx
- B: Moggy
- C: Moke
- D: Mutt

50:50 Go to page 456 · Go to page 480 · ? Answers on page 496

8 ◆ £8,000

81

What was the first name of former US President Eisenhower?

A: Dwayne
B: Dwight
C: Delroy
D: Duke

82

Which process takes the salt out of seawater?

A: Desalination
B: Infiltration
C: Decompression
D: Infusion

83

On which continent is the River Niger?

A: Asia
B: North America
C: Africa
D: Australia

84

A 'derrick' is a type of what?

A: Crane
B: Code
C: Curry
D: Chisel

85

Who starred with Brad Pitt in the 2001 film 'The Mexican'?

A: Sandra Bullock
B: Penélope Cruz
C: Julia Roberts
D: Cameron Diaz

50:50 Go to page 456 Go to page 480 ? Answers on page 496

8 ◆ £8,000

86

Carol Smillie joined which TV show as an assistant in 1989?

- A: Blockbusters
- B: Wheel of Fortune
- C: The Krypton Factor
- D: The Generation Game

87

Which musical features the song 'All That Jazz'?

- A: Chicago
- B: New York
- C: Orlando
- D: Las Vegas

88

Which of these horse races is traditionally run at Doncaster?

- A: The Derby
- B: St Leger
- C: Grand National
- D: One Thousand Guineas

89

Francis Rossi and Rick Parfitt are members of which rock group?

- A: Deep Purple
- B: Status Quo
- C: Slade
- D: Def Leppard

90

Which town is the home of Whipsnade Zoo?

- A: Dunstable
- B: Dover
- C: Dartford
- D: Doncaster

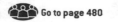

50:50 Go to page 456 Go to page 480 ? Answers on page 496

8 ◆ £8,000

91

As what is Chris Bonington most famous?

A: Cyclist
B: Mountaineer
C: Swimmer
D: Yachtsman

92

In which of these years was a census not done in the UK?

A: 1911
B: 1921
C: 1931
D: 1941

93

Charles Ryder is the central character in which novel?

A: The Heart of Midlothian
B: The Old Curiosity Shop
C: Wuthering Heights
D: Brideshead Revisited

94

In which country was Audrey Hepburn born?

A: France
B: Russia
C: Italy
D: Belgium

95

From which creature does the pigment 'sepia' come?

A: Red-spotted newt
B: Sea anemone
C: Ladybird
D: Cuttlefish

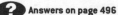

50:50 Go to page 456 Go to page 480 ? Answers on page 496

96

What is the accepted abbreviation for Oxfordshire?

A: Oxol
B: Oxot
C: Oxod
D: Oxon

97

What is the meaning of the adjective 'noxious'?

A: Pretty
B: Arrogant
C: Poisonous
D: Loud

98

Which term means to laugh at an inopportune moment whilst acting on stage?

A: Body
B: Torso
C: Cadaver
D: Corpse

99

What was the subject of the long-running TV show 'Pot Black'?

A: Cookery
B: Potholing
C: Bowls
D: Snooker

100

Which of these won an Oscar for the 1977 film 'Julia'?

A: Julie Walters
B: Glenda Jackson
C: Julie Christie
D: Vanessa Redgrave

50:50 Go to page 456 Go to page 480 ? Answers on page 496

8 ◆ £8,000

101

Grace Van Owen and Victor Sifuentes were characters in which TV show?

A: Philadelphia Police
B: Detroit Dentistry
C: Massachusetts Medicine
D: LA Law

102

In which country did balsamic vinegar originate?

A: France
B: Japan
C: India
D: Italy

103

Which line on the London Underground map is yellow?

A: Bakerloo
B: Central
C: Circle
D: Northern

104

What type of creature is a 'basenji'?

A: Rabbit
B: Dog
C: Tortoise
D: Parrot

105

Mark Phillips is the ex-husband of which member of the royal family?

A: Princess Margaret
B: Duchess of Kent
C: Princess Royal
D: Duchess of York

50:50 Go to page 456 · Go to page 480 · ? Answers on page 496

8 ◆ £8,000

106

What is the first year of Samuel Pepys's famous diary?

- A: 1460
- B: 1560
- C: 1660
- D: 1760

107

Which of these was a hit for Frankie Goes to Hollywood?

- A: Two Hearts
- B: Two People
- C: Two Tribes
- D: Two Thoughts

108

'Gone With The Wind' is a novel about which Civil War?

- A: American
- B: Spanish
- C: English
- D: Russian

109

Which of these is a Russian prison camp?

- A: Guilder
- B: Gulf
- C: Gulag
- D: Gully

110

Britain's M62 motorway crosses which range of hills?

- A: Cheviots
- B: Malverns
- C: Pennines
- D: Quantocks

50:50 Go to page 456 Go to page 480 ? Answers on page 496

8 ◆ £8,000

111

Which of these US Presidents served only one term of office?

A: Bill Clinton
B: George Bush
C: Ronald Reagan
D: Dwight Eisenhower

112

Who played Mrs Slocombe in 'Are You Being Served?'?

A: Beryl Reid
B: Mollie Sugden
C: Dora Bryan
D: Sheila Hancock

113

Benny the Ball was a companion of which cartoon character?

A: Deputy Dawg
B: Penelope Pitstop
C: Top Cat
D: Yogi Bear

114

What is the name for the conducting wire in an electric light bulb?

A: Condiment
B: Filament
C: Ligament
D: Sentiment

115

Which fabric is often used to describe a series of lies?

A: Gauze
B: Silk
C: Lace
D: Tissue

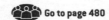

50:50 Go to page 456 Go to page 480 ? Answers on page 496

8 ◆ £8,000

116

Who played Bobbie in the 1970 film of 'The Railway Children'?

A: Jenny Agutter
B: Susan George
C: Lesley-Anne Down
D: Liza Goddard

117

In Shakespeare's play, how is Macbeth's wife referred to?

A: Queen Macbeth
B: Lady Macbeth
C: Dame Macbeth
D: Mrs Macbeth

118

Which English county had its own language which was closely related to Welsh?

A: Cornwall
B: Durham
C: Warwickshire
D: Yorkshire

119

Who starred in the Billy Wilder film 'Sunset Boulevard'?

A: Greta Garbo
B: Jean Harlow
C: Gloria Swanson
D: Hedy Lamarr

120

What does the word 'feasible' mean?

A: Edible
B: Readable
C: Possible
D: Liveable

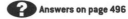

50:50 Go to page 456 · Go to page 480 · ? Answers on page 496

8 ◆ £8,000

121

Which of these would a barrister be most likely to do in a court of law?

A: Cross-hatch
B: Cross reference
C: Cross-examine
D: Cross-dress

122

What kind of wine are port, sherry and marsala?

A: Fortified
B: Petrified
C: Dignified
D: Sanctified

123

Complete the title of the classic American novel: 'The Last of the...'?

A: Apaches
B: Cherokees
C: Mohicans
D: Sioux

124

Which group is best known as the backing singers for Gladys Knight?

A: Crystals
B: Pips
C: Supremes
D: Vandellas

50:50 Go to page 456 · Go to page 480 · Answers on page 496

15		£1 MILLION
14		£500,000
13		£250,000
12		£125,000
11		£64,000
10		£32,000
9	◆	£16,000
8	◆	£8,000
7	◆	£4,000
6	◆	£2,000
5	◆	£1,000
4	◆	£500
3	◆	£300
2	◆	£200
1	◆	£100

9 ◆ £16,000

1

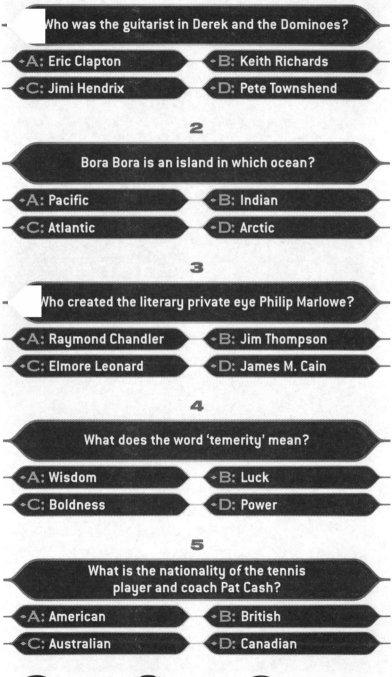

Who was the guitarist in Derek and the Dominoes?

- A: Eric Clapton
- B: Keith Richards
- C: Jimi Hendrix
- D: Pete Townshend

2

Bora Bora is an island in which ocean?

- A: Pacific
- B: Indian
- C: Atlantic
- D: Arctic

3

Who created the literary private eye Philip Marlowe?

- A: Raymond Chandler
- B: Jim Thompson
- C: Elmore Leonard
- D: James M. Cain

4

What does the word 'temerity' mean?

- A: Wisdom
- B: Luck
- C: Boldness
- D: Power

5

What is the nationality of the tennis player and coach Pat Cash?

- A: American
- B: British
- C: Australian
- D: Canadian

50:50 Go to page 458 · Go to page 482 · ? Answers on page 496

9 ◆ £16,000

6

Which actor won an Oscar for his role in 'Rain Man'?

A: Robert De Niro
B: Gene Hackman
C: Al Pacino
D: Dustin Hoffman

7

Rip Van Winkle is the creation of which author?

A: Washington Irving
B: Jack London
C: William Faulkner
D: Ernest Hemingway

8

'Coward of the County' was a 1980 UK number one single for which singer?

A: Dolly Parton
B: Kenny Rogers
C: Tammy Wynette
D: Patsy Cline

9

In music, what does the word 'pianissimo' mean?

A: Very loud
B: Very fast
C: Very quiet
D: Very late

10

Who played the role of Margaret in 'One Foot in the Grave'?

A: Annette Crosbie
B: Patricia Routledge
C: Prunella Scales
D: Judi Dench

50:50 Go to page 458 Go to page 482 ? Answers on page 496

9 ◆ £16,000

11

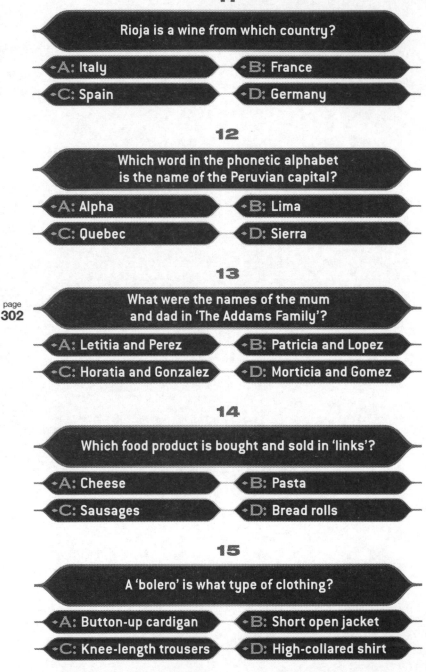

Rioja is a wine from which country?

- A: Italy
- B: France
- C: Spain
- D: Germany

12

Which word in the phonetic alphabet is the name of the Peruvian capital?

- A: Alpha
- B: Lima
- C: Quebec
- D: Sierra

13

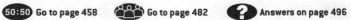

What were the names of the mum and dad in 'The Addams Family'?

- A: Letitia and Perez
- B: Patricia and Lopez
- C: Horatia and Gonzalez
- D: Morticia and Gomez

14

Which food product is bought and sold in 'links'?

- A: Cheese
- B: Pasta
- C: Sausages
- D: Bread rolls

15

A 'bolero' is what type of clothing?

- A: Button-up cardigan
- B: Short open jacket
- C: Knee-length trousers
- D: High-collared shirt

50:50 Go to page 458 Go to page 482 ? Answers on page 496

9 ◆ £16,000

16

What is the name of the submarine structure used as a bridge when the vessel is on the surface?

- A: Crow's nest
- B: Funnel
- C: Periscope
- D: Conning tower

17

Which of these flowers is the name of a marine animal, if prefixed by the word 'sea'?

- A: Daffodil
- B: Anemone
- C: Foxglove
- D: Dandelion

18

What type of fish is a 'beluga'?

- A: Trout
- B: Shark
- C: Sturgeon
- D: Pike

19

Which nickname was given to bulky rock singer Marvin Lee Aday by his high school football coach?

- A: Beef Cake
- B: Meat Loaf
- C: Pork Chop
- D: Buffalo Foot

20

In badminton, what must the shuttlecock hit on the opposite side to score?

- A: The net
- B: The ceiling
- C: Opponent's racquet
- D: The floor

50:50 Go to page 458 Go to page 482 ? Answers on page 496

9 ◆ £16,000

21

A true Cockney is someone who is born within the sound of what?

- A: Bow Bells
- B: Big Ben's Bells
- C: Bells of St Clements
- D: Jingle Bells

22

Which animals are associated with anything 'equestrian'?

- A: Dogs
- B: Horses
- C: Camels
- D: Cattle

23

A Muscovite resides in the capital city of which country?

- A: Austria
- B: Hungary
- C: Russia
- D: Spain

24

How high above the table is the net in table tennis?

- A: Six millimetres
- B: Six centimetres
- C: Six inches
- D: Six feet

25

What was the title of the first UK hit single for the Jimi Hendrix Experience?

- A: Hey Tim
- B: Hey Liz
- C: Hey Joe
- D: Hey Mike

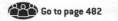

50:50 Go to page 458 Go to page 482 ? Answers on page 496

26

How many children feature in the title of a TV sitcom about the Porter family?

- A: 1 Point 5
- B: 2 Point 4
- C: 3 Point 3
- D: 4 Point 2

27

The name of which tool goes after 'Shepton' to make the placename of a Somerset town?

- A: Mallet
- B: Brace
- C: Clamp
- D: Sander

28

What is the star sign of someone born on Leap Year Day?

- A: Aquarius
- B: Capricorn
- C: Pisces
- D: Taurus

29

With which sport do you associate the name 'Aintree'?

- A: Formula 1
- B: Horse racing
- C: Cricket
- D: Golf

30

Samurai were members of a military caste in which country?

- A: Japan
- B: Egypt
- C: Mongolia
- D: Macedonia

50:50 Go to page 458 Go to page 482 ? Answers on page 496

9 ◆ £16,000

31

In 1984, Rajiv Gandhi succeeded his mother Indira as prime minister of which country?

- A: Afghanistan
- B: Pakistan
- C: Sri Lanka
- D: India

32

In which sport is a drop goal worth three points?

- A: Football
- B: Hockey
- C: Rugby union
- D: Basketball

33

Egypt is part of which continent?

- A: Europe
- B: Asia
- C: Africa
- D: South America

34

What was the subject of the theory formulated by Charles Darwin?

- A: Probability
- B: Evolution
- C: Big Bang
- D: Relativity

35

Which of these words is the surname of a former Yorkshire and England cricketer?

- A: Boycott
- B: Campaign
- C: Sanction
- D: Embargo

50:50 Go to page 458 Go to page 482 ? Answers on page 496

9 ◆ £16,000

36

In 'Star Wars', what species is Obi-Wan Kenobi?

A: Human
B: Anzati
C: Twi'lek
D: Firrereon

37

In which of these Bond movies did Ursula Andress appear as Honey Ryder?

A: Dr No
B: From Russia With Love
C: Tomorrow Never Dies
D: Goldfinger

38

'Platoon' is the title of a film set in which war?

A: World War II
B: Korean War
C: Vietnam War
D: Gulf War

39

Which breed of dog is a favourite of the Queen and her mother?

A: Cocker spaniel
B: Toy poodle
C: Welsh corgi
D: Jack Russell

40

What shape is the 'World' in the Terry Pratchett series of fantasy stories?

A: Oval
B: Ellipse
C: Disc
D: Geodesic dome

50:50 Go to page 458 Go to page 482 ? Answers on page 496

9 ◆ £16,000

41

How much wine is normally in a standard magnum bottle?

- A: 0.5 litre
- B: 1 litre
- C: 1.5 litres
- D: 2 litres

42

Fair Isle is a traditional design used in what?

- A: Bricklaying
- B: Stained glass windows
- C: Knitting
- D: Parquet flooring

43

Which of these is a play by George Bernard Shaw?

- A: Androcles and the Lion
- B: Androcles and the Tiger
- C: Androcles and the Gorilla
- D: Androcles and the Badger

44

'House of the Rising Sun' was a hit single for which group in the 1960s?

- A: Monsters
- B: Animals
- C: People
- D: Children

45

Which Shakespeare play is set in Denmark?

- A: Othello
- B: The Tempest
- C: Hamlet
- D: Romeo and Juliet

50:50 Go to page 458 Go to page 482 ? Answers on page 496

9 ◆ £16,000

46

'Urchin' is a dialect word for which creature?

- A: Shrew
- B: Hedgehog
- C: Tortoise
- D: Bat

47

What was the first name of the English physicist Faraday?

- A: James
- B: Graham
- C: David
- D: Michael

48

As what is John Tavener best known?

- A: Chef
- B: Racing driver
- C: Composer
- D: Journalist

49

Which of these is the name of a US state capital?

- A: Florida City
- B: Missouri City
- C: Oklahoma City
- D: Iowa City

50

Who plays the role of Fox Mulder in 'The X-Files'?

- A: David Duchovny
- B: Gillian Anderson
- C: Mitch Pileggi
- D: William B. Davis

50:50 Go to page 458 Go to page 482 Answers on page 496

9 ◆ £16,000

51

Which female's name is a county in the Republic of Ireland?

- A: Clare
- B: Shannon
- C: Bridie
- D: Kelly

52

Who wrote the TV sitcom 'Butterflies'?

- A: Carla Lane
- B: Johnny Speight
- C: John Sullivan
- D: Eric Chappell

53

'Retroussé' is a word used to describe which specific part of the body?

- A: Ear
- B: Nose
- C: Chin
- D: Thumb

54

In the US, what is the name for an ex-serviceman or woman, especially one who has seen active service?

- A: Vintager
- B: Venerable
- C: Vintner
- D: Veteran

55

What is the meaning of 'Papillon', the title of the famous novel by Henri Charrière?

- A: Butterfly
- B: Swallow
- C: Grasshopper
- D: Eel

50:50 Go to page 458 Go to page 482 ? Answers on page 496

9 ◆ £16,000

56

What was the former English name of Beijing, the capital of China?

- A: Peking
- B: Shenyang
- C: Shanghai
- D: Kunming

57

Who played Mr Hudson the butler in 'Upstairs, Downstairs'?

- A: Ian Bannen
- B: Gordon Jackson
- C: Kenneth More
- D: Derek Jacobi

58

What was the nickname for a fan of heavy-metal music?

- A: Hand-clapper
- B: Foot-stomper
- C: Head-banger
- D: Body-rocker

59

Which vegetable has a head formed by close-packed 'florets'?

- A: Cabbage
- B: Cauliflower
- C: Celery
- D: Lettuce

60

What is the title of Willy Russell's stage musical about a separated family?

- A: Blood Brothers
- B: Foster Parents
- C: Step Sisters
- D: God's Children

50:50 Go to page 458 Go to page 482 ? Answers on page 496

9 ◆ £16,000

61

Which 20th-century British king reigned without being crowned?

A: George V
B: George VI
C: Edward VII
D: Edward VIII

62

Napoleon was born in Ajaccio, the capital of which island?

A: Cyprus
B: Sardinia
C: Crete
D: Corsica

63

Which two rivers formed the name of a franchised ITV company that merged with YTV?

A: Tyne Tees
B: Tay Tweed
C: Thames Trent
D: Tamar Test

64

Who had a UK number one single in 2001 with 'It's Raining Men'?

A: Emma Bunton
B: S Club 7
C: Geri Halliwell
D: Destiny's Child

65

What do the letters in the magazine title 'GQ' stand for?

A: Gentlemen's Quarterly
B: Gentlemen's Quandary
C: Gentlemen's Query
D: Gentlemen's Quality

50:50 Go to page 458 · Ask the audience: Go to page 482 · ? Answers on page 496

9 ◆ £16,000

66

Which of these TV shows starred David Janssen?

A: Harry and the Hendersons
B: Harry Enfield and Chums
C: Harry O
D: Harry's Game

67

Bill Hickok is the principal male in which musical?

A: Calamity Jane
B: Sweet Charity
C: Annie Get Your Gun
D: Kiss Me Kate

68

What is the subtitle to Helen Fielding's second Bridget Jones book?

A: The Power of Reason
B: The Voice of Reason
C: The Edge of Reason
D: The Gift of Reason

69

Which Robbie Williams song contains the line 'We've got stars directing our faith'?

A: No Regrets
B: Angels
C: Millennium
D: Let Me Entertain You

70

In which county is the town of Bury St Edmunds?

A: Kent
B: Suffolk
C: West Sussex
D: Buckinghamshire

50:50 Go to page 458 Go to page 482 ? Answers on page 496

9 ◆ £16,000

71

'A Mother's Gift', published in 2001, is a novel by which singer and her mother?

- A: Britney Spears
- B: Billie Piper
- C: Christina Aguilera
- D: Geri Halliwell

72

What is an 'oystercatcher'?

- A: Plant
- B: Fish
- C: Bird
- D: Tree

73

Who is the husband of 'Cheers' actress Rhea Perlman?

- A: Bob Hoskins
- B: Jeremy Irons
- C: Danny DeVito
- D: Steven Spielberg

74

In DIY, what is the main purpose of a bradawl?

- A: Forming right angles
- B: Removing paint
- C: Boring holes
- D: Strengthening joints

75

On which county's coast is the ruined castle of Tintagel?

- A: Kent
- B: Northumberland
- C: Lancashire
- D: Cornwall

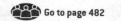

50:50 Go to page 458 Go to page 482 ? Answers on page 496

9 ◆ £16,000

76

With which of these TV series is Henry Winkler most associated?

A: Happy Days
B: Bewitched
C: Who's The Boss?
D: Diff'rent Strokes

77

Which of these is a play by Mike Leigh?

A: Agatha's Party
B: Andrea's Party
C: Adelaide's Party
D: Abigail's Party

78

In which county is Luton airport?

A: Hertfordshire
B: Northamptonshire
C: Essex
D: Bedfordshire

79

Which of these literary characters is associated with the game 'quidditch'?

A: Billy Bunter
B: Harry Potter
C: Charlie Bucket
D: Christopher Robin

80

In the 'Peanuts' cartoon strip, who is the brother of Lucy?

A: Charlie Brown
B: Linus
C: Pig Pen
D: Schroeder

50:50 Go to page 458 Go to page 482 ? Answers on page 496

9 ◆ £16,000

81

With which London theatre is Shakespeare most associated?

A: The Orb | B: The Sphere
C: The Ball | D: The Globe

82

Tara Newley is the daughter of which British actress?

A: Jane Birkin | B: Julie Christie
C: Joan Collins | D: Judi Dench

83

Which of these lines of latitude runs through the Galapagos Islands?

A: Antarctic Circle | B: Tropic of Cancer
C: Equator | D: Arctic Circle

84

What type of living thing is bamboo?

A: Grass | B: Fern
C: Fungus | D: Conifer

85

In which country was the sitcom 'It Ain't Half Hot, Mum' set?

A: Burma | B: India
C: Malaysia | D: Vietnam

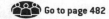

50:50 Go to page 458 Go to page 482 ? Answers on page 496

9 ◆ £16,000

86

On a musical score, 'p' is the abbreviation for what?

A: Pizzicato
B: Piano
C: Pianissimo
D: Pedalo

87

What did the 'R' of 'USSR' stand for?

A: Regions
B: Royal
C: Russia
D: Republics

88

Which of the Beatles composed the classical work 'Standing Stone'?

A: George Harrison
B: John Lennon
C: Paul McCartney
D: Ringo Starr

89

The abbreviation CAD stands for 'computer-aided...' what?

A: Digitalisation
B: Design
C: Diskettes
D: Downloading

90

Which TV presenter had a series of 'Weird Weekends'?

A: Melvyn Bragg
B: John Craven
C: Bob Monkhouse
D: Louis Theroux

50:50 Go to page 458 · Go to page 482 · ? Answers on page 496

9 ◆ £16,000

91

What goes after 'Hello' to make the title of a musical based on Thornton Wilder's play 'The Matchmaker'?

- A: Dolly
- B: Polly
- C: Holly
- D: Molly

92

Which spirit is the basis of a mai tai cocktail?

- A: Gin
- B: Rum
- C: Whisky
- D: Vodka

93

What is required to play a game of 'pinochle'?

- A: Marbles
- B: Dice
- C: Cards
- D: Dominoes

94

Who wrote 'The Children of the New Forest'?

- A: C. S. Forester
- B: C. S. Lewis
- C: Captain W. E. Johns
- D: Captain Marryat

95

In Britain, what is the maximum length of a parliament before a general election must be called?

- A: Three years
- B: Four years
- C: Five years
- D: Six years

50:50 Go to page 458 Go to page 482 ? Answers on page 496

9 ◆ £16,000

96

Which of these is essential for the Japanese pastime of 'ikebana'?

A: Paper
B: Teapot
C: Flowers
D: Pen

97

What is the US equivalent of the game show 'Family Fortunes'?

A: Family Feud
B: Family Friendships
C: Family Fate
D: Family Fling

98

Which of these words means 'urgent'?

A: Exigent
B: Evident
C: Elegant
D: Erudite

99

Which first name is shared by the wives of Tim Henman and Greg Rusedski?

A: Bunty
B: Lucy
C: Mary
D: Daisy

100

What was the surname of the American frontiersman known by the first name Davy?

A: Earp
B: Crockett
C: Boone
D: Clanton

50:50 Go to page 458 · Go to page 482 · ? Answers on page 496

9 ◆ £16,000

101

Which Beatles song was issued as a double A-side with 'Something'?

- A: Come Together
- B: Get Back
- C: Hey Jude
- D: Paperback Writer

102

The young of which of these birds is known as a 'poult'?

- A: Eagle
- B: Ostrich
- C: Seagull
- D: Turkey

103

Which word is used to denote things from the reign of James I?

- A: Jacobian
- B: Jacobean
- C: Jacobite
- D: Jamesian

104

What kind of object is most likely to be described as 'clinker-built'?

- A: Boat
- B: Cake
- C: Bridge
- D: Wall

105

Ngorongoro in Tanzania is known for which specific feature?

- A: Crater
- B: Glacier
- C: Forest
- D: Waterfall

50:50 Go to page 458 · Go to page 482 · ? Answers on page 496

9 ◆ £16,000

106

In which century did Cleopatra, the lover of Mark Antony, live?

- A: 10th century BC
- B: 1st century BC
- C: 1st century AD
- D: 10th century AD

107

In the TV series 'Friends', what is the name of Phoebe's twin sister?

- A: Agatha
- B: Joanna
- C: Ursula
- D: Fiona

108

What is the capital of the US state of Nevada?

- A: Carson City
- B: Manning City
- C: Tarbuck City
- D: Forsyth City

109

From which Disney animation did the song 'When You Wish Upon A Star' originally come?

- A: Pinocchio
- B: Cinderella
- C: Dumbo
- D: The Jungle Book

110

Which of these countries does not share a border with the Czech Republic?

- A: Hungary
- B: Poland
- C: Germany
- D: Austria

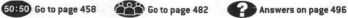

50:50 Go to page 458 Go to page 482 ? Answers on page 496

9 ◆ £16,000

111

Who set up the company Maverick Records in 1992?

A: Celine Dion
B: Madonna
C: Dolly Parton
D: Whitney Houston

112

Which US president shares a name with a major port in Ohio?

A: Jackson
B: Cleveland
C: Polk
D: Tyler

113

What nationality is the actress Penélope Cruz?

A: Cuban
B: Spanish
C: Mexican
D: Costa Rican

114

Which of these Shakespeare tragedies is set chiefly in Verona?

A: Othello
B: Cymbeline
C: Romeo and Juliet
D: Troilus and Cressida

115

What is a 'corniche'?

A: Centre of a flower
B: Coastal road
C: Cattle ranch
D: Circus horse

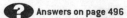

50:50 Go to page 458 Go to page 482 ? Answers on page 496

9 ◆ £16,000

116

Which royal event occurred in the same year that Virginia Wade won her Wimbledon singles title?

- A: Queen's Coronation
- B: Queen's Silver Jubilee
- C: Prince Edward's birth
- D: Prince Charles's marriage

50:50 Go to page 458 Go to page 482 ? Answers on page 496

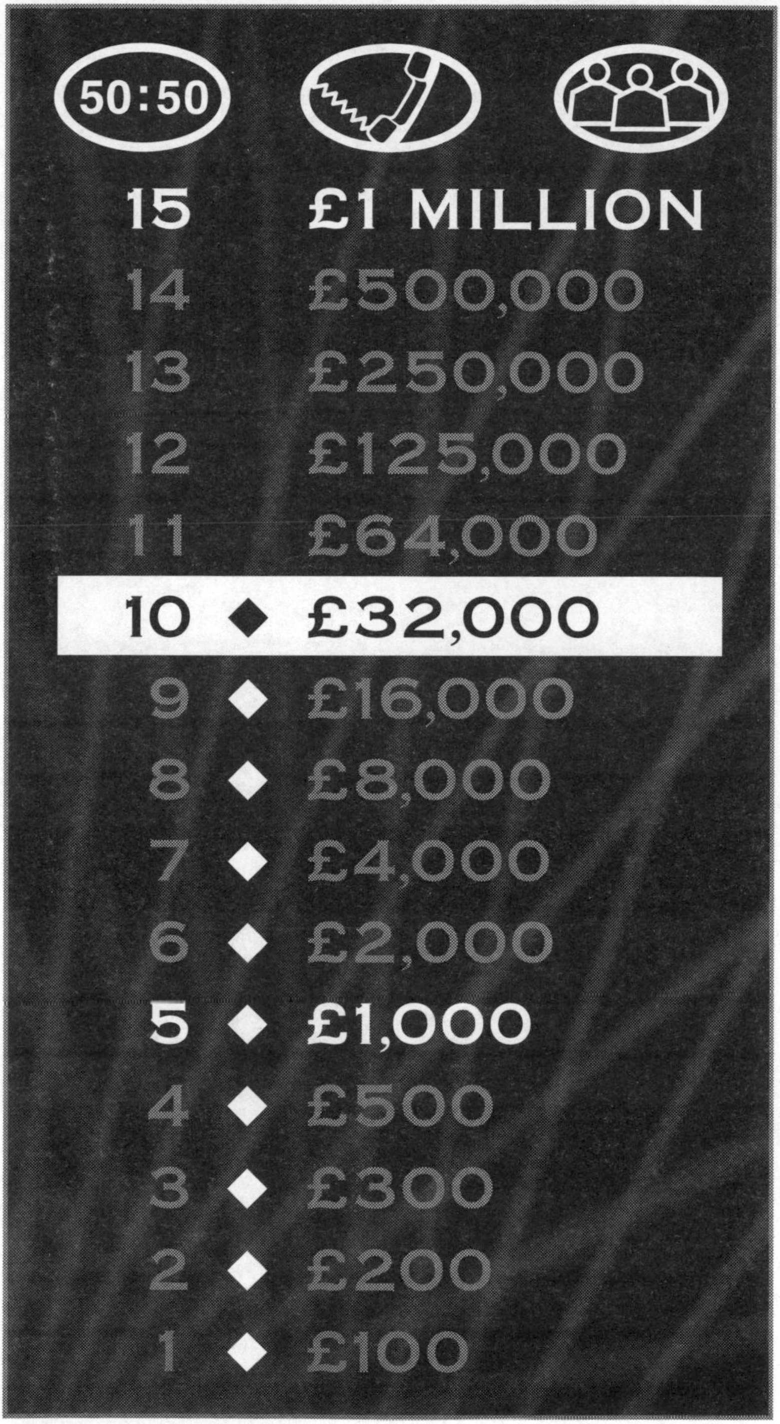
50:50
15 £1 MILLION
14 £500,000
13 £250,000
12 £125,000
11 £64,000
10 ◆ £32,000
9 ◆ £16,000
8 ◆ £8,000
7 ◆ £4,000
6 ◆ £2,000
5 ◆ £1,000
4 ◆ £500
3 ◆ £300
2 ◆ £200
1 ◆ £100

10 ◆ £32,000

1

Which of these is a film written, produced and directed by the Coen brothers?

- A: The Big Sleep
- B: The Big Easy
- C: The Big Red One
- D: The Big Lebowski

2

In Hawaii, what is Mauna Loa?

- A: Airport
- B: Volcano
- C: Parliament
- D: Coral reef

3

If you 'repugn' an idea, you...?

- A: Agree with it
- B: Expand upon it
- C: Write it down
- D: Disagree with it

4

On which continent was Queen Anne's War fought?

- A: North America
- B: Antarctica
- C: Africa
- D: Asia

5

What does the Latin phrase 'tempus fugit' mean?

- A: Know your enemy
- B: Mind and body
- C: Time flies
- D: For the gods

50:50 Go to page 459 Go to page 483 ? Answers on page 497

10 ◆ £32,000

6

John Inverdale is a TV presenter specialising in which type of programme?

A: Politics
B: Sport
C: Music
D: Food

7

What is the first name of the Shakespeare character named Falstaff?

A: James
B: Jonah
C: John
D: Jason

8

Which song topped the charts for the Wurzels in 1976?

A: Combine Harvester
B: Tractor
C: Crop Sprayer
D: Ditch Digger

9

The Ligurian Sea is part of which larger body of water?

A: South China Sea
B: Tasman Sea
C: Mediterranean Sea
D: North Sea

10

Who played Jim Hacker in the TV sitcom 'Yes, Minister'?

A: Nigel Hawthorne
B: Derek Fowlds
C: Paul Eddington
D: Nigel Havers

50:50 Go to page 459 Go to page 483 ? Answers on page 497

11

Margaret Court was a major 1960s star in which sport?

A: Squash
B: Athletics
C: Tennis
D: Swimming

12

Which cake is a marzipan-covered sponge that cuts into pink and yellow chequered squares?

A: Strasbourg
B: Nuremburg
C: Hamburg
D: Battenberg

13

How many sides has a trapezium?

A: Three
B: Four
C: Six
D: Ten

14

According to the saying, what 'repeats itself'?

A: Geography
B: Biology
C: History
D: Chemistry

15

Which type of pan do Americans call a 'skillet'?

A: Steamer
B: Saucepan
C: Frying pan
D: Pressure cooker

50:50 Go to page 459 Go to page 483 ? Answers on page 497

10 ◆ £32,000

16

The College of Cardinals is the group that elects whom?

A: Primate of All England
B: The Pope
C: King of Morocco
D: Sheik of Araby

17

What type of ingredient is 'rocket'?

A: Root vegetable
B: Podded vegetable
C: Green vegetable
D: Tuberous vegetable

18

Which abbreviation identifies a UK representative elected to the EU Parliament?

A: EMP
B: PEM
C: MPE
D: MEP

19

With what do you associate the name Billy Butlin?

A: Travelling circus
B: Stage musicals
C: Holiday camps
D: Beauty contests

20

Dunes are mounds and ridges of drifted... what?

A: Snow
B: Ash
C: Sand
D: Dust

50:50 Go to page 459 · Go to page 483 · ? Answers on page 497

10 ◆ £32,000

21

Which of these is the name of the Royal Highland Regiment of the British Army?

A: The Black Watch
B: The Tartan Guard
C: The Red Hussars
D: The Blue Lancers

22

Mike Brearley captained England in which sport?

A: Golf
B: Yachting
C: Tennis
D: Cricket

23

What is a 'bittern'?

A: Harbour bollard
B: Gold tooth filling
C: Wading bird
D: Hard-shelled nut

24

What is the chemical symbol for the metallic element of the medal given to an Olympic champion?

A: Au
B: Or
C: Go
D: Ag

25

Which Martin Scorsese film features the life of the FBI informant Henry Hill?

A: Raging Bull
B: GoodFellas
C: Mean Streets
D: Casino

50:50 Go to page 459 Go to page 483 ? Answers on page 497

10 ◆ £32,000

26

What do the two letter 'F's stand for in the acronym MAFF?

- A: Food and Farming
- B: Farming and Fuel
- C: Fuel and Fisheries
- D: Fisheries and Food

27

Germany has a coastline on the Baltic and which other Sea?

- A: Norwegian Sea
- B: North Sea
- C: Barents Sea
- D: Mediterranean Sea

28

Who was the lead singer of the pop group Roxy Music?

- A: Barry Clipper
- B: Byron Liner
- C: Billy Tanker
- D: Bryan Ferry

29

Which former 'EastEnders' actress had a 'Perfect Moment' chart hit in 1999?

- A: Letitia Dean
- B: Susan Tully
- C: Martine McCutcheon
- D: Gillian Taylforth

30

What does the phrase 'Auld lang syne' refer to?

- A: James VI
- B: Church of Scotland
- C: Old times
- D: Old Father Time

50:50 Go to page 459 | Go to page 483 | ? Answers on page 497

10 ◆ £32,000

31

Who played Lurcio in 'Up Pompeii'?

A: Frankie Howerd
B: Charles Hawtrey
C: Kenneth Williams
D: Sid James

32

What is the first name of the communist who led the coup in Cuba in 1959?

A: Manuel
B: Miguel
C: Fidel
D: Rafael

33

The young of which bird are always brought up by foster-parents?

A: Warbler
B: Ostrich
C: Penguin
D: Cuckoo

34

What is the technical name for an insect's feeler?

A: Spiracle
B: Proboscis
C: Carapace
D: Antenna

35

Sark is part of which British island group?

A: Channel Islands
B: Hebrides
C: Shetlands
D: Scilly Isles

50:50 Go to page 459 Go to page 483 ? Answers on page 497

10 ◆ £32,000

36

What is a 'chorizo'?

- A: Polish dog breed
- B: Desert cactus
- C: Spanish sausage
- D: Russian fur hat

37

Who was Larry Grayson's assistant on 'The Generation Game' in the 1970s and 1980s?

- A: Pam St Clement
- B: Jill St John
- C: Susan St James
- D: Isla St Clair

38

If a drink is described 'au lait', what has it got in it?

- A: Sugar
- B: Ice cubes
- C: Milk
- D: Slice of lemon

39

Which of these is the correct English spelling?

- A: Bazaar
- B: Baazar
- C: Bazzar
- D: Baazzar

40

What nationality was the three-times World Champion Formula 1 driver Ayrton Senna?

- A: Belgian
- B: Austrian
- C: Italian
- D: Brazilian

50:50 Go to page 459 Go to page 483 ? Answers on page 497

10 ◆ £32,000

41

In word processing, which term is used for changing the position of a block of text?

A: Trim and stick
B: Cut and paste
C: Snip and glue
D: Chop and change

42

Complete the title of the Willam Golding book about a group of boys: 'Lord of the…'?

A: Rings
B: Flies
C: Isles
D: Dance

43

Harwich, the ferry port, is in which English county?

A: Kent
B: Suffolk
C: Essex
D: East Sussex

44

Which of these is the name of a Channel Island?

A: Olderney
B: Ulderney
C: Alderney
D: Elderney

45

Henry Higgins is a character in which stage musical?

A: Miss Saigon
B: My Fair Lady
C: Cats
D: Chicago

50:50 Go to page 459 Go to page 483 ? Answers on page 497

10 ◆ £32,000

46

Competitors in the Olympic 4000 metre 'pursuit' utilise which mode of transportation?

A: Speedboat
B: Car
C: Bicycle
D: Yacht

47

Who played Mr Abbott in the TV sitcom 'Bless This House'?

A: Terry Scott
B: Sid James
C: William Gaunt
D: Warren Mitchell

48

What nationality is the tennis player Goran Ivanisevic?

A: Bulgarian
B: Russian
C: Croatian
D: Czech

49

In which county is the famous headland Beachy Head?

A: Kent
B: Suffolk
C: East Sussex
D: Dorset

50

What is the meaning of the prefix 'pseudo-'?

A: Mental
B: Winged
C: Itchy
D: False

50:50 Go to page 459 Go to page 483 ? Answers on page 497

10 ◆ £32,000

51

Which character in 'EastEnders' is played by June Brown?

- A: Peggy Mitchell
- B: Melanie Owen
- C: Dot Cotton
- D: Laura Beale

52

Which Biblical character wrestled with God in Genesis 32:22?

- A: Esau
- B: Isaac
- C: Jacob
- D: Abraham

53

Founded in 1917, the Politburo was the policy-forming body of which country?

- A: France
- B: Soviet Union
- C: United States
- D: Great Britain

54

Which of these creatures does a Portuguese man-of-war most closely resemble?

- A: Snake
- B: Jellyfish
- C: Fly
- D: Weevil

55

Elizabeth I, daughter of Henry VIII, reigned mainly in which century?

- A: 14th
- B: 15th
- C: 16th
- D: 17th

50:50 Go to page 459   Go to page 483   ? Answers on page 497

56

Which of these is the film title of an Alfred Hitchcock thriller?

A: The Birds
B: The Bees
C: The Flowers
D: The Trees

57

In the TV series 'Happy Days', what is the full name of the Fonz?

A: Arthur Fonzaloni
B: Arthur Fonzaretta
C: Arthur Fonzanoza
D: Arthur Fonzarelli

58

In which US state is Phoenix?

A: Arizona
B: Texas
C: Colorado
D: Georgia

59

Somebody who believes that it is impossible to know whether God exists is... what?

A: Atheist
B: Agonist
C: Agnostic
D: Augur

60

Which ball is the highest scoring colour on the snooker table?

A: Brown
B: Black
C: Pink
D: Blue

50:50 Go to page 459 Go to page 483 ? Answers on page 497

10 ◆ £32,000

61

Boris Godunov was a ruler of which country?

A: Turkey
B: Russia
C: Germany
D: France

62

Who released the album 'This Is Where I Came In' in 2001?

A: The Beautiful South
B: The Boo Radleys
C: The Bee Gees
D: The Backstreet Boys

63

Which poet wrote 'The Charge of the Light Brigade' in 1854?

A: Tennyson
B: Browning
C: Byron
D: Shelley

64

From which country do the members of the group Destiny's Child come?

A: Australia
B: United States
C: Ireland
D: South Africa

65

What was the name of the ship's computer in the TV sitcom 'Red Dwarf'?

A: Holly
B: Polly
C: Hal
D: Pal

50:50 Go to page 459 Go to page 483 ? Answers on page 497

10 ◆ £32,000

66

In which state is Silicon Valley, the centre of the US information technology industry?

- A: Nevada
- B: Alabama
- C: California
- D: Illinois

67

Which of these means to decrease or fade gradually before coming to an end?

- A: Peter
- B: Paul
- C: Patrick
- D: Percy

68

What equipment do competitors on the 'Cresta Run' require?

- A: Toboggan
- B: Roller skates
- C: Skateboard
- D: Snowboard

69

During World War II, Anderson and Morrison were types of what?

- A: Aeroplane
- B: Bomb
- C: Gas mask
- D: Air-raid shelter

70

In which TV sitcom did Caroline Quentin play Dorothy?

- A: Drop the Dead Donkey
- B: Father Ted
- C: Men Behaving Badly
- D: The Vicar of Dibley

50:50 Go to page 459 Go to page 483 ? Answers on page 497

10 ◆ £32,000

71

Complete the name of the character from 'Star Wars: Episode 1 - The Phantom Menace': Jar Jar...?

- A: Binks
- B: Tinks
- C: Links
- D: Jinks

72

H_2SO_4 is the chemical symbol for which acid?

- A: Sulphuric acid
- B: Acetic acid
- C: Hydrochloric acid
- D: Ascorbic acid

73

In which county is the town of Tamworth?

- A: Shropshire
- B: Staffordshire
- C: Warwickshire
- D: Leicestershire

74

During the 17th century, Molière was a famous what?

- A: Violin manufacturer
- B: Opera singer
- C: Ballet dancer
- D: Playwright

75

Which 'EastEnders' character shot Phil Mitchell in 2001?

- A: Pauline
- B: Dot
- C: Lisa
- D: Laura

50:50 Go to page 459 · Go to page 483 · ? Answers on page 497

10 ◆ £32,000

76

Who created the animation sequences for 'Monty Python's Flying Circus'?

A: Eric Idle
B: Terry Jones
C: Terry Gilliam
D: Graham Chapman

77

The Royal Albert Hall is situated in which part of London?

A: Bloomsbury
B: Kensington
C: Lambeth
D: Marylebone

78

Which of these places is a British crown colony sometimes known as 'The Rock'?

A: The Falklands
B: Gibraltar
C: Hong Kong
D: Jersey

79

The film 'The Deer Hunter' is set during which war?

A: World War I
B: World War II
C: Korean War
D: Vietnam War

80

What is the opposite of 'concave'?

A: Convex
B: Concise
C: Converse
D: Concane

50:50 Go to page 459 Go to page 483 ? Answers on page 497

10 ◆ £32,000

81

With which field of the arts is Gérard Depardieu most associated?

A: Ballet
B: Opera
C: Film
D: Literature

82

In which city was footballer Eric Cantona born?

A: Cherbourg
B: Lyons
C: Marseilles
D: Paris

83

A 'beater' would be involved in which outdoor activity?

A: Orienteering
B: Skiing
C: Shooting
D: Potholing

84

In which religion is a 'mufti' a legal expert?

A: Hinduism
B: Judaism
C: Islam
D: Buddhism

85

In pre-decimal currency, a crown was worth how many shillings?

A: 20
B: 10
C: 5
D: 2

50:50 Go to page 459 Go to page 483 ? Answers on page 497

86

Which of these French authors had the first name Marcel?

A: Camus
B: Proust
C: Sartre
D: Zola

87

In which country did Colonel Gaddafi overthrow King Idris?

A: Iraq
B: Saudi Arabia
C: Libya
D: Tunisia

88

In a book, what would be printed on the flyleaf?

A: Author's name
B: Index
C: Nothing
D: Title

89

What were the real first names of the musician Duke Ellington?

A: Edward Kennedy
B: Albert Gore
C: Hillary Clinton
D: John Rockefeller

90

Which character in the US sitcom 'Cheers' was played by Shelley Long?

A: Rebecca
B: Carla
C: Diane
D: Lilith

50:50 Go to page 459 Go to page 483 ? Answers on page 497

10 ◆ £32,000

91

What kind of animal is a 'reebok'?

A: Fish
B: Monkey
C: Antelope
D: Marsupial

92

Willie John McBride is best known for playing which sport?

A: Cricket
B: Golf
C: Football
D: Rugby union

93

'Guga' is the nickname of which top tennis player?

A: Andre Agassi
B: Gustavo Kuerten
C: Magnus Norman
D: Patrick Rafter

94

Which Beatles 1995 UK hit single featured George, Paul and Ringo and a pre-recorded vocal by John?

A: Cry For A Shadow
B: You Know What To Do
C: Leave My Kitten Alone
D: Free As A Bird

95

The painting 'Bubbles', by John Millais, was used to advertise which brand of soap?

A: Imperial Leather
B: Lifebuoy
C: Pears
D: Lux

50:50 Go to page 459 Go to page 483 ? Answers on page 497

10 ◆ £32,000

96

In the TV comedy 'My Hero', which superhero is played by Ardal O'Hanlon?

A: Silicoman
B: Turboman
C: Microman
D: Thermoman

97

What kind of creature is a mudskipper?

A: Bird
B: Fish
C: Insect
D: Reptile

98

Which of these was a political party founded in the United States in the 1960s?

A: Black Lions
B: Black Panthers
C: Black Leopards
D: Black Pumas

99

What kind of fabric is 'chino'?

A: Cotton
B: Linen
C: Silk
D: Wool

100

In 2001, who replaced Robin Cook as Foreign Secretary?

A: Gordon Brown
B: Jack Straw
C: David Blunkett
D: John Prescott

50:50 Go to page 459 · Go to page 483 · ? Answers on page 497

10 ◆ £32,000

101

Which member of the pop group Hear'Say has the surname Foster?

A: Noel
B: Danny
C: Kym
D: Myleene

102

All Take That singles were recorded on which label?

A: London
B: Polydor
C: RCA
D: Virgin

103

In which country is the volcano Krakatoa?

A: Mexico
B: Italy
C: Indonesia
D: Japan

104

What was the surname of the 1st Viscount Nuffield, the car manufacturer?

A: Ford
B: Morgan
C: Austin
D: Morris

105

In the Bible, who interpreted the dreams of King Nebuchadnezzar?

A: Adam
B: Daniel
C: Jacob
D: Noah

50:50 Go to page 459 Go to page 483 ? Answers on page 497

10 ◆ £32,000

106

What nationality was the artist Edvard Munch?

A: Danish
B: German
C: Norwegian
D: Swedish

107

Ham Gravy was the first boyfriend of which cartoon character?

A: Wilma Flintstone
B: Olive Oyl
C: Betty Boop
D: Daisy Duck

108

Which year does the Roman numeral MIX represent?

A: 991
B: 999
C: 1009
D: 1011

50:50 Go to page 459 Go to page 483 Answers on page 497

50:50

15		£1 MILLION
14		£500,000
13		£250,000
12		£125,000
11	◆	£64,000
10	◆	£32,000
9	◆	£16,000
8	◆	£8,000
7	◆	£4,000
6	◆	£2,000
5	◆	£1,000
4	◆	£500
3	◆	£300
2	◆	£200
1	◆	£100

11 ◆ £64,000

1

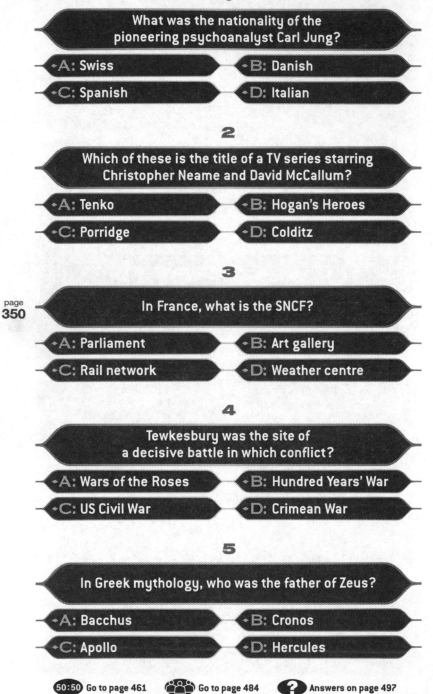

What was the nationality of the pioneering psychoanalyst Carl Jung?

A: Swiss
B: Danish
C: Spanish
D: Italian

2

Which of these is the title of a TV series starring Christopher Neame and David McCallum?

A: Tenko
B: Hogan's Heroes
C: Porridge
D: Colditz

3

In France, what is the SNCF?

A: Parliament
B: Art gallery
C: Rail network
D: Weather centre

4

Tewkesbury was the site of a decisive battle in which conflict?

A: Wars of the Roses
B: Hundred Years' War
C: US Civil War
D: Crimean War

5

In Greek mythology, who was the father of Zeus?

A: Bacchus
B: Cronos
C: Apollo
D: Hercules

50:50 Go to page 461 Go to page 484 ? Answers on page 497

11 ◆ £64,000

6

Which of these French ports is the nearest to England?

A: Calais
B: Le Havre
C: Le Touquet
D: Cherbourg

7

The Glorious Revolution of 1688 occurred in which country?

A: Russia
B: France
C: United States
D: England

8

Matt Dawson has captained England in which sport?

A: Football
B: Cricket
C: Rugby union
D: Hockey

9

Which philosopher had the first names John Stuart?

A: Hobbes
B: Bentham
C: Mill
D: Locke

10

What type of fish is an 'albacore'?

A: Sild
B: Shark
C: Tuna
D: Brill

50:50 Go to page 461 Go to page 484 ? Answers on page 497

11 ◆ £64,000

11

The Taurus Mountains are a feature of which country?

- A: Egypt
- B: Turkey
- C: Romania
- D: Italy

12

What does the 'mere' of the names Windermere, Grasmere and Buttermere mean?

- A: River
- B: Lake
- C: Hill
- D: Fell

13

Who played the lead role in the TV sitcom 'Shelley'?

- A: Hywel Bennett
- B: Leonard Rossiter
- C: Ronnie Barker
- D: David Jason

14

What was the nickname of the actress Lily Langtry?

- A: Guernsey Lily
- B: Sark Lily
- C: Alderney Lily
- D: Jersey Lily

15

In Greek mythology, who was the father of Icarus?

- A: Daedalus
- B: Perseus
- C: Chiron
- D: Tantalus

50:50 Go to page 461 · Go to page 484 · ? Answers on page 497

16

Fritz Lang was best known as a director of what?

A: Plays | B: Stage musicals
C: Films | D: Traffic

17

What type of creature is the 'ptarmigan'?

A: Fox | B: Bear
C: Seal | D: Bird

18

What is the 'Little Bighorn', where General Custer was killed in battle in 1876?

A: River | B: Mountain
C: Cattle ranch | D: Open plain

19

How often is 'diurnally'?

A: Every day | B: Every week
C: Every other week | D: Every decade

20

What is the meaning of the Latin name 'Magna Carta'?

A: Giant map | B: Magic diploma
C: Huge postcard | D: Great charter

50:50 Go to page 461 · Go to page 484 · ? Answers on page 497

11 ◆ £64,000

21

Charlie Fairhead is a character in which medical drama series?

A: Casualty
B: ER
C: Doctors
D: A & E

22

What do you lose if you suffer from amnesia?

A: Your voice
B: Your hair
C: Your sense of taste
D: Your memory

23

If a ship is 'rounding the Horn', in which part of the world is it sailing?

A: North America
B: South America
C: North Africa
D: South Africa

24

Which country split up into its fifteen constituent republics in 1991?

A: Yugoslavia
B: Czechoslovakia
C: Pakistan
D: Soviet Union

25

'A Doll's House' is a play by which writer?

A: Strindberg
B: Ibsen
C: Chekhov
D: Beckett

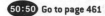

50:50 Go to page 461 Go to page 484 ? Answers on page 497

11 ◆ £64,000

26

Which Shakespeare play contains a famous balcony scene?

A: Twelfth Night
B: As You Like It
C: The Tempest
D: Romeo and Juliet

27

São Paulo is the largest city in which South American country?

A: Chile
B: Argentina
C: Brazil
D: Colombia

28

The song 'I Whistle a Happy Tune' comes from which musical?

A: South Pacific
B: Showboat
C: My Fair Lady
D: The King And I

29

The royal family of the Netherlands belongs to which royal House?

A: Orange
B: Damson
C: Bramble
D: Quince

30

'Old man's beard' is the name of a what?

A: Climbing plant
B: Strong beer
C: Spider's web
D: Long-sleeved vest

50:50 Go to page 461 · Go to page 484 · ? Answers on page 497

11 ◆ £64,000

31

In the UK, a barrister who becomes a QC is known as a what?

A: Satin
B: Silk
C: Gauze
D: Taffeta

32

What is the name of Michael Schumacher's brother, who also drives in Formula 1 racing?

A: Randolf
B: Ralf
C: Ranulf
D: Rolf

33

Complete the title of the E. M. Forster novel: 'A Passage to...'?

A: China
B: Hawaii
C: America
D: India

34

A 'Springbok' is a person representing which country in a sport?

A: Argentina
B: South Africa
C: Mexico
D: Kenya

35

In which royal building is the Queen's Gallery?

A: Buckingham Palace
B: Hampton Court
C: Windsor Castle
D: Sandringham House

50:50 Go to page 461 Go to page 484 ? Answers on page 497

11 ◆ £64,000

36

Where would you look for a monk's tonsure?

- A: On his habit
- B: On his belt
- C: On his head
- D: On his feet

37

Which Shakespeare play features a loan of three thousand ducats?

- A: The Merchant of Venice
- B: Much Ado About Nothing
- C: Measure for Measure
- D: A Midsummer Night's Dream

38

In the saying that means the attraction has been destroyed, 'the gilt is knocked off the...' what?

- A: Gingerbread
- B: Flapjack
- C: Sponge cake
- D: Malt loaf

39

'Peptic' is the adjective that refers to which bodily function?

- A: Healing
- B: Respiration
- C: Blood circulation
- D: Digestion

40

Which mythological creature was half horse and half eagle?

- A: Hippogriff
- B: Hydra
- C: Gorgon
- D: Basilisk

50:50 Go to page 461 Go to page 484 ? Answers on page 497

11 ◆ £64,000

41

In chemistry, what name is given to some fatty acids that are insoluble in water?

- A: Lipids
- B: Moles
- C: Alkalis
- D: Magnesia

42

Who was the alleged assassin of President Kennedy?

- A: Lee Harvey Oswald
- B: Jack Ruby
- C: Sirhan Sirhan
- D: James Earl Ray

43

What is the alternative name of the Shakespearean character Robin Goodfellow?

- A: The Merchant of Venice
- B: The Moor of Venice
- C: Puck
- D: Ariel

44

In Greek mythology, what is the name of the river that surrounds the Underworld?

- A: Alpheus
- B: Styx
- C: Xanthus
- D: Achelous

45

Stalingrad was the name of a battle fought in which conflict?

- A: Crimean War
- B: World War I
- C: Russian Revolution
- D: World War II

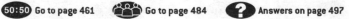

50:50 Go to page 461 Go to page 484 ? Answers on page 497

11 ◆ £64,000

46

Which subjects comprise the university course PPE?

A: Polemics Poetry Existentialism
B: Philosophy Politics Economics
C: Psychiatry Photography Education
D: Physics Psychology Ergonomics

47

In biblical terms, anything described as 'evangelical' is based on what?

A: Pentateuch
B: Ten Commandments
C: Apocrypha
D: Four Gospels

48

Which zodiac sign is represented by an animal that is a relative of spiders?

A: Scorpio
B: Sagittarius
C: Cancer
D: Aquarius

49

What is the nickname for a cricketer sent in to bat at the end of play, to hold the wicket till the next day?

A: Guardsman
B: Dark horse
C: Nightwatchman
D: Shift manager

50

Which legendary ghost ship is the title of an opera by Wagner?

A: The Phantom Corsair
B: The Travelling Galleon
C: The Flying Dutchman
D: The Spectral Clipper

50:50 Go to page 461 Go to page 484 ? Answers on page 497

11 ◆ £64,000

51

Flavio Briatore became the director of which Formula 1 racing team in 2000?

A: Ferrari
B: Arrows
C: Jaguar
D: Benetton

52

In 1984, Prince Charles called a new wing design for which London building a 'monstrous carbuncle'?

A: National Gallery
B: Victoria and Albert Museum
C: Mansion House
D: Old Bailey

53

What was the first UK number one single for the Pet Shop Boys?

A: It's A Sin
B: Suburbia
C: Rent
D: West End Girls

54

'Leaving Patrick' was the first novel by which food writer?

A: Nigella Lawson
B: Prue Leith
C: Delia Smith
D: Sophie Grigson

55

What is the first name of the fictional pilot known as 'Biggles'?

A: William
B: James
C: Henry
D: Edward

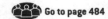

50:50 Go to page 461 Go to page 484 ? Answers on page 497

11 ◆ £64,000

56

The Scottish cheese 'caboc' is shaped into logs and rolled in what?

A: Sesame seeds
B: Lemon juice
C: Oatmeal
D: Pig fat

57

With which team did James Hunt win the 1976 Formula 1 World Championship?

A: Ferrari
B: Lotus
C: McLaren
D: Renault

58

Ronnie Scott, founder of a famous jazz club, is most associated with which instrument?

A: Double bass
B: Piano
C: Trumpet
D: Saxophone

59

Which religious movement publishes a periodical called 'The Watchtower'?

A: Salvation Army
B: Church of Latterday Saints
C: Jehovah's Witnesses
D: Seventh Day Adventists

60

'Shoat' is a term applied to the young of which creature?

A: Pig
B: Sheep
C: Cow
D: Chicken

50:50 Go to page 461 · Go to page 484 · ? Answers on page 497

11 ◆ £64,000

61

In finance, what does the letter 'P' stand for in the abbreviation P and L?

A: Payment
B: Public
C: Profit
D: Postings

62

With which of these groups are the musicians Peter Hook and Bernard Sumner associated?

A: Divine Comedy
B: New Order
C: Prefab Sprout
D: Boo Radleys

63

What was the full first name of the author Bram Stoker?

A: Bertram
B: Bramwell
C: Abraham
D: Graham

64

Which of these is not one of the noble gases?

A: Krypton
B: Chlorine
C: Xenon
D: Helium

65

On what date in 2001 was the General Election held?

A: 7th June
B: 9th June
C: 11th June
D: 13th June

50:50 Go to page 461 Go to page 484 ? Answers on page 497

11 ◆ £64,000

66

Which of these is a song from Irving Berlin's musical 'White Christmas'?

A: Sisters
B: Brothers
C: Mothers
D: Fathers

67

What is the term for the spawn of shellfish?

A: Chat
B: Spat
C: Drat
D: Plat

68

With which sport is Austrian Barbara Schett most associated?

A: Athletics
B: Golf
C: Tennis
D: Figure skating

69

What nationality is racing driver Jean Alesi?

A: French
B: Canadian
C: Italian
D: Swiss

70

What type of musical instruments do the quartet Bond play?

A: Wind
B: Percussion
C: String
D: Brass

50:50 Go to page 461 Go to page 484 ? Answers on page 497

11 ◆ £64,000

71

In which TV series did Neil Pearson play Dave Charnley?

A: Heaven on Earth
B: Between The Lines
C: Drop the Dead Donkey
D: The Whistle-Blower

72

Which actor directed the Arnold Schwarzenegger film 'The Running Man'?

A: James Garner
B: Tom Selleck
C: Peter Falk
D: Paul Michael Glaser

73

Uppsala is a city in which country?

A: Estonia
B: Latvia
C: Norway
D: Sweden

74

What was the title of Stephen King's first novel?

A: It
B: Carrie
C: The Shining
D: Christine

75

The word 'taboo' comes from which language?

A: Hindi
B: Flemish
C: Afrikaans
D: Tongan

50:50 Go to page 461 Go to page 484 ? Answers on page 497

11 ◆ £64,000

76

Which of these words refers to the twinkling of stars?

A: Oscillation
B: Scintillation
C: Titillation
D: Vacillation

77

Bikini Atoll belongs to which island group?

A: Azores
B: Grenadines
C: Marshalls
D: Solomons

78

In which county is Sunbury-on-Thames?

A: Berkshire
B: Essex
C: Oxfordshire
D: Surrey

79

The navigator John Cabot is best known for his journey to which continent?

A: Asia
B: North America
C: Australia
D: Africa

80

Which town lies across the Firth of Forth from Edinburgh?

A: Oban
B: Thurso
C: Dunfermline
D: Fort William

50:50 Go to page 461 Go to page 484 ? Answers on page 497

11 ◆ £64,000

81

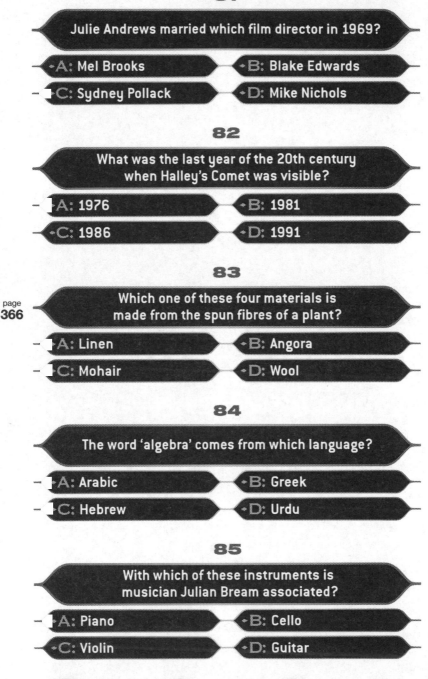

Julie Andrews married which film director in 1969?

A: Mel Brooks
B: Blake Edwards
C: Sydney Pollack
D: Mike Nichols

82

What was the last year of the 20th century when Halley's Comet was visible?

A: 1976
B: 1981
C: 1986
D: 1991

83

Which one of these four materials is made from the spun fibres of a plant?

A: Linen
B: Angora
C: Mohair
D: Wool

84

The word 'algebra' comes from which language?

A: Arabic
B: Greek
C: Hebrew
D: Urdu

85

With which of these instruments is musician Julian Bream associated?

A: Piano
B: Cello
C: Violin
D: Guitar

50:50 Go to page 461 Go to page 484 ? Answers on page 497

11 ◆ £64,000

86

What is the meaning of the female name 'Ruth'?

- A: Happiness
- B: Pity
- C: Love
- D: Devotion

87

Who would be most likely to use a Rorschach test?

- A: Obstetrician
- B: Psychologist
- C: Oculist
- D: Haematologist

88

At which British university do Rhodes scholars study?

- A: Oxford
- B: Cambridge
- C: St Andrews
- D: London

89

Which major company is known as 'Big Blue'?

- A: Ford
- B: IBM
- C: Pearson
- D: ICI

90

Tattenham Corner is a feature of which racecourse?

- A: Newmarket
- B: Epsom
- C: Sandown
- D: Market Rasen

50:50 Go to page 461 Go to page 484 ? Answers on page 497

11 ◆ £64,000

91

What is a 'lugger'?

A: Boat
B: Miner
C: Lumberjack
D: Fish

92

On a ship, what is a hawser?

A: Rope
B: Deck
C: Sail
D: Anchor

93

Pashmina is a fabric made from the coat of which animal?

A: Goat
B: Llama
C: Rabbit
D: Sheep

94

What is the name of the president played by Martin Sheen in 'The West Wing'?

A: Adam Stevenson
B: Josiah Bartlet
C: Caleb Mason
D: Daniel Webster

95

In which country was the tennis player Monica Seles born?

A: Czechoslovakia
B: East Germany
C: Soviet Union
D: Yugoslavia

50:50 Go to page 461 Go to page 484 ? Answers on page 497

11 ◆ £64,000

96

Ghee is a clarified butter popular in the cuisine of which country?

A: Italy | B: India
C: Israel | D: Ireland

97

In which county is the University of Keele based?

A: Leicestershire | B: Nottinghamshire
C: Staffordshire | D: Derbyshire

98

Accra is the capital city of which African country?

A: Ghana | B: Gabon
C: Gambia | D: Guinea

99

What nationality was the writer Thomas Mann?

A: Russian | B: Italian
C: French | D: German

100

In Greek mythology, who gave fire to Man?

A: Paris | B: Poseidon
C: Prometheus | D: Perseus

50:50 Go to page 461 · Go to page 484 · ? Answers on page 497

50:50

15	£1 MILLION
14	£500,000
13	£250,000
12	£125,000
11	£64,000
10	£32,000
9	£16,000
8	£8,000
7	£4,000
6	£2,000
5	£1,000
4	£500
3	£300
2	£200
1	£100

12 ◆ £125,000

1

Monte Cervino is the Italian name for which mountain?

- A: Mont Blanc
- B: Eiger
- C: Matterhorn
- D: Jungfrau

2

What was the profession of Humphry Repton?

- A: Landscape gardener
- B: Scientist
- C: Executioner
- D: Highwayman

3

In Greek mythology, Priam was the king of which city?

- A: Colchis
- B: Troy
- C: Carthage
- D: Syracuse

4

Who wrote 'The Talented Mr Ripley'?

- A: Iris Murdoch
- B: Patricia Highsmith
- C: P.D. James
- D: Daphne Du Maurier

5

'Portrait of a Lady' is a work by which author?

- A: Edith Wharton
- B: Nathaniel Hawthorne
- C: Henry James
- D: F. Scott Fitzgerald

50:50 Go to page 462 · Go to page 486 · ? Answers on page 498

12 ◆ £125,000

6

The 'contras' were a guerrilla fighting force in which country during the 1980s?

A: Egypt
B: Nicaragua
C: Mexico
D: Chile

7

Who traditionally sits on a 'donkey stool'?

A: Driver
B: Yachtsman
C: Artist
D: Teacher

8

Henry the Navigator was a prince of which sea-faring nation?

A: Spain
B: Portugal
C: Italy
D: Netherlands

9

Who founded Singapore in 1819?

A: Rhodes
B: Raffles
C: Wellington
D: Salisbury

10

The word 'teutonic' describes people from which country?

A: France
B: Germany
C: Spain
D: Italy

50:50 Go to page 462 Go to page 486 ? Answers on page 498

12 ◆ £125,000

11

Van Morrison was a member of which band in the 1960s?

A: Them
B: Us
C: Me
D: You

12

Helvetia is the Latin name for which country?

A: Switzerland
B: Greece
C: Denmark
D: Ireland

13

Dundee cake is traditionally decorated with which type of nut?

A: Almond
B: Peanut
C: Cashew
D: Walnut

14

What is an alternative name for the Limpopo River?

A: Hippo River
B: Piranha River
C: Crocodile River
D: Snake River

15

In Greek mythology, Phrixus flew to Colchis on what type of creature?

A: Golden Hind
B: Golden Ram
C: Golden Bull
D: Golden Cow

50:50 Go to page 462
Go to page 486
Answers on page 498

12 ◆ £125,000

16

Who wrote the 'Ars Poetica'?

A: Ovid
B: Sallust
C: Horace
D: Pliny

17

What was the first name of Machiavelli?

A: Romano
B: Niccolò
C: Antonio
D: Gasparo

18

Walter Raleigh was executed during the reign of which monarch?

A: Elizabeth I
B: Henry VIII
C: James I
D: William III

19

Which French artist was known as the 'Douanier'?

A: Matisse
B: Monet
C: Gauguin
D: Rousseau

20

Paul Henri Spaak was the premier of which country?

A: Holland
B: Belgium
C: France
D: Luxembourg

50:50 Go to page 462 Go to page 486 ? Answers on page 498

12 ◆ £125,000

21

Swaledale is a variety of which farmyard animal?

A: Pig
B: Goat
C: Sheep
D: Cow

22

Fox Talbot was a pioneer in which field?

A: Poetry
B: Photography
C: Theatre
D: Nuclear power

23

What type of weather does Shakespeare specify for the opening scene of Macbeth?

A: Ice and snow
B: Wind and rain
C: Thunder and lightning
D: Mist and fog

24

Which plantation mansion is the main home of Scarlett O'Hara in 'Gone With The Wind'?

A: Lara
B: Mara
C: Cara
D: Tara

25

Stevenage, the first New Town established in Britain, is in which county?

A: Bedfordshire
B: Berkshire
C: Hertfordshire
D: Northamptonshire

50:50 Go to page 462 Go to page 486 ? Answers on page 498

12 ◆ £125,000

26

Joe DiMaggio, Marilyn Monroe's second husband, was a famous player in which sport?

A: American Football
B: Basketball
C: Ice hockey
D: Baseball

27

Where is the natural habitat of penguins?

A: Arctic circle
B: Southern oceans
C: Labrador coast
D: Bay of Biscay

28

Gozo is a small island that belongs to which larger Mediterranean island?

A: Sicily
B: Cyprus
C: Malta
D: Corsica

29

Which of these musicians plays the 'timpani' in the orchestra?

A: Cellist
B: Flautist
C: Trumpeter
D: Drummer

30

'Digger' was a nickname given to World War II Allied soldiers of which country?

A: Australia
B: Poland
C: USA
D: Belgium

50:50 Go to page 462 Go to page 486 ? Answers on page 498

12 ◆ £125,000

31

Who wrote the poem 'Night Mail', as a commentary for a GPO film?

A: John Betjeman
B: Cecil Day Lewis
C: Philip Larkin
D: W. H. Auden

32

What is the title of the anthem that begins 'And did those feet in ancient time'?

A: Antioch
B: Jerusalem
C: Canaan
D: Babylon

33

Which sportsmen traditionally wear 'silks', whatever the material?

A: Swimmers
B: Boxers
C: Golfers
D: Jockeys

34

What is the highest age of a 'quinquagenarian'?

A: 50
B: 55
C: 59
D: 60

35

Which of these theatres is sometimes called 'Covent Garden', as that is where it is situated?

A: London Palladium
B: Royal Opera House
C: Old Vic
D: Theatre Royal

50:50 Go to page 462 Go to page 486 ? Answers on page 498

12 ◆ £125,000

36

Which US President had the middle name Milhous?

A: Dwight Eisenhower
B: Richard Nixon
C: Ronald Reagan
D: Jimmy Carter

37

What was the surname of Leonard, the composer who wrote the music for 'West Side Story'?

A: Goldstein
B: Feinstein
C: Bernstein
D: Einstein

38

Which of these is a synonym for the word 'spartan'?

A: Brave
B: Austere
C: Talented
D: Harassed

39

Whose names would you most associate with Debrett's?

A: Members of the MCC
B: Members of Parliament
C: Members of the Peerage
D: Members of the Freemasons

40

The PLO is a political organisation in which part of the world?

A: Papua
B: Philippines
C: Poland
D: Palestine

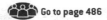

50:50 Go to page 462 Go to page 486 ? Answers on page 498

12 ◆ £125,000

41

What do the letters 'S' and 'C' stand for in the acronym 'scuba'?

A: Self-contained
B: Sailing club
C: Standard course
D: Swimming certificate

42

In 'The Simpsons', what colour is Bart's mum's beehive hairdo?

A: Green
B: Yellow
C: Red
D: Blue

43

Which of these is the correct spelling?

A: Minescule
B: Minascule
C: Minuscule
D: Miniescule

44

What was the stage name of classic blues singer McKinley Morganfield?

A: Mississippi Micky
B: Stoney Creek
C: Muddy Waters
D: Marshall River

45

In which year did Valentina Tereshkova become the first woman to fly in space?

A: 1963
B: 1965
C: 1967
D: 1969

50:50 Go to page 462 Go to page 486 ? Answers on page 498

12 ◆ £125,000

46

Hay on Wye, famous for its bookshops and annual literary festival, is in which Welsh county?

A: Dyfed
B: Gwynedd
C: Powys
D: Gwent

47

What is affected if you crack a 'carnassial'?

A: Nail
B: Tooth
C: Knuckle
D: Tendon

48

Which of these is a stylised form of classic Japanese drama?

A: Noh
B: Yeseh
C: Ayeh
D: Nayh

49

In Greek mythology, what did the nymph Daphne become to save her from the attentions of Apollo?

A: Gold statue
B: Daffodil
C: Bear
D: Laurel tree

50

During which century was French writer Cyrano de Bergerac born?

A: 16th
B: 17th
C: 18th
D: 19th

50:50 Go to page 462 Go to page 486 ? Answers on page 498

12 ◆ £125,000

51

On television, American Alvin Hall is an expert in which area?

A: Finance
B: Property
C: Interior design
D: Men's health

52

Which of these countries has horizontal, not vertical, stripes on its national flag?

A: France
B: Belgium
C: Germany
D: Italy

53

The phrase 'brave new world' comes from a work by which playwright?

A: Shakespeare
B: Milton
C: Marlowe
D: Pinter

54

How is Beatrix Potter's Peter Rabbit related to Benjamin Bunny?

A: Cousin
B: Father
C: Brother
D: Uncle

55

What was the first name of the founder of the luxury car company Lamborghini?

A: Fernando
B: Ferdinando
C: Fabrizio
D: Ferruccio

50:50 Go to page 462 · Go to page 486 · Answers on page 498

12 ◆ £125,000

56

Which of these sea creatures belongs to the class Asteroidea?

A: Periwinkle
B: Conch
C: Starfish
D: Sea urchin

57

What were the names of the brothers who became known as 'the princes in the tower'?

A: Edward and Richard
B: Henry and Edward
C: James and Henry
D: Charles and Richard

58

In which country is the seaport of Chittagong?

A: Afghanistan
B: Pakistan
C: Bangladesh
D: India

59

What is the name of the character played by Natalie Wood in the film 'Rebel Without A Cause'?

A: Janet
B: Jackie
C: Judy
D: Joy

60

With which rock group is Gavin Rossdale associated?

A: Tree
B: Shrub
C: Bush
D: Hedge

50:50 Go to page 462 Go to page 486 ? Answers on page 498

12 ◆ £125,000

61

'Dysphemia' is the medical term for which of these conditions?

- A: Low blood pressure
- B: Long-sightedness
- C: Indigestion
- D: Stammering

62

What is the name of the Prince who is heir to the throne in Monaco?

- A: Pierre
- B: Honoré
- C: Albert
- D: Anton

63

Russell Crowe won a Best Actor Oscar for his role as which character?

- A: Germanicus
- B: Maximus
- C: Minimus
- D: Octavius

64

The Manzanares River flows through which European capital?

- A: Athens
- B: Lisbon
- C: Madrid
- D: Bucharest

65

The ITV series 'Survivor', shown in 2001, was set on which island?

- A: Pulau Besar
- B: Pulau Midai
- C: Pulau Subi
- D: Pulau Tiga

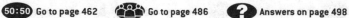

50:50 Go to page 462 Go to page 486 ? Answers on page 498

12 ◆ £125,000

66

What kind of fruit is a Ribstone pippin?

A: Cherry
B: Pear
C: Apple
D: Blackcurrant

67

The 'riyal' is the unit of currency in which of these countries?

A: Kuwait
B: Saudi Arabia
C: Iraq
D: Morocco

68

With which sport is the Ponds Forge venue in Sheffield most associated?

A: Athletics
B: Football
C: Ice hockey
D: Swimming

69

Malic acid is found in what kind of foods?

A: Fruit
B: Dairy products
C: Wheat products
D: Red meats

70

The Space Needle is a major tourist attraction in which US city?

A: Cleveland
B: Saint Louis
C: Orlando
D: Seattle

50:50 Go to page 462 Go to page 486 ? Answers on page 498

12 ◆ £125,000

71

What is the name Van short for, in the rock singer's name Van Morrison?

A: Vivian
B: Vaughan
C: Vance
D: Ivan

72

Bhangra developed from the music of which region?

A: Asia Minor
B: Mesopotamia
C: Punjab
D: Patagonia

73

Who was Time Magazine's Person of the Century for the 20th century?

A: Mandela
B: Einstein
C: Churchill
D: Gandhi

74

Which authors are eligible for the Orange Prize for fiction?

A: First-time novelists
B: Authors under 35
C: British
D: Women

75

Which city is the capital of the Piedmont region of Italy?

A: Bologna
B: Cagliari
C: Perugia
D: Turin

50:50 Go to page 462 Go to page 486 ? Answers on page 498

12 ◆ £125,000

76

Which cheese is most associated with the town of Melton Mowbray?

- A: Caerphilly
- B: Double Gloucester
- C: Sage Derby
- D: Stilton

77

What kind of creature is a 'hawksbill'?

- A: Lizard
- B: Turtle
- C: Moth
- D: Owl

78

In medieval times, what was the occupation of a 'chapman'?

- A: Gamekeeper
- B: Innkeeper
- C: Trader
- D: Woodcutter

79

In which country was the ancient Mycenaean civilization centred?

- A: Egypt
- B: Greece
- C: Italy
- D: Turkey

80

What is a 'jorum'?

- A: Drinking vessel
- B: Spanish dance
- C: Woman's coat
- D: Sub-atomic particle

50:50 Go to page 462 · Go to page 486 · ? Answers on page 498

12 ◆ £125,000

81

Which war began with an attack on Fort Sumter?

A: American Civil War
B: Spanish Civil War
C: American War of Independence
D: Maori Wars

82

What would a 'whetstone' be used for?

A: Carrying bricks
B: Retreading tyres
C: Sharpening tools
D: Training horses

83

During World War I, who appeared on the 'Your Country Needs You' recruitment poster?

A: Haig
B: Baden-Powell
C: Roberts
D: Kitchener

84

Who created the fictional detective Aurelio Zen?

A: Michael Dibdin
B: Donna Leon
C: Iain Pears
D: Reginald Hill

85

Which actor starred in the 1998 film 'Croupier'?

A: Joseph Fiennes
B: Clive Owen
C: Jude Law
D: Rupert Graves

50:50 Go to page 462 · Go to page 486 · Answers on page 498

12 ◆ £125,000

86

The Hausa people live mainly in which African country?

- A: Algeria
- B: Ethiopia
- C: Nigeria
- D: Angola

87

Who wrote the song 'A Fine Romance'?

- A: Jerome Kern
- B: George Gershwin
- C: Irving Berlin
- D: Kurt Weill

88

In which city was musician Jimi Hendrix born?

- A: Birmingham
- B: Detroit
- C: Indianapolis
- D: Seattle

89

Who wrote the play 'The Winslow Boy'?

- A: Manuel Pinero
- B: Terence Rattigan
- C: Sean O'Casey
- D: Oscar Wilde

90

Which of these is a type of past tense?

- A: Improper
- B: Imperfect
- C: Important
- D: Impecunious

50:50 Go to page 462 Go to page 486 ? Answers on page 498

12 ◆ £125,000

91

Which of these is the title of a 1981 U2 album?

A: July
B: August
C: September
D: October

92

Of which Caribbean country was Michael Manley prime minister?

A: Antigua
B: Barbados
C: Jamaica
D: St Lucia

50:50 Go to page 462 Go to page 486 ? Answers on page 498

50:50

15		£1 MILLION
14		£500,000
13	◆	£250,000
12	◆	£125,000
11	◆	£64,000
10	◆	£32,000
9	◆	£16,000
8	◆	£8,000
7	◆	£4,000
6	◆	£2,000
5	◆	£1,000
4	◆	£500
3	◆	£300
2	◆	£200
1	◆	£100

13 ◆ £250,000

1

Who wrote the novel 'Jamaica Inn'?

- A: Susan Hill
- B: Iris Murdoch
- C: Daphne Du Maurier
- D: Patricia Highsmith

2

Which of these is the title of an album by the Beach Boys?

- A: Pet Rumbles
- B: Pet Noises
- C: Pet Sounds
- D: Pet Shrieks

3

The word 'rubáiyát' is a term most commonly used in relation to which branch of the arts?

- A: Sculpture
- B: Classical music
- C: Poetry
- D: Ballet

4

What was the profession of Alberto Giacometti?

- A: Politician
- B: Sculptor
- C: Sportsman
- D: Pop star

5

Liam Howlett and Keith Flint are members of which dance group?

- A: Prodigy
- B: Moby
- C: Faithless
- D: Shamen

50:50 Go to page 463 · Go to page 487 · ? Answers on page 498

13 ◆ £250,000

6

Where would a Hindu woman traditionally wear a 'bindi'?

A: Elbow
B: Ankle
C: Forehead
D: Neck

7

Etruria was once a region of which modern day country?

A: France
B: Germany
C: Spain
D: Italy

8

In which year did Edmund Hillary first reach the summit of Everest?

A: 1950
B: 1953
C: 1956
D: 1959

9

Bobby Fischer is a former world champion in which game?

A: Backgammon
B: Darts
C: Snooker
D: Chess

10

What famous landmark is located on the island of Staffa?

A: Giant's Causeway
B: Blarney Stone
C: Fingal's Cave
D: Scott Monument

50:50 Go to page 463 Go to page 487 ? Answers on page 498

13 ◆ £250,000

11

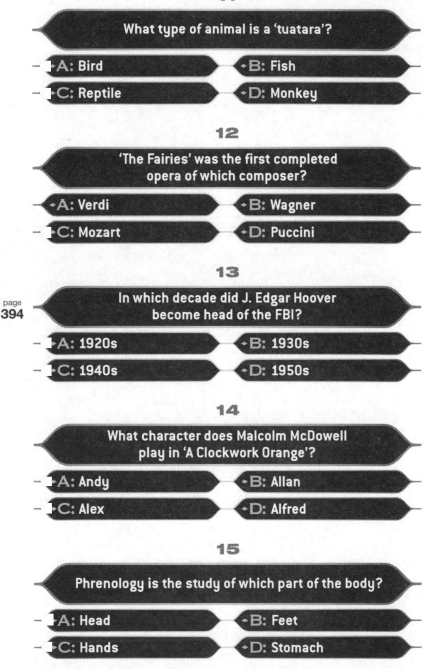

What type of animal is a 'tuatara'?

A: Bird
B: Fish
C: Reptile
D: Monkey

12

'The Fairies' was the first completed opera of which composer?

A: Verdi
B: Wagner
C: Mozart
D: Puccini

13

In which decade did J. Edgar Hoover become head of the FBI?

A: 1920s
B: 1930s
C: 1940s
D: 1950s

14

What character does Malcolm McDowell play in 'A Clockwork Orange'?

A: Andy
B: Allan
C: Alex
D: Alfred

15

Phrenology is the study of which part of the body?

A: Head
B: Feet
C: Hands
D: Stomach

50:50 Go to page 463 Go to page 487 ? Answers on page 498

13 ◆ £250,000

16

The word 'pilgarlic' describes a person with which physical characteristic?

- A: Large ears
- B: Big nose
- C: Fat fingers
- D: Bald head

17

What was the profession of Grace Darling's father?

- A: Lighthouse keeper
- B: Smuggler
- C: Policeman
- D: Magistrate

18

In Australia, the Sheffield Shield is a competition in which sport?

- A: Rugby league
- B: Australian rules football
- C: Cricket
- D: Tennis

19

What was the first name of the astronomer after whom Halley's comet is named?

- A: Lionel
- B: Gilbert
- C: Charles
- D: Edmund

20

Talca is a city in which country?

- A: Brazil
- B: Chile
- C: Ecuador
- D: Argentina

50:50 Go to page 463 · Go to page 487 · ? Answers on page 498

13 ◆ £250,000

21

Tallahassee is the capital of which US state?

A: California
B: Alabama
C: Florida
D: Texas

22

Which US state is named after the wife of England's Charles I?

A: Virginia
B: Maryland
C: North Carolina
D: Louisiana

23

Benghazi and Tripoli are the two main cities in which Mediterranean country?

A: Libya
B: Lebanon
C: Tunisia
D: Syria

24

Which African country changed its name to Zambia when it gained independence in 1964?

A: Abyssinia
B: Northern Rhodesia
C: Southern Rhodesia
D: Nyasaland

25

In history, who was known as the Maid of Orleans?

A: Marie Antoinette
B: St Bernadette
C: Joan of Arc
D: Empress Josephine

50:50 Go to page 463 Go to page 487 ? Answers on page 498

13 ◆ £250,000

26

Which of these events featured in the American Civil War?

- A: Battle of Gettysburg
- B: Boston Tea Party
- C: Custer's Last Stand
- D: Siege of the Alamo

27

What was the first name of the French artist Chagall?

- A: Henri
- B: Antoine
- C: Marc
- D: Jean-Claude

28

Who was the leader of the Liberal Party when it merged with the SDP in 1988?

- A: Paddy Ashdown
- B: David Steel
- C: Joe Grimmond
- D: David Owen

29

What is Clyde, who stars with Clint Eastwood in 'Every Which Way But Loose'?

- A: Baby elephant
- B: St Bernard dog
- C: Orphaned calf
- D: Orang-utan

30

Which of these was a Scottish title of rank, used by Shakespeare in his play 'Macbeth'?

- A: Thane
- B: Provost
- C: Laird
- D: Chief

50:50 Go to page 463 Go to page 487 ? Answers on page 498

31

Who was the first British sovereign to be 'Elector of Hanover'?

A: George I
B: Victoria
C: William IV
D: Edward V

32

The boll weevil is an insect that attacks which American crop?

A: Cotton
B: Tobacco
C: Sweetcorn
D: Grapes

33

What is the literal meaning of the Latin phrase 'Quid pro quo'?

A: Something for something
B: Something for nothing
C: Something for everything
D: Something for anything

34

Which of these American cities is on the Mississippi River?

A: Atlanta
B: Kansas City
C: Chicago
D: Memphis

35

Which of these British servicemen are members of the 'Senior Service'?

A: Airmen
B: Soldiers
C: Sailors
D: TA volunteers

50:50 Go to page 463 Go to page 487 ? Answers on page 498

13 ◆ £250,000

36

Which of these is a cricket term for a delivery by a left-handed spin bowler to a right-handed batsman?

A: Chinaman
B: Prussian
C: Antipodean
D: Laplander

37

What was the profession of Auguste Escoffier?

A: Chef
B: Composer
C: Engineer
D: Sportsman

38

Which US state is appropriately nicknamed 'The Last Frontier'?

A: Wyoming
B: Alaska
C: Montana
D: Hawaii

39

What nationality was the 20th century artist Paul Klee?

A: French
B: Swiss
C: Belgian
D: Dutch

40

Berry Gordy was the founder of which record company?

A: Motown
B: Paisley Park
C: Maverick
D: Chess

50:50 Go to page 463 Go to page 487 ? Answers on page 498

13 ◆ £250,000

41

Glaucoma is a disease that affects which part of the body?

A: Hair
B: Eyes
C: Gums
D: Muscles

42

In area, which is the largest country in the European Union?

A: France
B: Germany
C: Spain
D: Italy

43

What is the word for Hoover, Biro or Jacuzzi, items named after the person who invented them?

A: Patronym
B: Acronym
C: Synonym
D: Eponym

44

Andorra is a country landlocked in which mountain range?

A: Pyrenees
B: Andes
C: Himalayas
D: Alps

45

Which Scandinavian country has never hosted a Winter or Summer Olympics?

A: Sweden
B: Norway
C: Finland
D: Denmark

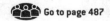

50:50 Go to page 463 Go to page 487 ? Answers on page 498

13 ◆ £250,000

46

What was the specific name for the coastal regions of Turkey, Lebanon, Syria and Israel?

A: Palestine
B: The Levant
C: Anatolia
D: Mesopotamia

47

'Paschal' is a word that relates to which festival in the Christian calendar?

A: Epiphany
B: Easter
C: Pentecost
D: Advent

48

In which London square is the US Embassy situated?

A: Eton Square
B: Grosvenor Square
C: Brunswick Square
D: Berkeley Square

49

In what type of rocks are stalagmites and stalactites formed?

A: Limestone
B: Granite
C: Sandstone
D: Slate

50

Who composed the music for the 1947 musical 'Brigadoon'?

A: Richard Rodgers
B: Jerry Bock
C: Cole Porter
D: Frederick Loewe

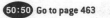

50:50 Go to page 463 · Go to page 487 · ? Answers on page 498

13 ◆ £250,000

51

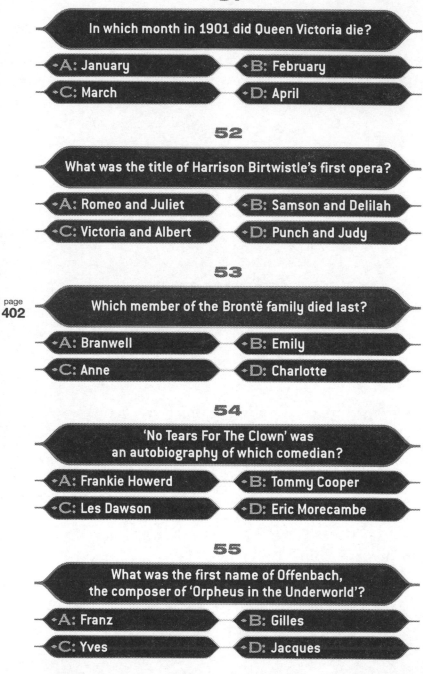

In which month in 1901 did Queen Victoria die?

- A: January
- B: February
- C: March
- D: April

52

What was the title of Harrison Birtwistle's first opera?

- A: Romeo and Juliet
- B: Samson and Delilah
- C: Victoria and Albert
- D: Punch and Judy

53

Which member of the Brontë family died last?

- A: Branwell
- B: Emily
- C: Anne
- D: Charlotte

54

'No Tears For The Clown' was an autobiography of which comedian?

- A: Frankie Howerd
- B: Tommy Cooper
- C: Les Dawson
- D: Eric Morecambe

55

What was the first name of Offenbach, the composer of 'Orpheus in the Underworld'?

- A: Franz
- B: Gilles
- C: Yves
- D: Jacques

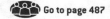

50:50 Go to page 463 · Go to page 487 · Answers on page 498

13 ◆ £250,000

56

In chemistry, on the pH scale which number is neutral?

- A: 3
- B: 5
- C: 7
- D: 9

57

To which family of flowers does the cyclamen belong?

- A: Lily
- B: Primrose
- C: Iris
- D: Magnolia

58

What type of bird is a flicker?

- A: Penguin
- B: Vulture
- C: Dove
- D: Woodpecker

59

Which of these colours does not appear on the flag of Iceland?

- A: Yellow
- B: White
- C: Blue
- D: Red

60

The town of Mafeking was besieged for seven months during which war?

- A: Boer War
- B: Hundred Years' War
- C: Vietnam War
- D: World War I

50:50 Go to page 463 Go to page 487 ? Answers on page 498

13 ◆ £250,000

61

Where in the body is the malar bone?

A: Ankle
B: Cheek
C: Elbow
D: Thumb

62

What are the names of George W. Bush's daughters?

A: Barbara and Jenna
B: Barbara and Ellie
C: Laura and Pam
D: Laura and Lucy

63

Which of these British Commonwealth countries has the highest population?

A: Canada
B: Australia
C: United Kingdom
D: Kenya

64

'Rennet' is particularly used in the making of which food or drink?

A: Beer
B: Bread
C: Cheese
D: Wine

65

Which of these creatures might suffer from the disease 'rinderpest'?

A: Horses
B: Cattle
C: Chickens
D: Dogs

50:50 Go to page 463 Go to page 487 ? Answers on page 498

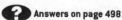

13 ◆ £250,000

66

'Wicca' is another term for what?

A: Water divining
B: Wind energy
C: Witchcraft
D: Wine tasting

67

Julius was the real name of which of the Marx Brothers?

A: Groucho
B: Chico
C: Harpo
D: Zeppo

68

What nationality was the composer Heitor Villa-Lobos?

A: Argentinian
B: Chilean
C: Venezuelan
D: Brazilian

69

In which film does Johnny Depp play Ichabod Crane?

A: Chocolat
B: Sleepy Hollow
C: Dead Man
D: Arizona Dream

70

In the army, which of these ranks would class as a subaltern?

A: 2nd lieutenant
B: Major
C: Colonel
D: Brigadier

50:50 Go to page 463 · Go to page 487 · ? Answers on page 498

13 ◆ £250,000

71

What chiefly takes place in the Lincoln Center in New York?

A: Shopping
B: Boxing
C: Artistic performances
D: Baseball

72

Which author created the Grinch?

A: Raymond Briggs
B: Allan Ahlberg
C: Dr Seuss
D: Maurice Sendak

73

Who are paid according to the Burnham scale?

A: Civil servants
B: Clergy
C: Nurses
D: Teachers

74

Which modern country is on the site of the biblical Sheba?

A: Iraq
B: Jordan
C: Lebanon
D: Yemen

75

In which field is Milton Friedman a famous name?

A: Medicine
B: Physics
C: Literature
D: Economics

50:50 Go to page 463 Go to page 487 ? Answers on page 498

13 ◆ £250,000

76

Who was chosen as George W. Bush's vice president in 2000?

A: Ralph Nader
B: Dick Cheney
C: Pat Buchanan
D: Newt Gingrich

77

In which musical does the song 'The Surrey With The Fringe On Top' feature?

A: Oklahoma!
B: State Fair
C: Carousel
D: Paint Your Wagon

78

What is a 'maelstrom'?

A: Sandstorm
B: Earthquake
C: Whirlpool
D: Tornado

79

Which of these Indian cities is on the coast?

A: Bangalore
B: Delhi
C: Hyderabad
D: Mumbai

80

Who trained the 2001 Derby winner Galileo?

A: Michael Stoute
B: Toby Balding
C: Aidan O'Brien
D: Martin Pipe

50:50 Go to page 463 Go to page 487 ? Answers on page 498

13 ◆ £250,000

81

What nationality was the man after whom the Richter scale is named?

- A: German
- B: Swiss
- C: American
- D: British

82

In the human body, what are the hamstrings?

- A: Bones
- B: Ligaments
- C: Muscles
- D: Tendons

83

What was the title of Elvis Costello's first British chart hit?

- A: Accidents Will Happen
- B: (I Don't Wanna Go To) Chelsea
- C: Oliver's Army
- D: Watching the Detectives

84

Which specific word means the examination of one's own mental and emotional processes?

- A: Inspection
- B: Introgression
- C: Introspection
- D: Inspiration

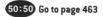

50:50 Go to page 463 Go to page 487 ? Answers on page 498

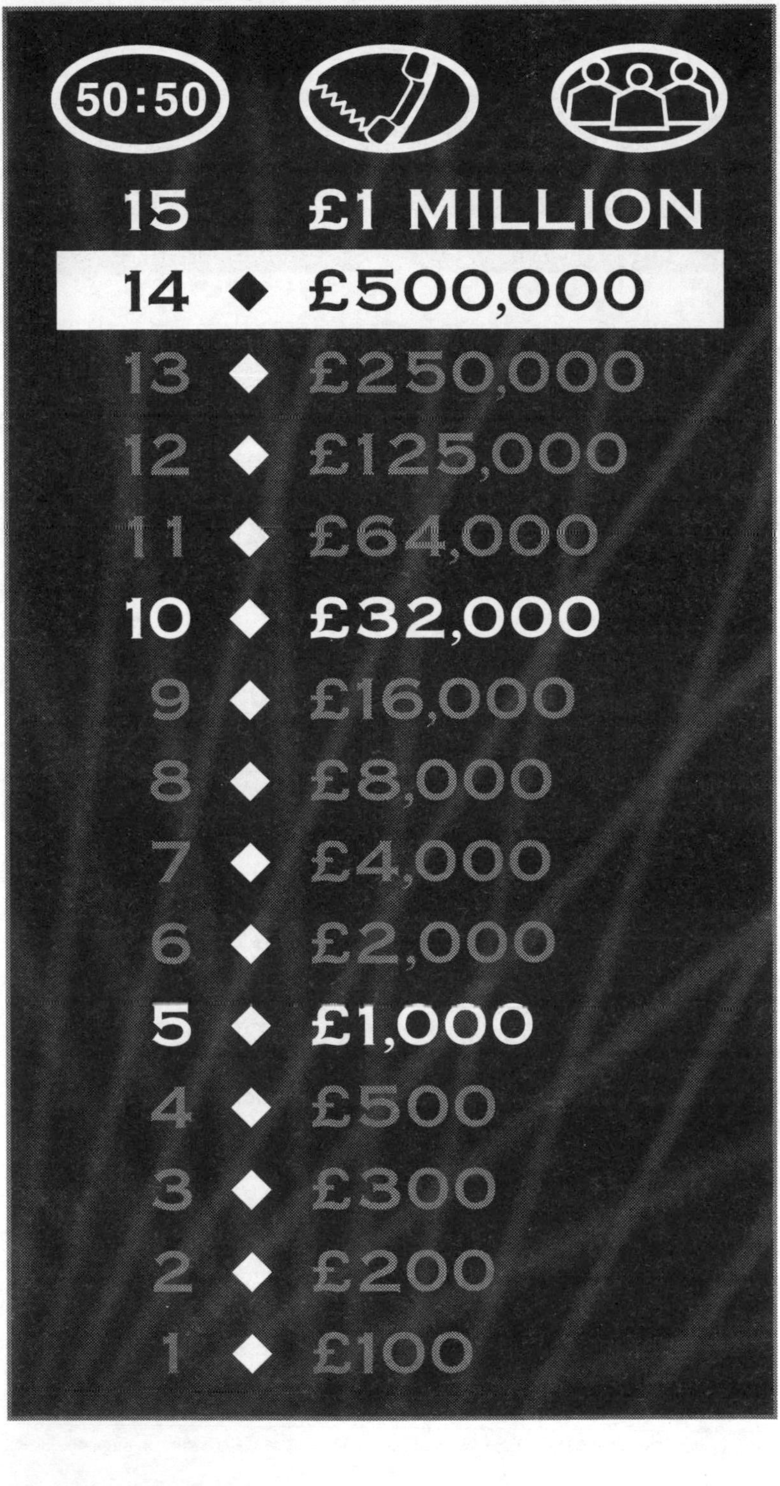
50:50
15 £1 MILLION
14 ◆ £500,000
13 ◆ £250,000
12 ◆ £125,000
11 ◆ £64,000
10 ◆ £32,000
9 ◆ £16,000
8 ◆ £8,000
7 ◆ £4,000
6 ◆ £2,000
5 ◆ £1,000
4 ◆ £500
3 ◆ £300
2 ◆ £200
1 ◆ £100

14 ◆ £500,000

1

What do the initials C.P. stand for in the name of the writer and physicist C.P. Snow?

- A: Charles Percy
- B: Courtney Powell
- C: Carlos Paolo
- D: Christopher Peter

2

Henrietta Maria was the wife of which English king?

- A: William I
- B: Henry I
- C: Charles I
- D: Edward I

3

Who attempted to steal the Crown Jewels in 1671?

- A: Thomas Gore
- B: Thomas Guts
- C: Thomas Blood
- D: Thomas Entrails

4

Portobello is a port in which country?

- A: Cuba
- B: Panama
- C: Surinam
- D: Venezuela

5

What is the deepest lake in the USA?

- A: Crater Lake
- B: Lake Superior
- C: Lake Winnipeg
- D: Great Salt Lake

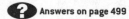

50:50 Go to page 464 Go to page 488 ? Answers on page 499

14 ◆ £500,000

6

What does the word 'blitzkrieg' mean when translated from the German?

A: Death from above
B: Lightning war
C: Sky plague
D: Heaven fire

7

If you were 'hornswoggling' someone, what would you be doing?

A: Praising them
B: Cheating them
C: Attacking them
D: Loving them

8

Dunedin is one of the biggest cities in which Commonwealth country?

A: Jamaica
B: Canada
C: Sri Lanka
D: New Zealand

9

In Greek mythology, who was the nephew of Daedalus?

A: Theseus
B: Talos
C: Actaeon
D: Narcissus

10

Harlean Carpenter was the real name of which Hollywood star?

A: Mary Pickford
B: Carole Lombard
C: Clara Bow
D: Jean Harlow

50:50 Go to page 464 Go to page 488 ? Answers on page 499

11

Which woman was Wimbledon champion from 1919 to 1925?

- A: Maureen Connolly
- B: Lottie Dodd
- C: Alice Marble
- D: Suzanne Lenglen

12

Lotte Lenya was the wife of which songwriter?

- A: Burt Bacharach
- B: Oscar Hammerstein
- C: Kurt Weill
- D: George Gershwin

13

Randle P. McMurphy is the central character in which book?

- A: One Flew Over The Cuckoo's Nest
- B: On The Road
- C: Naked Lunch
- D: Catch-22

14

Ljubljana is the capital of which country?

- A: Macedonia
- B: Ukraine
- C: Slovenia
- D: Albania

15

Which of these British prime ministers was Lord Palmerston?

- A: Sir Charles Grey
- B: Sir Henry John Temple
- C: Sir George Hamilton Gordon
- D: Sir William Lamb

50:50 Go to page 464 Go to page 488 ? Answers on page 499

14 ◆ £500,000

16

'Pedology' is the study of what?

- A: Soils
- B: Education
- C: Feet
- D: Cycling

17

What was the name of General Grant, the soldier who became the 18th President of the USA?

- A: Odysseus
- B: Achilles
- C: Ulysses
- D: Hercules

18

The Klondike, to which gold prospectors rushed in 1896, is a region of which country?

- A: USA
- B: South Africa
- C: Russia
- D: Canada

19

The Hermitage is a major art museum in which European city?

- A: Amsterdam
- B: Brussels
- C: St Petersburg
- D: Copenhagen

20

'Some Day My Prince Will Come' is a song from which animated Disney feature film?

- A: Cinderella
- B: Snow White
- C: Sleeping Beauty
- D: Beauty and the Beast

50:50 Go to page 464 Go to page 488 ? Answers on page 499

14 ◆ £500,000

21

Which parliament of Charles I governed before and into the English Civil War?

- A: Fleet Parliament
- B: Great Parliament
- C: Short Parliament
- D: Long Parliament

22

Enniskillen is the county town of which county in Northern Ireland?

- A: Fermanagh
- B: Down
- C: Tyrone
- D: Armagh

23

What is the name of the idyllic utopia in James Hilton's novel 'Lost Horizon'?

- A: Eldorado
- B: Shangri-la
- C: Brigadoon
- D: Celador

24

Which of these planets does not have a radioactive element named after it?

- A: Pluto
- B: Uranus
- C: Saturn
- D: Neptune

25

'My word is my bond' is the motto of which British institution?

- A: London Stock Exchange
- B: House of Lords
- C: Inns of Court
- D: MI6

50:50 Go to page 464 Go to page 488 ? Answers on page 499

14 ◆ £500,000

26

World War I started after the assassination of Franz Ferdinand, Archduke of which country?

A: Prussia
B: Russia
C: Latvia
D: Austria

27

What is the meaning of the prefix 'halo-'?

A: Ring
B: Water
C: Salt
D: Gas

28

Which of these American states is part of the region called New England?

A: New Hampshire
B: Maryland
C: New York
D: Washington

29

What follows the Tan-tan-tara in the song that signals the approach of the Lord Chancellor's procession in Gilbert and Sullivan's 'Iolanthe'?

A: Tzing! Boom!
B: Bang! Crash!
C: Ching! Thump!
D: Bing! Bong!

30

Who assumed the US Presidency after the assassination of William McKinley in 1901?

A: Woodrow Wilson
B: Grover Cleveland
C: Calvin Coolidge
D: Theodore Roosevelt

50:50 Go to page 464 Go to page 488 ? Answers on page 499

14 ◆ £500,000

31

Oona, Charlie Chaplin's fourth and last wife, was the daughter of which famous American writer?

- A: F. Scott Fitzgerald
- B: Henry James
- C: Tennessee Williams
- D: Eugene O'Neill

32

Triton is a satellite of which planet?

- A: Neptune
- B: Saturn
- C: Uranus
- D: Jupiter

33

A 'columbarium' is another name for... what?

- A: Chicken coop
- B: Kitten basket
- C: Dovecote
- D: Rabbit run

34

The American Robert Frost was famous for writing... what?

- A: Poetry
- B: Detective stories
- C: Biographies
- D: Plays

35

Pakapoo is a Chinese form of what?

- A: Water feature
- B: Japanese
- C: Lottery
- D: Hopscotch

50:50 Go to page 464 Go to page 488 ? Answers on page 499

14 ◆ £500,000

36

Which creature belongs to the family Castoridae?

A: Shrew
B: Beaver
C: Dormouse
D: Marmot

37

Which fashion designer married sculptor Stephan Weiss?

A: Donna Karan
B: Mary Quant
C: Vivienne Westwood
D: Zandra Rhodes

38

Alf Ramsey was manager of which football team from 1955 to 1963?

A: Aston Villa
B: Southampton
C: Middlesbrough
D: Ipswich Town

39

In which city was the ballerina Anna Pavlova born?

A: St Petersburg
B: Volgograd
C: Moscow
D: Yekaterinburg

40

'Dysphagia' is a difficulty in doing what?

A: Sleeping
B: Spelling
C: Swallowing
D: Speaking

50:50 Go to page 464 Go to page 488 ? Answers on page 499

14 ◆ £500,000

41

The Marshalsea debtors' prison was situated in which part of London?

- A: Fulham
- B: Leyton
- C: Pimlico
- D: Southwark

42

A shellback is an informal term for a sailor who has done what?

- A: Served in a war
- B: Sailed round Cape Horn
- C: Crossed the Equator
- D: Drunk a gallon of rum

43

Which parts of the body are affected by myositis?

- A: Joints
- B: Bones
- C: Veins
- D: Muscles

44

The Camorra is a secret society originally from which Italian city?

- A: Modena
- B: Naples
- C: Rome
- D: Venice

45

The word 'Messiah' comes from a Hebrew word meaning what?

- A: Anointed
- B: Believer
- C: Devout
- D: Teacher

50:50 Go to page 464 | Go to page 488 | ? Answers on page 499

46

What kind of mineral is aquamarine?

- A: Beryl
- B: Corundum
- C: Garnet
- D: Quartz

47

McGill University is based in which Canadian city?

- A: Montreal
- B: Toronto
- C: Vancouver
- D: Winnipeg

48

Stalactites consist of which mineral?

- A: Silicon hydroxide
- B: Calcium carbonate
- C: Magnesium sulphate
- D: Sodium silicate

49

The Maghrib is a region of which continent?

- A: Africa
- B: Asia
- C: North America
- D: South America

50

In which industry is a machine called a 'nodding donkey' used?

- A: Film
- B: Oil
- C: Fishing
- D: Shipbuilding

50:50 Go to page 464 Go to page 488 ? Answers on page 499

51

Who composed the opera 'Tristan and Isolde'?

A: Beethoven
B: Strauss
C: Wagner
D: Weber

52

In the Christian calendar, in which month is Innocents' Day?

A: September
B: October
C: November
D: December

53

Madame du Barry was the mistress of which French king?

A: Louis XIII
B: Louis XIV
C: Louis XV
D: Louis XVI

54

William Wallace led an uprising against which king of England?

A: Edward I
B: Edward II
C: Henry I
D: Henry II

55

What nationality was Maurice Maeterlinck, the winner of the 1911 Nobel Literature Prize?

A: Belgian
B: Dutch
C: French
D: German

50:50 Go to page 464 Go to page 488 ? Answers on page 499

14 ◆ £500,000

56

The Waikato is the longest river in which country?

A: Papua New Guinea
B: New Zealand
C: Australia
D: Chile

57

In Vanuatu, in the Pacific, who or what is 'Bislama'?

A: A religion
B: A language
C: A rain god
D: A stew

58

In Greek myth, the nymph Arethusa was changed into a...what?

A: Cloud
B: Rainbow
C: Spring
D: Waterfall

59

Which insects belong to the order Coleoptera?

A: Wasps
B: Ants
C: Grasshoppers
D: Beetles

60

Which item of clothing shares its name with a timber joint?

A: Hat
B: Coat
C: Scarf
D: Sock

50:50 Go to page 464 Go to page 488 ? Answers on page 499

14 ◆ £500,000

61

Koplick's spots are a feature of which disease?

A: Mumps
B: Measles
C: Whooping-cough
D: Chickenpox

62

Who was the first man to win the Nobel Prize for Physics?

A: Pierre Curie
B: Wilhelm Röntgen
C: Henri Becquerel
D: Gabriel Lippmann

63

Which country lies immediately to the north of Chad?

A: Algeria
B: Egypt
C: Libya
D: Morocco

64

How many players are there on a shinty team?

A: Six
B: Eight
C: Nine
D: Twelve

65

Launceston is the chief port of which island?

A: Jamaica
B: Prince Edward Island
C: Tasmania
D: Zanzibar

50:50 Go to page 464 · Go to page 488 · ? Answers on page 499

14 ◆ £500,000

66

With which field of the arts was Adelina Patti associated?

A: Ballet
B: Opera
C: Poetry
D: Sculpture

67

The city of Avignon stands on which river?

A: Seine
B: Loire
C: Isère
D: Rhône

68

A Parmentier dish is garnished with which vegetable?

A: Carrot
B: Onion
C: Potato
D: Aubergine

69

Which American Civil War general was accidentally shot by his own soldiers in 1863?

A: Robert E. Lee
B: Thomas 'Stonewall' Jackson
C: James Longstreet
D: Pierre Beauregard

70

Who had a UK hit single with Sarah Brightman in 1997 with 'Time To Say Goodbye'?

A: Luciano Pavarotti
B: Paul Miles-Kingston
C: Andrea Bocelli
D: Placido Domingo

50:50 Go to page 464 Go to page 488 ? Answers on page 499

14 ◆ £500,000

71

In which county are Pinewood studios?

A: Hertfordshire
B: Berkshire
C: Surrey
D: Buckinghamshire

72

Who published his 'American Dictionary of the English Language' in 1828?

A: John Collins
B: William Chambers
C: Noah Webster
D: Samuel Johnson

73

An 'okta' is a measure of what?

A: Star magnitude
B: Cloud cover
C: Soil saturation
D: Wind intensity

74

What is the capital of Haiti?

A: Port Louis
B: Port-of-Spain
C: Port Moresby
D: Port-au-Prince

75

In which century did the building of Pisa's Leaning Tower begin?

A: 8th
B: 10th
C: 12th
D: 14th

50:50 Go to page 464 Go to page 488 ? Answers on page 499

14 ◆ £500,000

76

Who plays the title role in TV's 'The Larry Sanders Show'?

A: Garry Shandling
B: Jerry Seinfeld
C: Paul Reiser
D: Charlie Sheen

50:50 Go to page 464 Go to page 488 ? Answers on page 499

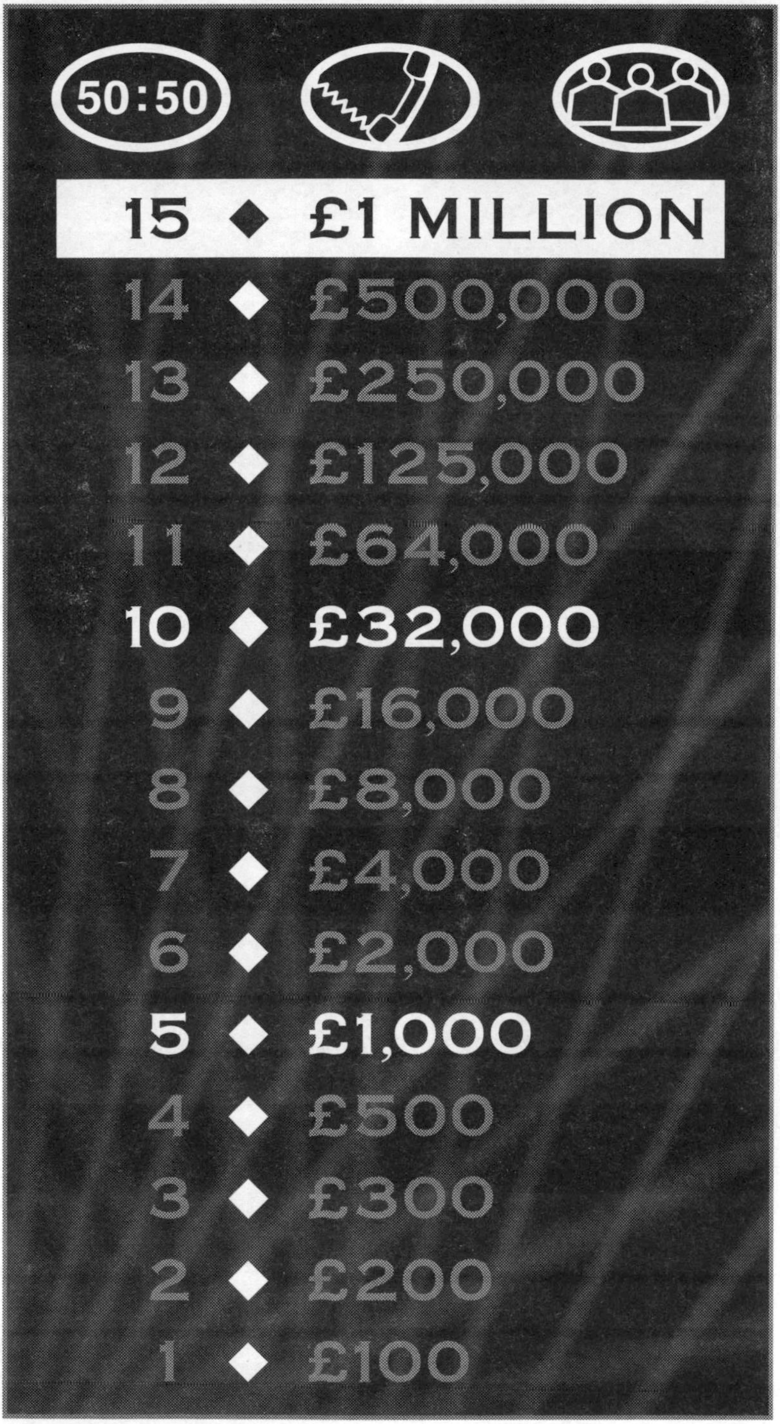
50:50
15 ◆ £1 MILLION
14 ◆ £500,000
13 ◆ £250,000
12 ◆ £125,000
11 ◆ £64,000
10 ◆ £32,000
9 ◆ £16,000
8 ◆ £8,000
7 ◆ £4,000
6 ◆ £2,000
5 ◆ £1,000
4 ◆ £500
3 ◆ £300
2 ◆ £200
1 ◆ £100

15 ◆ £1 MILLION

1

What type of animal was the extinct 'aurochs'?

A: Ox | B: Eagle
C: Monkey | D: Lion

2

Which of these is another name for the plant known as the scarlet pimpernel?

A: Farmer's Weatherglass | B: Doctor's Weatherglass
C: Shepherd's Weatherglass | D: Boatman's Weatherglass

3

Who wrote the 1779 play 'The Critic'?

A: Oliver Goldsmith | B: George Farquhar
C: Richard Brinsley Sheridan | D: William Congreve

4

In Norse mythology, what was Fafnir?

A: Dragon | B: Dwarf
C: Goddess | D: Horse

5

The Society Islands are located in which ocean?

A: Indian | B: Pacific
C: Atlantic | D: Arctic

50:50 Go to page 465 Go to page 489 ? Answers on page 499

15 ◆ £1 MILLION

6

In Indonesia, what is a 'songkok'?

A: Water buffalo
B: Hat
C: Boat
D: Government

7

Reuben Haredale appears in which Charles Dickens novel?

A: Hard Times
B: Barnaby Rudge
C: Nicholas Nickleby
D: Oliver Twist

8

The dish called 'spitchcock' is made from which animal?

A: Shark
B: Octopus
C: Eel
D: Manatee

9

What is the capital of Fiji?

A: Nadi
B: Labasa
C: Levuku
D: Suva

10

3-D, Daddy G and Mushroom are members of which pop group?

A: Portishead
B: Massive Attack
C: Wu-Tang Clan
D: Beastie Boys

50:50 Go to page 465 · Go to page 489 · ? Answers on page 499

15 ◆ £1 MILLION

11

By what name is the rock star James Jewel Osterberg better known?

A: Beck
B: Iggy Pop
C: Bono
D: Lemmy

12

Bart Starr was a leading figure in which sport?

A: Ice hockey
B: Basketball
C: American football
D: Baseball

13

The jazz musician Art Blakey was an expert on which instrument?

A: Guitar
B: Drums
C: Saxophone
D: Trumpet

14

Which of these writers was born in Bromley, Kent, in 1866?

A: Rudyard Kipling
B: H.G. Wells
C: Thomas Hardy
D: P.G. Wodehouse

15

In which country is the Order of the Paulownia Sun awarded?

A: Brazil
B: France
C: Japan
D: Germany

50:50 Go to page 465 Go to page 489 ? Answers on page 499

15 ◆ £1 MILLION

16

George Orwell wrote 'Nineteen Eighty-Four' in 1949, but who wrote '1985' in 1978?

A: Kingsley Amis
B: Anthony Burgess
C: Ian Fleming
D: John Osborne

17

A tercel is the male of which bird?

A: Partridge
B: Hawk
C: Crow
D: Peacock

18

What is the literal meaning of 'Eskimo'?

A: Family of the cold
B: Eater of raw meat
C: Seal hunter
D: Ice house maker

19

Lot, whose wife was turned into a pillar of salt, was what relation to Abraham?

A: Uncle
B: Brother
C: Grandson
D: Nephew

20

If something is described as 'pavonine', which bird does it resemble?

A: Parrot
B: Peacock
C: Pigeon
D: Penguin

50:50 Go to page 465 Go to page 489 ? Answers on page 499

15 ◆ £1 MILLION

21

Grumio and Gremio are two characters in which Shakespeare play?

- A: Love's Labour's Lost
- B: The Taming of the Shrew
- C: The Comedy of Errors
- D: Measure for Measure

22

In the USA, President's Day is celebrated on the third Monday of which month?

- A: February
- B: May
- C: August
- D: October

23

What was the botanical emblem of the Plantagenets?

- A: Two oak leaves
- B: Sprig of broom
- C: Holly twig and berries
- D: Wild violet

24

Which Rodgers and Hammerstein musical was based on Lynn Riggs's play 'Green Grow the Lilacs'?

- A: State Fair
- B: Oklahoma!
- C: Carousel
- D: South Pacific

25

Why was Brian Trubshaw a famous name in Britain?

- A: Concorde test pilot
- B: Produced first Bond film
- C: Internet inventor
- D: Designer of the Mini

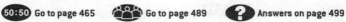

50:50 Go to page 465 | Go to page 489 | ? Answers on page 499

15 ◆ £1 MILLION

26

What is the collective word for a flock of geese in flight?

A: Muster
B: Skein
C: Wisp
D: Sedge

27

Yerevan is the capital of which country, once a republic of the Soviet Union?

A: Belarus
B: Armenia
C: Kazakhstan
D: Moldavia

28

Tashkent and Samarkand are two cities in which independent republic?

A: Turkmenistan
B: Kazakhstan
C: Azerbaijan
D: Uzbekistan

29

Which of these novels did D. H. Lawrence write first?

A: The Plumed Serpent
B: Lady Chatterley's Lover
C: The Rainbow
D: The White Peacock

30

What is the diet of 'limivorous' animals?

A: Bark
B: Mud
C: Bracken
D: Lichen

50:50 Go to page 465 Go to page 489 ? Answers on page 499

15 ◆ £1 MILLION

31

Which region of Russia, surrounded by Poland, Lithuania and Belarus, is an enclave 600km from Russia itself?

A: Novgorod
B: Kaliningrad
C: Sakhalin
D: Stavropol

32

On which continent is the country of Surinam?

A: Asia
B: Africa
C: South America
D: Europe

33

In Greek mythology, who built the Labyrinth in which the Minotaur lived?

A: Prometheus
B: Daedalus
C: Perseus
D: Theseus

34

What was the name of the federal investigation into the assassination of President Kennedy?

A: Operation Eagle
B: Manhattan Project
C: Warren Commission
D: Brady Board

35

Bjorn Borg won five Wimbledon Singles Championships in a row, but who stopped him taking his sixth?

A: John Newcombe
B: Roscoe Tanner
C: Jimmy Connors
D: John McEnroe

50:50 Go to page 465 Go to page 489 ? Answers on page 499

15 ◆ £1 MILLION

36

Who contested the Tory leadership with Major and Heseltine after Mrs Thatcher's resignation?

- A: Norman Fowler
- B: Douglas Hurd
- C: Willie Whitelaw
- D: Geoffrey Howe

37

In which South American country are the granite peaks known as Paine Towers?

- A: Brazil
- B: Chile
- C: Argentina
- D: Peru

38

Which poison is obtained from the seeds of the nux vomica tree?

- A: Arsenic
- B: Hemlock
- C: Aconitine
- D: Strychnine

39

Lady Dedlock is a character in which Charles Dickens novel?

- A: Hard Times
- B: Bleak House
- C: Oliver Twist
- D: Great Expectations

40

In which year was Karl Marx born?

- A: 1808
- B: 1818
- C: 1828
- D: 1838

50:50 Go to page 465 · Go to page 489 · ? Answers on page 499

15 ◆ £1 MILLION

41

If something is described as 'marmoreal', what does it resemble?

- A: Marble
- B: Marshland
- C: Monkeys
- D: Meadowland

42

The name of which public place comes from the Latin meaning 'sand'?

- A: Arena
- B: Colosseum
- C: Field
- D: Stadium

43

Which post was held in India by Sir George Everest, the official after whom the mountain is named?

- A: Governor General
- B: Viceroy
- C: Surveyor General
- D: Commander-in-Chief

44

GSK is a leading company in which field?

- A: Publishing
- B: Software
- C: Pharmaceuticals
- D: Food

45

In Greek mythology, who was the mother of Orestes?

- A: Electra
- B: Iphigenia
- C: Andromache
- D: Clytemnestra

50:50 Go to page 465 Go to page 489 ? Answers on page 499

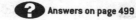

15 ◆ £1 MILLION

46

What is the more common name for the tree Araucaria araucana?

A: Baobab
B: Judas
C: Monkey puzzle
D: Sago palm

47

What kind of creature is a 'bilby'?

A: Fish
B: Amphibian
C: Marsupial
D: Insect

48

In ancient Greece, Sparta was the capital of which country?

A: Boeotia
B: Argolis
C: Laconia
D: Macedon

49

In which US state is Rutgers University?

A: New Hampshire
B: New Jersey
C: New Mexico
D: New York

50

In Norse mythology, which creatures lived in Jotunheim?

A: Dwarves
B: Gods
C: Men
D: Giants

50:50 Go to page 465 · Go to page 489 · ? Answers on page 499

15 ◆ £1 MILLION

51

Which French author wrote the satirical work 'Candide'?

A: Corneille
B: Molière
C: Rabelais
D: Voltaire

52

The Negus was the title of the ruler of which African country?

A: Benin
B: Ethiopia
C: Libya
D: Zimbabwe

53

What was the first novel in John Galsworthy's 'Forsyte Saga'?

A: In Chancery
B: The White Monkey
C: Swan Song
D: The Man of Property

54

In which century did the Chinese emperor Kublai Khan live?

A: 11th
B: 12th
C: 13th
D: 14th

55

Which man won a gold medal when tennis was re-introduced into the Olympics in 1988?

A: Marc Rosset
B: Miloslav Mečíř
C: Anders Jarryd
D: Slobodan Zivojinovic

50:50 Go to page 465 Go to page 489 ? Answers on page 499

56

Where in a church would a 'reredos' be found'?

A: Altar
B: Belfry
C: Choir stalls
D: Pulpit

57

Which symbol appears on the national flag of Nauru?

A: Palm tree
B: Star
C: Crescent moon
D: Bird

58

What was the name of the first space probe to hit the Moon?

A: Viking
B: Ranger 4
C: Luna 2
D: Voyager

59

Hero is a character in which Shakespeare play?

A: Love's Labour's Lost
B: Much Ado About Nothing
C: The Tempest
D: The Winter's Tale

60

Which of these spices is obtained from the Myristica fragrans tree?

A: Clove
B: Cinnamon
C: Nutmeg
D: Paprika

50:50 Go to page 465 Go to page 489 ? Answers on page 499

15 ◆ £1 MILLION

61

A Landseer is a black and white variety of which dog?

- A: Corgi
- B: Newfoundland
- C: Doberman pinscher
- D: Irish wolfhound

62

In Greek mythology, Niobe was turned into what by Zeus?

- A: Stone
- B: Tree
- C: Spider
- D: Stream

63

Which US state has 'The Sagebrush State' as a nickname?

- A: Montana
- B: Nevada
- C: Minnesota
- D: Nebraska

64

The city of Chennai is the capital of which Indian state?

- A: Assam
- B: Kerala
- C: Rajasthan
- D: Tamil Nadu

65

Where in the body is the Bowman's capsule?

- A: Brain
- B: Ear
- C: Kidney
- D: Liver

50:50 Go to page 465 Go to page 489 ? Answers on page 499

15 ◆ £1 MILLION

66

Which Kurt Weill work features the song 'My Ship'?

- A: Knickerbocker Holiday
- B: Lady in the Dark
- C: One Touch of Venus
- D: Street Scene

67

By what name is the Roman emperor born Lucius Domitius Ahenobarbus better known?

- A: Commodus
- B: Hadrian
- C: Caligula
- D: Nero

68

Which American composer wrote the film score for the 1939 film 'Of Mice and Men'?

- A: George Gershwin
- B: Aaron Copland
- C: Samuel Barber
- D: Philip Glass

50:50 Go to page 465 Go to page 489 ? Answers on page 499

50:50

£100

1 Options remaining are A and B
2 Options remaining are A and C
3 Options remaining are A and C
4 Options remaining are B and D
5 Options remaining are A and B
6 Options remaining are B and C
7 Options remaining are B and C
8 Options remaining are A and C
9 Options remaining are B and C
10 Options remaining are A and C
11 Options remaining are A and B
12 Options remaining are A and D
13 Options remaining are A and B
14 Options remaining are A and B
15 Options remaining are C and D
16 Options remaining are B and C
17 Options remaining are A and B
18 Options remaining are A and C
19 Options remaining are A and C
20 Options remaining are B and D
21 Options remaining are C and D
22 Options remaining are B and C
23 Options remaining are A and C
24 Options remaining are B and D
25 Options remaining are A and B
26 Options remaining are B and D
27 Options remaining are A and B
28 Options remaining are C and D
29 Options remaining are A and D
30 Options remaining are A and C
31 Options remaining are B and C
32 Options remaining are A and B
33 Options remaining are A and B
34 Options remaining are B and D
35 Options remaining are A and C
36 Options remaining are B and C
37 Options remaining are A and C
38 Options remaining are C and D
39 Options remaining are C and D
40 Options remaining are A and B
41 Options remaining are B and C
42 Options remaining are B and C
43 Options remaining are A and D
44 Options remaining are A and C
45 Options remaining are C and D
46 Options remaining are A and B
47 Options remaining are B and C
48 Options remaining are A and C
49 Options remaining are A and B
50 Options remaining are A and D
51 Options remaining are A and C
52 Options remaining are A and D
53 Options remaining are A and D
54 Options remaining are A and C
55 Options remaining are A and D
56 Options remaining are A and D
57 Options remaining are A and D
58 Options remaining are C and D
59 Options remaining are A and D
60 Options remaining are A and D
61 Options remaining are A and D
62 Options remaining are A and C
63 Options remaining are C and D
64 Options remaining are A and D
65 Options remaining are A and C
66 Options remaining are A and D
67 Options remaining are B and D
68 Options remaining are C and D
69 Options remaining are A and D
70 Options remaining are A and D
71 Options remaining are A and D
72 Options remaining are A and D
73 Options remaining are A and B
74 Options remaining are A and C

75 Options remaining are A and B
76 Options remaining are A and D
77 Options remaining are A and D
78 Options remaining are A and D
79 Options remaining are A and D
80 Options remaining are A and D
81 Options remaining are B and C
82 Options remaining are A and D
83 Options remaining are A and B
84 Options remaining are A and C
85 Options remaining are B and D
86 Options remaining are A and D
87 Options remaining are A and D
88 Options remaining are C and D
89 Options remaining are C and D
90 Options remaining are A and D
91 Options remaining are A and C
92 Options remaining are A and D
93 Options remaining are A and C
94 Options remaining are B and C
95 Options remaining are A and C
96 Options remaining are A and C
97 Options remaining are A and D
98 Options remaining are A and D
99 Options remaining are A and B
100 Options remaining are A and C
101 Options remaining are A and D
102 Options remaining are A and D
103 Options remaining are A and C
104 Options remaining are A and B
105 Options remaining are A and C
106 Options remaining are B and D
107 Options remaining are A and C
108 Options remaining are A and D
109 Options remaining are A and D
110 Options remaining are A and C
111 Options remaining are B and C
112 Options remaining are B and C
113 Options remaining are A and B
114 Options remaining are A and C
115 Options remaining are B and D
116 Options remaining are C and D
117 Options remaining are A and B
118 Options remaining are B and D
119 Options remaining are C and D
120 Options remaining are A and B
121 Options remaining are B and C
122 Options remaining are A and C
123 Options remaining are A and C
124 Options remaining are A and D
125 Options remaining are A and B
126 Options remaining are A and C
127 Options remaining are A and D
128 Options remaining are A and C
129 Options remaining are B and C
130 Options remaining are A and B
131 Options remaining are B and C
132 Options remaining are A and B
133 Options remaining are A and C
134 Options remaining are B and D
135 Options remaining are C and D
136 Options remaining are B and C
137 Options remaining are A and D
138 Options remaining are A and C
139 Options remaining are A and B
140 Options remaining are B and C
141 Options remaining are A and D
142 Options remaining are A and D
143 Options remaining are A and D
144 Options remaining are A and D
145 Options remaining are A and D
146 Options remaining are A and B
147 Options remaining are A and C
148 Options remaining are B and D
149 Options remaining are A and D
150 Options remaining are B and D
151 Options remaining are A and C
152 Options remaining are B and C
153 Options remaining are A and B
154 Options remaining are A and B
155 Options remaining are A and C
156 Options remaining are B and D
157 Options remaining are B and C
158 Options remaining are A and B
159 Options remaining are B and C
160 Options remaining are A and C

161 Options remaining are A and D
162 Options remaining are A and B
163 Options remaining are A and D
164 Options remaining are A and B
165 Options remaining are B and C
166 Options remaining are A and C
167 Options remaining are B and C
168 Options remaining are A and B
169 Options remaining are A and B
170 Options remaining are B and D
171 Options remaining are A and B
172 Options remaining are A and B
173 Options remaining are A and B
174 Options remaining are A and B
175 Options remaining are A and B
176 Options remaining are A and C
177 Options remaining are B and C
178 Options remaining are B and C
179 Options remaining are B and C
180 Options remaining are A and B

£200

1 Options remaining are A and C
2 Options remaining are A and C
3 Options remaining are A and B
4 Options remaining are A and C
5 Options remaining are A and C
6 Options remaining are B and D
7 Options remaining are B and C
8 Options remaining are A and D
9 Options remaining are C and D
10 Options remaining are B and D
11 Options remaining are B and D
12 Options remaining are A and C
13 Options remaining are A and B
14 Options remaining are B and D
15 Options remaining are C and D
16 Options remaining are A and C
17 Options remaining are B and C
18 Options remaining are A and D
19 Options remaining are B and C
20 Options remaining are A and C
21 Options remaining are B and C
22 Options remaining are A and C
23 Options remaining are B and C
24 Options remaining are C and D
25 Options remaining are B and C
26 Options remaining are C and D
27 Options remaining are B and C
28 Options remaining are A and C
29 Options remaining are C and D
30 Options remaining are A and C
31 Options remaining are B and D
32 Options remaining are A and B
33 Options remaining are A and D
34 Options remaining are A and C
35 Options remaining are A and C
36 Options remaining are C and D
37 Options remaining are A and D
38 Options remaining are A and B
39 Options remaining are A and D
40 Options remaining are A and D
41 Options remaining are B and D
42 Options remaining are A and B
43 Options remaining are A and D
44 Options remaining are B and D
45 Options remaining are B and C
46 Options remaining are A and C
47 Options remaining are A and B
48 Options remaining are A and C
49 Options remaining are A and B
50 Options remaining are A and D
51 Options remaining are A and B
52 Options remaining are A and D
53 Options remaining are A and D
54 Options remaining are A and D
55 Options remaining are A and C
56 Options remaining are A and D

57 Options remaining are C and D
58 Options remaining are A and D
59 Options remaining are A and B
60 Options remaining are A and C
61 Options remaining are A and D
62 Options remaining are A and D
63 Options remaining are A and D
64 Options remaining are A and C
65 Options remaining are C and D
66 Options remaining are A and D
67 Options remaining are A and D
68 Options remaining are A and C
69 Options remaining are A and D
70 Options remaining are A and D
71 Options remaining are A and D
72 Options remaining are A and B
73 Options remaining are A and D
74 Options remaining are A and D
75 Options remaining are A and D
76 Options remaining are A and D
77 Options remaining are A and D
78 Options remaining are A and B
79 Options remaining are A and D
80 Options remaining are A and D
81 Options remaining are A and B
82 Options remaining are A and D
83 Options remaining are A and C
84 Options remaining are A and C
85 Options remaining are B and D
86 Options remaining are A and D
87 Options remaining are C and D
88 Options remaining are A and C
89 Options remaining are A and B
90 Options remaining are A and C
91 Options remaining are A and C
92 Options remaining are B and C
93 Options remaining are A and C
94 Options remaining are B and C
95 Options remaining are A and C
96 Options remaining are B and C
97 Options remaining are A and B
98 Options remaining are B and C
99 Options remaining are A and B
100 Options remaining are A and B
101 Options remaining are B and C
102 Options remaining are B and C
103 Options remaining are A and D
104 Options remaining are A and D
105 Options remaining are C and D
106 Options remaining are A and B
107 Options remaining are A and C
108 Options remaining are A and B
109 Options remaining are C and D
110 Options remaining are C and D
111 Options remaining are A and C
112 Options remaining are A and D
113 Options remaining are B and C
114 Options remaining are B and D
115 Options remaining are A and D
116 Options remaining are A and D
117 Options remaining are A and B
118 Options remaining are B and C
119 Options remaining are A and B
120 Options remaining are B and D
121 Options remaining are B and D
122 Options remaining are A and B
123 Options remaining are C and D
124 Options remaining are A and D
125 Options remaining are A and C
126 Options remaining are A and C
127 Options remaining are A and B
128 Options remaining are B and D
129 Options remaining are C and D
130 Options remaining are C and D
131 Options remaining are A and D
132 Options remaining are B and C
133 Options remaining are C and D
134 Options remaining are B and D
135 Options remaining are C and D
136 Options remaining are B and D
137 Options remaining are A and B
138 Options remaining are B and C
139 Options remaining are A and D
140 Options remaining are B and C
141 Options remaining are A and B
142 Options remaining are A and C

143 Options remaining are A and B
144 Options remaining are B and D
145 Options remaining are A and B
146 Options remaining are A and C
147 Options remaining are A and D
148 Options remaining are B and D
149 Options remaining are B and D
150 Options remaining are A and B
151 Options remaining are A and B
152 Options remaining are A and B
153 Options remaining are A and B
154 Options remaining are B and D
155 Options remaining are A and B
156 Options remaining are A and B
157 Options remaining are A and C
158 Options remaining are B and C
159 Options remaining are C and D
160 Options remaining are B and D
161 Options remaining are A and B
162 Options remaining are A and C
163 Options remaining are B and D
164 Options remaining are A and D
165 Options remaining are B and D
166 Options remaining are A and C
167 Options remaining are B and C
168 Options remaining are A and C
169 Options remaining are A and C
170 Options remaining are A and B
171 Options remaining are A and C
172 Options remaining are A and C

£300

1 Options remaining are C and D
2 Options remaining are A and D
3 Options remaining are A and C
4 Options remaining are A and C
5 Options remaining are A and C
6 Options remaining are A and B
7 Options remaining are B and D
8 Options remaining are B and D
9 Options remaining are A and B
10 Options remaining are B and D
11 Options remaining are C and D
12 Options remaining are A and B
13 Options remaining are A and B
14 Options remaining are B and D
15 Options remaining are B and D
16 Options remaining are B and C
17 Options remaining are C and D
18 Options remaining are B and C
19 Options remaining are B and D
20 Options remaining are A and B
21 Options remaining are C and D
22 Options remaining are A and C
23 Options remaining are B and D
24 Options remaining are A and D
25 Options remaining are A and B
26 Options remaining are B and C
27 Options remaining are A and C
28 Options remaining are B and D
29 Options remaining are A and D
30 Options remaining are B and D
31 Options remaining are A and C
32 Options remaining are A and D
33 Options remaining are B and D
34 Options remaining are C and D
35 Options remaining are A and D
36 Options remaining are B and C
37 Options remaining are A and C
38 Options remaining are A and B
39 Options remaining are B and D
40 Options remaining are A and C
41 Options remaining are B and C
42 Options remaining are A and B
43 Options remaining are B and D
44 Options remaining are A and C
45 Options remaining are A and C
46 Options remaining are A and D

47 Options remaining are A and C
48 Options remaining are A and D
49 Options remaining are B and D
50 Options remaining are A and D
51 Options remaining are A and C
52 Options remaining are A and C
53 Options remaining are A and D
54 Options remaining are A and D
55 Options remaining are B and D
56 Options remaining are B and D
57 Options remaining are A and B
58 Options remaining are A and D
59 Options remaining are A and C
60 Options remaining are A and B
61 Options remaining are A and D
62 Options remaining are A and C
63 Options remaining are A and B
64 Options remaining are A and D
65 Options remaining are A and C
66 Options remaining are A and B
67 Options remaining are A and D
68 Options remaining are A and D
69 Options remaining are A and D
70 Options remaining are A and D
71 Options remaining are A and D
72 Options remaining are A and D
73 Options remaining are A and D
74 Options remaining are A and B
75 Options remaining are A and D
76 Options remaining are B and D
77 Options remaining are A and C
78 Options remaining are A and B
79 Options remaining are B and C
80 Options remaining are A and C
81 Options remaining are B and D
82 Options remaining are B and C
83 Options remaining are A and D
84 Options remaining are B and C
85 Options remaining are A and D
86 Options remaining are B and C
87 Options remaining are A and C
88 Options remaining are A and B
89 Options remaining are A and C
90 Options remaining are A and D
91 Options remaining are A and C
92 Options remaining are A and B
93 Options remaining are A and C
94 Options remaining are A and B
95 Options remaining are B and D
96 Options remaining are C and D
97 Options remaining are A and B
98 Options remaining are B and C
99 Options remaining are B and D
100 Options remaining are A and B
101 Options remaining are A and C
102 Options remaining are A and D
103 Options remaining are C and D
104 Options remaining are B and C
105 Options remaining are A and C
106 Options remaining are A and C
107 Options remaining are A and D
108 Options remaining are A and B
109 Options remaining are A and C
110 Options remaining are A and C
111 Options remaining are A and D
112 Options remaining are A and B
113 Options remaining are A and C
114 Options remaining are A and D
115 Options remaining are A and C
116 Options remaining are A and C
117 Options remaining are C and D
118 Options remaining are A and B
119 Options remaining are B and C
120 Options remaining are A and D
121 Options remaining are A and B
122 Options remaining are C and D
123 Options remaining are A and B
124 Options remaining are B and C
125 Options remaining are A and C
126 Options remaining are A and B
127 Options remaining are B and C
128 Options remaining are A and B
129 Options remaining are A and D
130 Options remaining are B and D
131 Options remaining are A and D
132 Options remaining are A and C

133 Options remaining are C and D
134 Options remaining are C and D
135 Options remaining are A and C
136 Options remaining are A and C
137 Options remaining are A and B
138 Options remaining are C and D
139 Options remaining are B and C
140 Options remaining are B and D
141 Options remaining are A and D
142 Options remaining are B and C
143 Options remaining are A and D
144 Options remaining are A and C
145 Options remaining are A and B
146 Options remaining are A and B
147 Options remaining are C and D
148 Options remaining are C and D
149 Options remaining are A and D
150 Options remaining are B and D
151 Options remaining are B and C
152 Options remaining are B and D
153 Options remaining are B and C
154 Options remaining are A and D
155 Options remaining are B and C
156 Options remaining are B and D
157 Options remaining are B and C
158 Options remaining are B and C
159 Options remaining are A and B
160 Options remaining are A and D
161 Options remaining are C and D
162 Options remaining are A and D
163 Options remaining are A and B
164 Options remaining are B and D

£500

1 Options remaining are A and B
2 Options remaining are B and D
3 Options remaining are A and D
4 Options remaining are B and D
5 Options remaining are A and B
6 Options remaining are A and B
7 Options remaining are B and D
8 Options remaining are A and C
9 Options remaining are A and C
10 Options remaining are B and C
11 Options remaining are A and C
12 Options remaining are B and C
13 Options remaining are A and D
14 Options remaining are A and C
15 Options remaining are B and C
16 Options remaining are B and C
17 Options remaining are A and C
18 Options remaining are B and D
19 Options remaining are A and B
20 Options remaining are A and C
21 Options remaining are B and D
22 Options remaining are A and D
23 Options remaining are C and D
24 Options remaining are B and C
25 Options remaining are C and D
26 Options remaining are A and C
27 Options remaining are B and C
28 Options remaining are B and C
29 Options remaining are A and B
30 Options remaining are A and D
31 Options remaining are B and C
32 Options remaining are A and B
33 Options remaining are B and D
34 Options remaining are A and B
35 Options remaining are A and D
36 Options remaining are A and B
37 Options remaining are A and B
38 Options remaining are A and D
39 Options remaining are B and D
40 Options remaining are B and D
41 Options remaining are A and D
42 Options remaining are B and D
43 Options remaining are A and D
44 Options remaining are A and D

45 Options remaining are A and D
46 Options remaining are A and C
47 Options remaining are C and D
48. Options remaining are A and D
49 Options remaining are C and D
50 Options remaining are A and D
51 Options remaining are C and D
52 Options remaining are A and D
53 Options remaining are B and D
54 Options remaining are A and D
55 Options remaining are A and D
56 Options remaining are B and D
57 Options remaining are A and B
58 Options remaining are C and D
59 Options remaining are A and B
60 Options remaining are A and B
61 Options remaining are B and D
62 Options remaining are B and D
63 Options remaining are A and D
64. Options remaining are B and C
65 Options remaining are C and D
66 Options remaining are A and D
67 Options remaining are C and D
68 Options remaining are C and D
69 Options remaining are A and D
70 Options remaining are A and B
71 Options remaining are A and D
72 Options remaining are A and C
73 Options remaining are B and C
74 Options remaining are A and D
75 Options remaining are B and D
76 Options remaining are B and D
77 Options remaining are B and D
78 Options remaining are B and C
79 Options remaining are A and C
80 Options remaining are A and B
81 Options remaining are A and B
82 Options remaining are C and D
83 Options remaining are B and C
84. Options remaining are C and D
85 Options remaining are A and B
86 Options remaining are A and C
87 Options remaining are A and D
88 Options remaining are B and C
89 Options remaining are B and D
90 Options remaining are A and D
91 Options remaining are B and D
92 Options remaining are B and D
93 Options remaining are B and D
94 Options remaining are B and C
95 Options remaining are A and C
96 Options remaining are A and B
97 Options remaining are A and D
98 Options remaining are A and C
99 Options remaining are A and D
100 Options remaining are B and D
101 Options remaining are C and D
102 Options remaining are A and B
103 Options remaining are A and B
104 Options remaining are C and D
105 Options remaining are B and D
106 Options remaining are A and B
107 Options remaining are A and D
108 Options remaining are C and D
109 Options remaining are B and D
110 Options remaining are A and D
111 Options remaining are B and D
112 Options remaining are B and C
113 Options remaining are A and B
114 Options remaining are A and C
115 Options remaining are A and C
116 Options remaining are B and D
117 Options remaining are A and C
118 Options remaining are B and D
119 Options remaining are A and D
120 Options remaining are A and B
121 Options remaining are A and C
122 Options remaining are A and D
123 Options remaining are B and C
124 Options remaining are B and D
125 Options remaining are C and D
126 Options remaining are A and B
127 Options remaining are A and D
128 Options remaining are B and D
129 Options remaining are A and C
130 Options remaining are C and D

131 Options remaining are C and D
132 Options remaining are C and D
133 Options remaining are B and D
134 Options remaining are C and D
135 Options remaining are A and B
136 Options remaining are A and B
137 Options remaining are B and D
138 Options remaining are A and C
139 Options remaining are A and C
140 Options remaining are C and D
141 Options remaining are A and D
142 Options remaining are A and D
143 Options remaining are A and C
144 Options remaining are A and D
145 Options remaining are C and D
146 Options remaining are A and C
147 Options remaining are A and B
148 Options remaining are B and C
149 Options remaining are B and D
150 Options remaining are A and C
151 Options remaining are B and C
152 Options remaining are B and D
153 Options remaining are A and D
154 Options remaining are B and C
155 Options remaining are A and D
156 Options remaining are A and D

£1,000

1 Options remaining are A and B
2 Options remaining are A and B
3 Options remaining are B and C
4 Options remaining are A and C
5 Options remaining are A and B
6 Options remaining are C and D
7 Options remaining are B and C
8 Options remaining are C and D
9 Options remaining are B and C
10 Options remaining are C and D
11 Options remaining are B and D
12 Options remaining are A and B
13 Options remaining are A and C
14 Options remaining are C and D
15 Options remaining are A and B
16 Options remaining are B and C
17 Options remaining are B and C
18 Options remaining are A and B
19 Options remaining are C and D
20 Options remaining are A and D
21 Options remaining are A and B
22 Options remaining are A and D
23 Options remaining are A and D
24 Options remaining are A and D
25 Options remaining are C and D
26 Options remaining are A and B
27 Options remaining are B and D
28 Options remaining are A and D
29 Options remaining are A and C
30 Options remaining are A and B
31 Options remaining are C and D
32 Options remaining are A and D
33 Options remaining are A and C
34 Options remaining are A and D
35 Options remaining are A and D
36 Options remaining are A and D
37 Options remaining are C and D
38 Options remaining are A and C
39 Options remaining are A and B
40 Options remaining are A and D
41 Options remaining are B and D
42 Options remaining are B and C
43 Options remaining are A and D
44 Options remaining are A and D
45 Options remaining are A and B
46 Options remaining are A and C
47 Options remaining are A and B
48 Options remaining are A and C
49 Options remaining are A and B
50 Options remaining are A and D

51 Options remaining are A and C
52 Options remaining are C and D
53 Options remaining are B and D
54 Options remaining are A and C
55 Options remaining are A and D
56 Options remaining are A and D
57 Options remaining are B and D
58 Options remaining are A and C
59 Options remaining are B and D
60 Options remaining are A and D
61 Options remaining are A and B
62 Options remaining are B and D
63 Options remaining are A and C
64 Options remaining are A and D
65 Options remaining are C and D
66 Options remaining are A and D
67 Options remaining are A and D
68 Options remaining are B and D
69 Options remaining are C and D
70 Options remaining are A and D
71 Options remaining are A and C
72 Options remaining are A and D
73 Options remaining are A and D
74 Options remaining are A and D
75 Options remaining are B and D
76 Options remaining are A and B
77 Options remaining are B and C
78 Options remaining are A and D
79 Options remaining are A and D
80 Options remaining are A and C
81 Options remaining are B and C
82 Options remaining are A and D
83 Options remaining are B and C
84 Options remaining are A and B
85 Options remaining are A and B
86 Options remaining are A and D
87 Options remaining are A and B
88 Options remaining are C and D
89 Options remaining are A and C
90 Options remaining are B and C
91 Options remaining are B and D
92 Options remaining are A and B
93 Options remaining are A and D
94 Options remaining are A and B
95 Options remaining are B and C
96 Options remaining are A and B
97 Options remaining are A and C
98 Options remaining are A and B
99 Options remaining are C and D
100 Options remaining are A and B
101 Options remaining are B and D
102 Options remaining are A and B
103 Options remaining are C and D
104 Options remaining are B and C
105 Options remaining are B and C
106 Options remaining are A and C
107 Options remaining are B and D
108 Options remaining are A and C
109 Options remaining are B and D
110 Options remaining are A and C
111 Options remaining are A and D
112 Options remaining are A and D
113 Options remaining are A and D
114 Options remaining are A and D
115 Options remaining are A and C
116 Options remaining are C and D
117 Options remaining are A and B
118 Options remaining are A and D
119 Options remaining are A and C
120 Options remaining are A and B
121 Options remaining are C and D
122 Options remaining are C and D
123 Options remaining are A and C
124 Options remaining are B and C
125 Options remaining are B and D
126 Options remaining are A and C
127 Options remaining are C and D
128 Options remaining are A and C
129 Options remaining are B and D
130 Options remaining are B and D
131 Options remaining are A and D
132 Options remaining are A and B
133 Options remaining are B and C
134 Options remaining are A and B
135 Options remaining are B and D
136 Options remaining are A and C

50:50

137 Options remaining are C and D
138 Options remaining are C and D
139 Options remaining are C and D
140 Options remaining are A and B
141 Options remaining are A and B
142 Options remaining are B and C
143 Options remaining are A and B
144 Options remaining are B and C
145 Options remaining are C and D
146 Options remaining are B and C
147 Options remaining are C and D
148 Options remaining are B and C

£2,000

1 Options remaining are A and D
2 Options remaining are C and D
3 Options remaining are B and D
4 Options remaining are B and D
5 Options remaining are A and C
6 Options remaining are B and C
7 Options remaining are A and C
8 Options remaining are B and D
9 Options remaining are B and D
10 Options remaining are C and D
11 Options remaining are A and B
12 Options remaining are B and C
13 Options remaining are A and B
14 Options remaining are B and D
15 Options remaining are A and C
16 Options remaining are B and C
17 Options remaining are A and D
18 Options remaining are B and C
19 Options remaining are A and C
20 Options remaining are A and D
21 Options remaining are B and D
22 Options remaining are B and D
23 Options remaining are A and C
24 Options remaining are A and D
25 Options remaining are A and B
26 Options remaining are A and C
27 Options remaining are A and B
28 Options remaining are A and B
29 Options remaining are B and C
30 Options remaining are A and C
31 Options remaining are A and B
32 Options remaining are B and C
33 Options remaining are A and D
34 Options remaining are A and B
35 Options remaining are A and B
36 Options remaining are B and D
37 Options remaining are A and D
38 Options remaining are B and D
39 Options remaining are B and C
40 Options remaining are A and D
41 Options remaining are A and D
42 Options remaining are A and D
43 Options remaining are B and D
44 Options remaining are B and D
45 Options remaining are A and D
46 Options remaining are A and D
47 Options remaining are C and D
48 Options remaining are B and D
49 Options remaining are A and D
50 Options remaining are B and D
51 Options remaining are B and D
52 Options remaining are A and D
53 Options remaining are A and D
54 Options remaining are B and D
55 Options remaining are A and D
56 Options remaining are A and D
57 Options remaining are A and B
58 Options remaining are A and D
59 Options remaining are A and B
60 Options remaining are A and D
61 Options remaining are A and D
62 Options remaining are A and C
63 Options remaining are B and D
64 Options remaining are C and D

65 Options remaining are C and D
66 Options remaining are A and D
67 Options remaining are A and D
68 Options remaining are A and D
69 Options remaining are A and C
70 Options remaining are A and D
71 Options remaining are A and D
72 Options remaining are C and D
73 Options remaining are B and D
74 Options remaining are C and D
75 Options remaining are B and D
76 Options remaining are A and C
77 Options remaining are A and D
78 Options remaining are A and B
79 Options remaining are B and D
80 Options remaining are A and C
81 Options remaining are A and D
82 Options remaining are A and C
83 Options remaining are C and D
84 Options remaining are A and D
85 Options remaining are B and D
86 Options remaining are B and D
87 Options remaining are A and D
88 Options remaining are A and C
89 Options remaining are A and B
90 Options remaining are A and D
91 Options remaining are A and B
92 Options remaining are A and C
93 Options remaining are B and C
94 Options remaining are A and B
95 Options remaining are A and C
96 Options remaining are A and C
97 Options remaining are A and B
98 Options remaining are A and B
99 Options remaining are A and D
100 Options remaining are A and B
101 Options remaining are A and D
102 Options remaining are A and B
103 Options remaining are A and C
104 Options remaining are B and D
105 Options remaining are B and D
106 Options remaining are A and C
107 Options remaining are B and D
108 Options remaining are B and C
109 Options remaining are C and D
110 Options remaining are A and D
111 Options remaining are A and D
112 Options remaining are B and C
113 Options remaining are C and D
114 Options remaining are A and C
115 Options remaining are A and B
116 Options remaining are A and D
117 Options remaining are B and D
118 Options remaining are A and D
119 Options remaining are C and D
120 Options remaining are A and B
121 Options remaining are A and D
122 Options remaining are B and D
123 Options remaining are A and C
124 Options remaining are B and C
125 Options remaining are A and D
126 Options remaining are C and D
127 Options remaining are A and B
128 Options remaining are B and C
129 Options remaining are B and C
130 Options remaining are A and B
131 Options remaining are C and D
132 Options remaining are A and B
133 Options remaining are C and D
134 Options remaining are A and B
135 Options remaining are A and C
136 Options remaining are B and D
137 Options remaining are B and C
138 Options remaining are B and C
139 Options remaining are B and D
140 Options remaining are B and D

£4,000

1 Options remaining are A and C
2 Options remaining are B and D
3 Options remaining are A and B
4 Options remaining are A and B
5 Options remaining are A and C
6 Options remaining are B and D
7 Options remaining are C and D
8 Options remaining are B and D
9 Options remaining are A and B
10 Options remaining are B and C
11 Options remaining are A and C
12 Options remaining are C and D
13 Options remaining are A and B
14 Options remaining are C and D
15 Options remaining are A and C
16 Options remaining are A and C
17 Options remaining are A and C
18 Options remaining are B and D
19 Options remaining are A and C
20 Options remaining are A and B
21 Options remaining are A and D
22 Options remaining are A and C
23 Options remaining are B and D
24 Options remaining are B and C
25 Options remaining are C and D
26 Options remaining are A and D
27 Options remaining are C and D
28 Options remaining are B and C
29 Options remaining are C and D
30 Options remaining are A and D
31 Options remaining are B and D
32 Options remaining are C and D
33 Options remaining are B and D
34 Options remaining are B and C
35 Options remaining are A and C
36 Options remaining are A and C
37 Options remaining are A and D
38 Options remaining are B and D
39 Options remaining are A and B
40 Options remaining are A and D
41 Options remaining are A and C
42 Options remaining are B and D
43 Options remaining are A and C
44 Options remaining are A and C
45 Options remaining are A and D
46 Options remaining are C and D
47 Options remaining are C and D
48 Options remaining are C and D
49 Options remaining are B and D
50 Options remaining are B and D
51 Options remaining are C and D
52 Options remaining are A and D
53 Options remaining are A and D
54 Options remaining are A and B
55 Options remaining are C and D
56 Options remaining are A and D
57 Options remaining are B and D
58 Options remaining are B and D
59 Options remaining are A and B
60 Options remaining are A and D
61 Options remaining are C and D
62 Options remaining are A and D
63 Options remaining are A and B
64 Options remaining are A and D
65 Options remaining are B and D
66 Options remaining are B and D
67 Options remaining are A and D
68 Options remaining are A and C
69 Options remaining are A and D
70 Options remaining are A and D
71 Options remaining are A and C
72 Options remaining are A and D
73 Options remaining are B and C
74 Options remaining are B and C
75 Options remaining are A and D
76 Options remaining are B and C
77 Options remaining are B and D
78 Options remaining are B and D
79 Options remaining are A and D
80 Options remaining are A and C
81 Options remaining are A and D
82 Options remaining are A and C
83 Options remaining are B and C
84 Options remaining are A and D

85 Options remaining are B and C
86 Options remaining are C and D
87 Options remaining are B and D
88 Options remaining are B and C
89 Options remaining are A and C
90 Options remaining are A and C
91 Options remaining are A and D
92 Options remaining are B and C
93 Options remaining are B and C
94 Options remaining are B and C
95 Options remaining are A and C
96 Options remaining are A and D
97 Options remaining are A and B
98 Options remaining are A and B
99 Options remaining are C and D
100 Options remaining are B and D
101 Options remaining are A and D
102 Options remaining are B and D
103 Options remaining are B and C
104 Options remaining are A and C
105 Options remaining are A and D
106 Options remaining are B and C
107 Options remaining are A and B
108 Options remaining are B and C
109 Options remaining are B and C
110 Options remaining are A and C
111 Options remaining are A and B
112 Options remaining are C and D
113 Options remaining are A and C
114 Options remaining are B and D
115 Options remaining are A and B
116 Options remaining are A and B
117 Options remaining are C and D
118 Options remaining are B and D
119 Options remaining are C and D
120 Options remaining are A and B
121 Options remaining are A and C
122 Options remaining are C and D
123 Options remaining are C and D
124 Options remaining are A and B
125 Options remaining are A and C
126 Options remaining are A and C
127 Options remaining are A and B
128 Options remaining are A and B
129 Options remaining are C and D
130 Options remaining are B and D
131 Options remaining are B and D
132 Options remaining are A and C

£8,000

1 Options remaining are B and C
2 Options remaining are B and D
3 Options remaining are B and D
4 Options remaining are A and B
5 Options remaining are A and D
6 Options remaining are B and D
7 Options remaining are A and C
8 Options remaining are B and D
9 Options remaining are A and C
10 Options remaining are A and B
11 Options remaining are B and C
12 Options remaining are A and C
13 Options remaining are B and C
14 Options remaining are B and C
15 Options remaining are A and B
16 Options remaining are B and D
17 Options remaining are A and C
18 Options remaining are A and C
19 Options remaining are C and D
20 Options remaining are B and D
21 Options remaining are B and D
22 Options remaining are A and B
23 Options remaining are B and D
24 Options remaining are A and D
25 Options remaining are A and C
26 Options remaining are A and D
27 Options remaining are B and D
28 Options remaining are A and D

29 Options remaining are C and D
30 Options remaining are B and D
31 Options remaining are B and D
32 Options remaining are B and D
33 Options remaining are C and D
34 Options remaining are A and B
35 Options remaining are B and C
36 Options remaining are A and D
37 Options remaining are B and D
38 Options remaining are A and D
39 Options remaining are B and D
40 Options remaining are A and D
41 Options remaining are A and B
42 Options remaining are B and D
43 Options remaining are A and D
44 Options remaining are B and C
45 Options remaining are A and D
46 Options remaining are A and C
47 Options remaining are A and D
48 Options remaining are B and D
49 Options remaining are B and D
50 Options remaining are A and D
51 Options remaining are A and C
52 Options remaining are B and D
53 Options remaining are A and D
54 Options remaining are A and D
55 Options remaining are A and D
56 Options remaining are B and D
57 Options remaining are A and D
58 Options remaining are A and C
59 Options remaining are A and D
60 Options remaining are C and D
61 Options remaining are B and D
62 Options remaining are A and D
63 Options remaining are B and D
64 Options remaining are A and D
65 Options remaining are A and D
66 Options remaining are C and D
67 Options remaining are A and B
68 Options remaining are B and D
69 Options remaining are B and D
70 Options remaining are C and D
71 Options remaining are C and D
72 Options remaining are A and D
73 Options remaining are B and D
74 Options remaining are A and C
75 Options remaining are B and D
76 Options remaining are B and C
77 Options remaining are B and C
78 Options remaining are B and C
79 Options remaining are A and B
80 Options remaining are C and D
81 Options remaining are B and C
82 Options remaining are A and D
83 Options remaining are A and C
84 Options remaining are A and B
85 Options remaining are A and C
86 Options remaining are B and D
87 Options remaining are A and C
88 Options remaining are B and D
89 Options remaining are B and D
90 Options remaining are A and B
91 Options remaining are A and B
92 Options remaining are A and D
93 Options remaining are A and D
94 Options remaining are A and D
95 Options remaining are B and D
96 Options remaining are A and D
97 Options remaining are B and C
98 Options remaining are B and D
99 Options remaining are A and D
100 Options remaining are A and D
101 Options remaining are A and D
102 Options remaining are B and D
103 Options remaining are A and C
104 Options remaining are B and C
105 Options remaining are C and D
106 Options remaining are C and D
107 Options remaining are A and C
108 Options remaining are A and C
109 Options remaining are A and C
110 Options remaining are A and C
111 Options remaining are B and D
112 Options remaining are B and D
113 Options remaining are A and C
114 Options remaining are B and C

115 Options remaining are A and D
116 Options remaining are A and C
117 Options remaining are B and C
118 Options remaining are A and B
119 Options remaining are A and C
120 Options remaining are C and D
121 Options remaining are B and C
122 Options remaining are A and C
123 Options remaining are B and C
124 Options remaining are B and D

£16,000

1 Options remaining are A and D
2 Options remaining are A and C
3 Options remaining are A and D
4 Options remaining are C and D
5 Options remaining are C and D
6 Options remaining are A and D
7 Options remaining are A and D
8 Options remaining are B and D
9 Options remaining are C and D
10 Options remaining are A and D
11 Options remaining are A and C
12 Options remaining are B and D
13 Options remaining are C and D
14 Options remaining are C and D
15 Options remaining are B and D
16 Options remaining are A and D
17 Options remaining are B and D
18 Options remaining are C and D
19 Options remaining are B and C
20 Options remaining are B and D
21 Options remaining are A and C
22 Options remaining are B and D
23 Options remaining are A and C
24 Options remaining are B and C
25 Options remaining are C and D
26 Options remaining are B and D
27 Options remaining are A and B
28 Options remaining are C and D
29 Options remaining are B and D
30 Options remaining are A and C
31 Options remaining are B and D
32 Options remaining are B and C
33 Options remaining are B and C
34 Options remaining are B and C
35 Options remaining are A and D
36 Options remaining are A and D
37 Options remaining are A and B
38 Options remaining are B and C
39 Options remaining are C and D
40 Options remaining are C and D
41 Options remaining are C and D
42 Options remaining are C and D
43 Options remaining are A and D
44 Options remaining are B and D
45 Options remaining are A and C
46 Options remaining are B and C
47 Options remaining are A and D
48 Options remaining are C and D
49 Options remaining are A and C
50 Options remaining are A and D
51 Options remaining are A and D
52 Options remaining are A and D
53 Options remaining are B and D
54 Options remaining are A and D
55 Options remaining are A and B
56 Options remaining are A and B
57 Options remaining are A and B
58 Options remaining are C and D
59 Options remaining are B and C
60 Options remaining are A and D
61 Options remaining are C and D
62 Options remaining are B and D
63 Options remaining are A and B
64 Options remaining are A and C
65 Options remaining are A and D
66 Options remaining are C and D

67 Options remaining are A and C
68 Options remaining are B and C
69 Options remaining are B and C
70 Options remaining are B and C
71 Options remaining are A and C
72 Options remaining are A and C
73 Options remaining are A and C
74 Options remaining are A and C
75 Options remaining are A and D
76 Options remaining are A and C
77 Options remaining are C and D
78 Options remaining are A and D
79 Options remaining are B and C
80 Options remaining are B and D
81 Options remaining are A and D
82 Options remaining are A and C
83 Options remaining are B and C
84 Options remaining are A and B
85 Options remaining are A and B
86 Options remaining are B and C
87 Options remaining are C and D
88 Options remaining are A and C
89 Options remaining are A and B
90 Options remaining are B and D
91 Options remaining are A and B
92 Options remaining are B and D
93 Options remaining are B and C
94 Options remaining are C and D
95 Options remaining are C and D
96 Options remaining are B and C
97 Options remaining are A and C
98 Options remaining are A and B
99 Options remaining are B and D
100 Options remaining are B and C
101 Options remaining are A and B
102 Options remaining are A and D
103 Options remaining are A and B
104 Options remaining are A and D
105 Options remaining are A and D
106 Options remaining are B and C
107 Options remaining are A and C
108 Options remaining are A and B
109 Options remaining are A and B
110 Options remaining are A and B
111 Options remaining are B and D
112 Options remaining are A and B
113 Options remaining are A and B
114 Options remaining are C and D
115 Options remaining are B and C
116 Options remaining are B and C

£32,000

1 Options remaining are A and D
2 Options remaining are B and D
3 Options remaining are A and D
4 Options remaining are A and D
5 Options remaining are C and D
6 Options remaining are B and D
7 Options remaining are C and D
8 Options remaining are A and D
9 Options remaining are C and D
10 Options remaining are A and C
11 Options remaining are C and D
12 Options remaining are A and D
13 Options remaining are A and B
14 Options remaining are B and C
15 Options remaining are B and C
16 Options remaining are A and B
17 Options remaining are B and C
18 Options remaining are A and D
19 Options remaining are C and D
20 Options remaining are A and C
21 Options remaining are A and B
22 Options remaining are C and D
23 Options remaining are A and C
24 Options remaining are A and D
25 Options remaining are B and D
26 Options remaining are A and D

27 Options remaining are B and C
28 Options remaining are A and D
29 Options remaining are A and C
30 Options remaining are C and D
31 Options remaining are A and D
32 Options remaining are B and C
33 Options remaining are A and D
34 Options remaining are C and D
35 Options remaining are A and D
36 Options remaining are A and C
37 Options remaining are B and D
38 Options remaining are C and D
39 Options remaining are A and B
40 Options remaining are C and D
41 Options remaining are B and D
42 Options remaining are A and B
43 Options remaining are B and C
44 Options remaining are A and C
45 Options remaining are B and D
46 Options remaining are A and C
47 Options remaining are B and D
48 Options remaining are C and D
49 Options remaining are C and D
50 Options remaining are C and D
51 Options remaining are C and D
52 Options remaining are C and D
53 Options remaining are B and D
54 Options remaining are B and D
55 Options remaining are B and C
56 Options remaining are A and B
57 Options remaining are B and D
58 Options remaining are A and B
59 Options remaining are A and C
60 Options remaining are B and C
61 Options remaining are B and C
62 Options remaining are A and C
63 Options remaining are A and C
64 Options remaining are A and B
65 Options remaining are A and B
66 Options remaining are A and C
67 Options remaining are A and D
68 Options remaining are A and C
69 Options remaining are A and D
70 Options remaining are C and D
71 Options remaining are A and D
72 Options remaining are A and C
73 Options remaining are A and B
74 Options remaining are A and D
75 Options remaining are C and D
76 Options remaining are B and C
77 Options remaining are A and B
78 Options remaining are B and D
79 Options remaining are B and D
80 Options remaining are A and C
81 Options remaining are B and C
82 Options remaining are B and D
83 Options remaining are A and C
84 Options remaining are A and C
85 Options remaining are C and D
86 Options remaining are B and D
87 Options remaining are A and C
88 Options remaining are C and D
89 Options remaining are A and B
90 Options remaining are A and C
91 Options remaining are B and C
92 Options remaining are A and D
93 Options remaining are A and B
94 Options remaining are A and D
95 Options remaining are C and D
96 Options remaining are B and D
97 Options remaining are B and C
98 Options remaining are A and B
99 Options remaining are A and B
100 Options remaining are B and C
101 Options remaining are A and B
102 Options remaining are B and C
103 Options remaining are A and C
104 Options remaining are C and D
105 Options remaining are B and C
106 Options remaining are C and D
107 Options remaining are B and C
108 Options remaining are B and C

£64,000

1 Options remaining are A and D
2 Options remaining are A and D
3 Options remaining are C and D
4 Options remaining are A and D
5 Options remaining are A and B
6 Options remaining are A and D
7 Options remaining are A and D
8 Options remaining are A and C
9 Options remaining are B and C
10 Options remaining are C and D
11 Options remaining are B and D
12 Options remaining are B and D
13 Options remaining are A and D
14 Options remaining are A and D
15 Options remaining are A and D
16 Options remaining are B and C
17 Options remaining are A and D
18 Options remaining are A and B
19 Options remaining are A and C
20 Options remaining are C and D
21 Options remaining are A and D
22 Options remaining are B and D
23 Options remaining are B and C
24 Options remaining are B and D
25 Options remaining are B and D
26 Options remaining are A and D
27 Options remaining are A and C
28 Options remaining are A and D
29 Options remaining are A and B
30 Options remaining are A and C
31 Options remaining are A and B
32 Options remaining are B and D
33 Options remaining are A and D
34 Options remaining are B and C
35 Options remaining are A and C
36 Options remaining are B and C
37 Options remaining are A and C
38 Options remaining are A and B
39 Options remaining are C and D
40 Options remaining are A and D
41 Options remaining are A and D
42 Options remaining are A and B
43 Options remaining are C and D
44 Options remaining are B and C
45 Options remaining are B and D
46 Options remaining are B and D
47 Options remaining are B and D
48 Options remaining are A and C
49 Options remaining are A and C
50 Options remaining are A and C
51 Options remaining are C and D
52 Options remaining are A and D
53 Options remaining are A and D
54 Options remaining are A and B
55 Options remaining are A and B
56 Options remaining are A and C
57 Options remaining are B and C
58 Options remaining are B and D
59 Options remaining are C and D
60 Options remaining are A and C
61 Options remaining are A and C
62 Options remaining are B and D
63 Options remaining are B and C
64 Options remaining are B and D
65 Options remaining are A and B
66 Options remaining are A and C
67 Options remaining are A and B
68 Options remaining are A and C
69 Options remaining are A and C
70 Options remaining are B and C
71 Options remaining are B and C
72 Options remaining are C and D
73 Options remaining are C and D
74 Options remaining are B and D
75 Options remaining are A and D
76 Options remaining are A and B
77 Options remaining are C and D
78 Options remaining are C and D
79 Options remaining are B and C
80 Options remaining are B and C
81 Options remaining are A and B
82 Options remaining are C and D
83 Options remaining are A and C
84 Options remaining are A and C

85 Options remaining are B and D
86 Options remaining are A and B
87 Options remaining are B and C
88 Options remaining are A and B
89 Options remaining are B and D
90 Options remaining are A and B
91 Options remaining are A and D
92 Options remaining are A and B
93 Options remaining are A and B
94 Options remaining are B and D
95 Options remaining are A and D
96 Options remaining are B and D
97 Options remaining are C and D
98 Options remaining are A and C
99 Options remaining are A and D
100 Options remaining are C and D

£125,000

1 Options remaining are C and D
2 Options remaining are A and D
3 Options remaining are B and D
4 Options remaining are B and D
5 Options remaining are C and D
6 Options remaining are B and D
7 Options remaining are A and C
8 Options remaining are B and D
9 Options remaining are B and D
10 Options remaining are B and D
11 Options remaining are A and D
12 Options remaining are A and D
13 Options remaining are A and D
14 Options remaining are C and D
15 Options remaining are B and D
16 Options remaining are C and D
17 Options remaining are A and B
18 Options remaining are C and D
19 Options remaining are C and D
20 Options remaining are B and D
21 Options remaining are C and D
22 Options remaining are B and D
23 Options remaining are B and C
24 Options remaining are B and D
25 Options remaining are A and C
26 Options remaining are A and D
27 Options remaining are B and C
28 Options remaining are A and C
29 Options remaining are A and D
30 Options remaining are A and B
31 Options remaining are A and D
32 Options remaining are B and D
33 Options remaining are A and D
34 Options remaining are B and C
35 Options remaining are B and D
36 Options remaining are B and C
37 Options remaining are B and C
38 Options remaining are B and D
39 Options remaining are A and C
40 Options remaining are A and D
41 Options remaining are A and D
42 Options remaining are A and D
43 Options remaining are B and C
44 Options remaining are B and C
45 Options remaining are A and C
46 Options remaining are B and C
47 Options remaining are B and C
48 Options remaining are A and C
49 Options remaining are B and D
50 Options remaining are B and C
51 Options remaining are A and C
52 Options remaining are C and D
53 Options remaining are A and C
54 Options remaining are A and B
55 Options remaining are A and D
56 Options remaining are C and D
57 Options remaining are A and B
58 Options remaining are C and D
59 Options remaining are A and C
60 Options remaining are A and C

50:50

61 Options remaining are A and D
62 Options remaining are B and C
63 Options remaining are A and B
64 Options remaining are B and C
65 Options remaining are C and D
66 Options remaining are B and C
67 Options remaining are A and B
68 Options remaining are C and D
69 Options remaining are A and C
70 Options remaining are B and D
71 Options remaining are A and D
72 Options remaining are A and C
73 Options remaining are A and B
74 Options remaining are B and D
75 Options remaining are C and D
76 Options remaining are B and D
77 Options remaining are B and C
78 Options remaining are C and D
79 Options remaining are B and D
80 Options remaining are A and C
81 Options remaining are A and C
82 Options remaining are A and C
83 Options remaining are A and D
84 Options remaining are A and B
85 Options remaining are B and C
86 Options remaining are B and C
87 Options remaining are A and B
88 Options remaining are C and D
89 Options remaining are A and B
90 Options remaining are A and B
91 Options remaining are A and D
92 Options remaining are B and C

£250,000

1 Options remaining are C and D
2 Options remaining are C and D
3 Options remaining are C and D
4 Options remaining are B and D
5 Options remaining are A and D
6 Options remaining are C and D
7 Options remaining are A and D
8 Options remaining are A and B
9 Options remaining are C and D
10 Options remaining are C and D
11 Options remaining are C and D
12 Options remaining are B and D
13 Options remaining are A and D
14 Options remaining are C and D
15 Options remaining are A and D
16 Options remaining are A and D
17 Options remaining are A and D
18 Options remaining are A and C
19 Options remaining are C and D
20 Options remaining are B and D
21 Options remaining are C and D
22 Options remaining are B and C
23 Options remaining are A and B
24 Options remaining are B and C
25 Options remaining are A and C
26 Options remaining are A and B
27 Options remaining are A and C
28 Options remaining are B and D
29 Options remaining are A and D
30 Options remaining are A and C
31 Options remaining are A and B
32 Options remaining are A and C
33 Options remaining are A and D
34 Options remaining are B and D
35 Options remaining are A and C
36 Options remaining are A and D
37 Options remaining are A and D
38 Options remaining are B and C
39 Options remaining are B and C
40 Options remaining are A and B
41 Options remaining are B and C
42 Options remaining are A and C
43 Options remaining are A and D
44 Options remaining are A and B

45 Options remaining are A and D
46 Options remaining are B and D
47 Options remaining are A and B
48 Options remaining are B and C
49 Options remaining are A and C
50 Options remaining are A and D
51 Options remaining are A and C
52 Options remaining are B and D
53 Options remaining are A and D
54 Options remaining are A and C
55 Options remaining are C and D
56 Options remaining are B and C
57 Options remaining are B and C
58 Options remaining are A and D
59 Options remaining are A and B
60 Options remaining are A and D
61 Options remaining are A and B
62 Options remaining are A and D
63 Options remaining are A and C
64 Options remaining are C and D
65 Options remaining are A and B
66 Options remaining are A and C
67 Options remaining are A and D
68 Options remaining are A and D
69 Options remaining are A and B
70 Options remaining are A and B
71 Options remaining are B and C
72 Options remaining are C and D
73 Options remaining are C and D
74 Options remaining are C and D
75 Options remaining are A and D
76 Options remaining are B and C
77 Options remaining are A and C
78 Options remaining are A and C
79 Options remaining are C and D
80 Options remaining are A and C
81 Options remaining are A and C
82 Options remaining are C and D
83 Options remaining are A and D
84 Options remaining are A and C

£500,000

1 Options remaining are A and D
2 Options remaining are C and D
3 Options remaining are A and C
4 Options remaining are A and B
5 Options remaining are A and C
6 Options remaining are B and D
7 Options remaining are B and D
8 Options remaining are C and D
9 Options remaining are B and D
10 Options remaining are A and D
11 Options remaining are A and D
12 Options remaining are C and D
13 Options remaining are A and D
14 Options remaining are C and D
15 Options remaining are B and D
16 Options remaining are A and D
17 Options remaining are C and D
18 Options remaining are C and D
19 Options remaining are A and C
20 Options remaining are B and C
21 Options remaining are B and D
22 Options remaining are A and B
23 Options remaining are A and B
24 Options remaining are C and D
25 Options remaining are A and C
26 Options remaining are A and D
27 Options remaining are C and D
28 Options remaining are A and C
29 Options remaining are A and D
30 Options remaining are A and D
31 Options remaining are A and D
32 Options remaining are A and B
33 Options remaining are B and C
34 Options remaining are A and D
35 Options remaining are C and D
36 Options remaining are B and D

50:50

37 Options remaining are A and D
38 Options remaining are C and D
39 Options remaining are A and D
40 Options remaining are C and D
41 Options remaining are C and D
42 Options remaining are B and C
43 Options remaining are B and D
44 Options remaining are B and C
45 Options remaining are A and C
46 Options remaining are A and B
47 Options remaining are A and B
48 Options remaining are B and C
49 Options remaining are A and B
50 Options remaining are B and D
51 Options remaining are C and D
52 Options remaining are C and D
53 Options remaining are B and C
54 Options remaining are A and B
55 Options remaining are A and B
56 Options remaining are A and B
57 Options remaining are A and B
58 Options remaining are C and D
59 Options remaining are C and D
60 Options remaining are C and D
61 Options remaining are B and D
62 Options remaining are B and C
63 Options remaining are A and C
64 Options remaining are C and D
65 Options remaining are B and C
66 Options remaining are A and B
67 Options remaining are B and D
68 Options remaining are B and C
69 Options remaining are B and D
70 Options remaining are A and C
71 Options remaining are B and D
72 Options remaining are B and C
73 Options remaining are B and D
74 Options remaining are B and D
75 Options remaining are C and D
76 Options remaining are A and D

£1 MILLION

1 Options remaining are A and D
2 Options remaining are C and D
3 Options remaining are C and D
4 Options remaining are A and D
5 Options remaining are A and B
6 Options remaining are B and D
7 Options remaining are B and D
8 Options remaining are C and D
9 Options remaining are A and D
10 Options remaining are B and D
11 Options remaining are B and D
12 Options remaining are A and C
13 Options remaining are B and D
14 Options remaining are B and D
15 Options remaining are C and D
16 Options remaining are A and B
17 Options remaining are B and D
18 Options remaining are A and B
19 Options remaining are B and D
20 Options remaining are B and C
21 Options remaining are A and B
22 Options remaining are A and C
23 Options remaining are B and C
24 Options remaining are B and C
25 Options remaining are A and D
26 Options remaining are B and D
27 Options remaining are B and D
28 Options remaining are B and D
29 Options remaining are A and D
30 Options remaining are A and B
31 Options remaining are B and C
32 Options remaining are A and C
33 Options remaining are A and B
34 Options remaining are C and D
35 Options remaining are A and D
36 Options remaining are B and D

37 Options remaining are B and C
38 Options remaining are C and D
39 Options remaining are B and D
40 Options remaining are B and C
41 Options remaining are A and B
42 Options remaining are A and D
43 Options remaining are A and C
44 Options remaining are A and C
45 Options remaining are C and D
46 Options remaining are C and D
47 Options remaining are A and C
48 Options remaining are C and D
49 Options remaining are B and D
50 Options remaining are A and D
51 Options remaining are B and D
52 Options remaining are A and B
53 Options remaining are A and D
54 Options remaining are C and D
55 Options remaining are B and D
56 Options remaining are A and C
57 Options remaining are B and C
58 Options remaining are B and C
59 Options remaining are A and B
60 Options remaining are B and C
61 Options remaining are B and C
62 Options remaining are A and D
63 Options remaining are B and D
64 Options remaining are C and D
65 Options remaining are A and C
66 Options remaining are B and C
67 Options remaining are A and D
68 Options remaining are A and B

Ask The Audience

£100

1	A:95%	B:2%	C:1%	D:2%
2	A:95%	B:2%	C:1%	D:2%
3	A:2%	B:5%	C:92%	D:1%
4	A:1%	B:91%	C:2%	D:6%
5	A:1%	B:91%	C:2%	D:6%
6	A:2%	B:94%	C:3%	D:1%
7	A:2%	B:5%	C:92%	D:1%
8	A:2%	B:5%	C:92%	D:1%
9	A:2%	B:94%	C:3%	D:1%
10	A:2%	B:5%	C:92%	D:1%
11	A:2%	B:94%	C:3%	D:1%
12	A:2%	B:7%	C:0%	D:91%
13	A:11%	B:81%	C:2%	D:6%
14	A:2%	B:94%	C:3%	D:1%
15	A:2%	B:5%	C:92%	D:1%
16	A:1%	B:91%	C:2%	D:6%
17	A:95%	B:2%	C:1%	D:2%
18	A:2%	B:5%	C:92%	D:1%
19	A:7%	B:4%	C:89%	D:0%
20	A:2%	B:2%	C:0%	D:91%
21	A:2%	B:5%	C:92%	D:1%
22	A:2%	B:94%	C:3%	D:1%
23	A:2%	B:5%	C:92%	D:1%
24	A:2%	B:94%	C:3%	D:1%
25	A:2%	B:94%	C:3%	D:1%
26	A:2%	B:7%	C:0%	D:91%
27	A:2%	B:94%	C:3%	D:1%
28	A:2%	B:5%	C:92%	D:1%
29	A:87%	B:5%	C:2%	D:6%
30	A:14%	B:1%	C:87%	D:2%
31	A:2%	B:94%	C:3%	D:1%
32	A:6%	B:83%	C:4%	D:7%
33	A:95%	B:2%	C:1%	D:2%
34	A:6%	B:83%	C:4%	D:7%
35	A:9%	B:2%	C:83%	D:6%
36	A:2%	B:5%	C:92%	D:1%
37	A:95%	B:2%	C:1%	D:2%
38	A:2%	B:7%	C:0%	D:91%
39	A:2%	B:5%	C:92%	D:1%
40	A:1%	B:91%	C:2%	D:6%
41	A:11%	B:81%	C:2%	D:6%
42	A:2%	B:5%	C:92%	D:1%
43	A:2%	B:7%	C:0%	D:91%
44	A:2%	B:5%	C:92%	D:1%
45	A:2%	B:7%	C:0%	D:91%
46	A:95%	B:2%	C:1%	D:2%
47	A:2%	B:5%	C:92%	D:1%
48	A:2%	B:5%	C:92%	D:1%
49	A:2%	B:94%	C:3%	D:1%
50	A:2%	B:7%	C:0%	D:91%
51	A:2%	B:5%	C:92%	D:1%
52	A:82%	B:4%	C:2%	D:2%
53	A:2%	B:7%	C:0%	D:91%
54	A:2%	B:5%	C:92%	D:1%
55	A:2%	B:7%	C:0%	D:91%
56	A:2%	B:7%	C:0%	D:91%
57	A:7%	B:2%	C:8%	D:83%
58	A:2%	B:5%	C:92%	D:1%
59	A:95%	B:2%	C:1%	D:2%
60	A:87%	B:4%	C:2%	D:7%
61	A:2%	B:7%	C:0%	D:91%
62	A:2%	B:5%	C:92%	D:1%
63	A:2%	B:5%	C:92%	D:1%
64	A:95%	B:2%	C:1%	D:2%
65	A:2%	B:5%	C:92%	D:1%
66	A:95%	B:2%	C:1%	D:2%
67	A:1%	B:91%	C:2%	D:6%
68	A:2%	B:5%	C:92%	D:1%
69	A:87%	B:5%	C:2%	D:6%
70	A:95%	B:2%	C:1%	D:2%
71	A:7%	B:2%	C:8%	D:83%
72	A:95%	B:2%	C:1%	D:2%
73	A:1%	B:91%	C:2%	D:6%
74	A:2%	B:5%	C:92%	D:1%

ASK THE AUDIENCE

75	A:11%	B:81%	C:2%	D:6%	118	A:2%	B:7%	C:0%	D:91%
76	A:95%	B:2%	C:1%	D:2%	119	A:9%	B:2%	C:83%	D:6%
77	A:2%	B:7%	C:0%	D:91%	120	A:95%	B:2%	C:1%	D:2%
78	A:7%	B:2%	C:8%	D:83%	121	A:1%	B:91%	C:2%	D:6%
79	A:2%	B:7%	C:0%	D:91%	122	A:2%	B:5%	C:92%	D:1%
80	A:2%	B:7%	C:0%	D:91%	123	A:95%	B:2%	C:1%	D:2%
81	A:2%	B:94%	C:3%	D:1%	124	A:95%	B:2%	C:1%	D:2%
82	A:95%	B:2%	C:1%	D:2%	125	A:6%	B:83%	C:4%	D:7%
83	A:2%	B:94%	C:3%	D:1%	126	A:2%	B:5%	C:92%	D:1%
84	A:4%	B:7%	C:87%	D:2%	127	A:87%	B:5%	C:2%	D:6%
85	A:2%	B:94%	C:3%	D:1%	128	A:2%	B:5%	C:92%	D:1%
86	A:2%	B:7%	C:0%	D:91%	129	A:2%	B:5%	C:92%	D:1%
87	A:2%	B:7%	C:0%	D:91%	130	A:1%	B:91%	C:2%	D:6%
88	A:2%	B:5%	C:92%	D:1%	131	A:16%	B:81%	C:1%	D:2%
89	A:2%	B:5%	C:92%	D:1%	132	A:2%	B:94%	C:3%	D:1%
90	A:95%	B:2%	C:1%	D:2%	133	A:2%	B:5%	C:92%	D:1%
91	A:2%	B:4%	C:89%	D:0%	134	A:2%	B:7%	C:0%	D:91%
92	A:2%	B:7%	C:3%	D:88%	135	A:4%	B:7%	C:87%	D:2%
93	A:7%	B:6%	C:81%	D:0%	136	A:2%	B:94%	C:3%	D:1%
94	A:2%	B:94%	C:3%	D:1%	137	A:95%	B:2%	C:1%	D:2%
95	A:2%	B:5%	C:92%	D:1%	138	A:7%	B:4%	C:89%	D:0%
96	A:2%	B:5%	C:92%	D:1%	139	A:95%	B:2%	C:1%	D:2%
97	A:95%	B:2%	C:1%	D:2%	140	A:2%	B:94%	C:3%	D:1%
98	A:2%	B:7%	C:0%	D:91%	141	A:2%	B:7%	C:0%	D:91%
99	A:2%	B:94%	C:3%	D:1%	142	A:2%	B:7%	C:3%	D:88%
100	A:2%	B:6%	C:87%	D:0%	143	A:2%	B:7%	C:0%	D:91%
101	A:95%	B:2%	C:1%	D:2%	144	A:95%	B:2%	C:1%	D:2%
102	A:2%	B:7%	C:0%	D:91%	145	A:2%	B:7%	C:0%	D:91%
103	A:2%	B:5%	C:92%	D:1%	146	A:95%	B:2%	C:1%	D:2%
104	A:2%	B:94%	C:3%	D:1%	147	A:95%	B:2%	C:1%	D:2%
105	A:95%	B:2%	C:1%	D:2%	148	A:2%	B:94%	C:3%	D:1%
106	A:3%	B:80%	C:17%	D:0%	149	A:2%	B:7%	C:3%	D:88%
107	A:95%	B:2%	C:1%	D:2%	150	A:2%	B:2%	C:0%	D:91%
108	A:2%	B:7%	C:0%	D:91%	151	A:95%	B:2%	C:1%	D:2%
109	A:2%	B:7%	C:0%	D:91%	152	A:2%	B:94%	C:3%	D:1%
110	A:2%	B:5%	C:92%	D:1%	153	A:95%	B:2%	C:1%	D:2%
111	A:2%	B:94%	C:3%	D:1%	154	A:95%	B:2%	C:1%	D:2%
112	A:2%	B:94%	C:3%	D:1%	155	A:95%	B:2%	C:1%	D:2%
113	A:95%	B:2%	C:1%	D:2%	156	A:2%	B:7%	C:0%	D:91%
114	A:2%	B:5%	C:92%	D:1%	157	A:2%	B:5%	C:92%	D:1%
115	A:2%	B:94%	C:3%	D:1%	158	A:95%	B:2%	C:1%	D:2%
116	A:2%	B:5%	C:92%	D:1%	159	A:7%	B:4%	C:89%	D:0%
117	A:95%	B:2%	C:1%	D:2%	160	A:95%	B:2%	C:1%	D:2%

161	A:95%	B:2%	C:1%	D:2%
162	A:16%	B:81%	C:1%	D:2%
163	A:100%	B:0%	C:0%	D:0%
164	A:12%	B:85%	C:13%	D:10%
165	A:2%	B:94%	C:3%	D:1%
166	A:2%	B:5%	C:92%	D:1%
167	A:2%	B:5%	C:92%	D:1%
168	A:95%	B:2%	C:1%	D:2%
169	A:95%	B:2%	C:1%	D:2%
170	A:2%	B:94%	C:3%	D:1%
171	A:87%	B:5%	C:2%	D:6%
172	A:95%	B:2%	C:1%	D:2%
173	A:11%	B:81%	C:2%	D:6%
174	A:95%	B:2%	C:1%	D:2%
175	A:16%	B:81%	C:1%	D:2%
176	A:95%	B:2%	C:1%	D:2%
177	A:2%	B:94%	C:3%	D:1%
178	A:2%	B:94%	C:3%	D:1%
179	A:2%	B:5%	C:92%	D:1%
180	A:2%	B:94%	C:3%	D:1%

£200

1	A:95%	B:2%	C:1%	D:2%
2	A:13%	B:11%	C:67%	D:9%
3	A:13%	B:77%	C:6%	D:4%
4	A:2%	B:5%	C:92%	D:1%
5	A:95%	B:2%	C:1%	D:2%
6	A:2%	B:94%	C:3%	D:1%
7	A:2%	B:94%	C:3%	D:1%
8	A:95%	B:2%	C:1%	D:2%
9	A:2%	B:7%	C:0%	D:91%
10	A:2%	B:7%	C:0%	D:91%
11	A:2%	B:2%	C:3%	D:88%
12	A:2%	B:5%	C:92%	D:1%
13	A:2%	B:94%	C:3%	D:1%
14	A:2%	B:94%	C:3%	D:1%
15	A:2%	B:7%	C:0%	D:91%
16	A:87%	B:5%	C:2%	D:6%
17	A:2%	B:5%	C:92%	D:1%
18	A:95%	D:2%	C:1%	D:2%
19	A:2%	B:7%	C:81%	D:10%
20	A:2%	B:7%	C:81%	D:10%
21	A:2%	B:5%	C:92%	D:1%
22	A:95%	B:2%	C:1%	D:2%
23	A:4%	B:7%	C:87%	D:2%
24	A:2%	B:5%	C:92%	D:1%
25	A:2%	B:5%	C:92%	D:1%
26	A:6%	B:4%	C:14%	D:76%
27	A:2%	B:94%	C:3%	D:1%
28	A:95%	B:2%	C:1%	D:2%
29	A:2%	B:5%	C:92%	D:1%
30	A:2%	B:5%	C:92%	D:1%
31	A:2%	B:7%	C:3%	D:88%
32	A:15%	B:65%	C:6%	D:14%
33	A:74%	B:5%	C:7%	D:14%
34	A:2%	B:5%	C:92%	D:1%
35	A:4%	B:7%	C:87%	D:2%
36	A:2%	B:5%	C:92%	D:1%
37	A:81%	B:2%	C:5%	D:12%
38	A:81%	B:2%	C:5%	D:12%
39	A:7%	B:2%	C:8%	D:83%
40	A:72%	B:21%	C:3%	D:4%
41	A:7%	B:7%	C:0%	D:91%
42	A:6%	B:83%	C:4%	D:2%
43	A:95%	B:2%	C:1%	D:2%
44	A:2%	B:7%	C:0%	D:91%
45	A:2%	B:94%	C:3%	D:1%
46	A:95%	B:2%	C:1%	D:2%
47	A:95%	B:2%	C:1%	D:2%
48	A:2%	B:5%	C:92%	D:1%
49	A:2%	B:94%	C:3%	D:1%
50	A:2%	B:7%	C:0%	D:91%
51	A:2%	B:94%	C:3%	D:1%
52	A:2%	B:7%	C:0%	D:91%
53	A 2%	B:7%	C:0%	D:91%
54	A:2%	B:7%	C:0%	D:91%
55	A:2%	B:5%	C:92%	D:1%
56	A:2%	B:7%	C:0%	D:91%
57	A:4%	B:7%	C:87%	D:2%
58	A:2%	B:7%	C:0%	D:91%

ASK THE AUDIENCE

59	A:3%	B:76%	C:12%	D:9%
60	A:7%	B:4%	C:89%	D:0%
61	A:87%	B:5%	C:2%	D:6%
62	A:2%	B:7%	C:0%	D:91%
63	A:6%	B:2%	C:11%	D:81%
64	A:2%	B:5%	C:92%	D:1%
65	A:2%	B:5%	C:92%	D:1%
66	A:2%	B:7%	C:0%	D:91%
67	A:95%	B:2%	C:1%	D:2%
68	A:2%	B:5%	C:92%	D:1%
69	A:2%	B:7%	C:0%	D:91%
70	A:95%	B:2%	C:1%	D:2%
71	A:18%	B:3%	C:2%	D:77%
72	A:13%	B:77%	C:6%	D:4%
73	A:5%	B:0%	C:14%	D:81%
74	A:87%	B:5%	C:2%	D:6%
75	A:2%	B:7%	C:0%	D:91%
76	A:2%	B:7%	C:0%	D:91%
77	A:2%	B:7%	C:0%	D:91%
78	A:2%	B:94%	C:3%	D:1%
79	A:95%	B:2%	C:1%	D:2%
80	A:2%	B:7%	C:0%	D:91%
81	A:2%	B:94%	C:3%	D:1%
82	A:95%	B:2%	C:1%	D:2%
83	A:2%	B:5%	C:92%	D:1%
84	A:4%	B:31%	C:49%	D:8%
85	A:4%	B:71%	C:12%	D:13%
86	A:95%	B:2%	C:1%	D:2%
87	A:2%	B:5%	C:92%	D:1%
88	A:95%	B:2%	C:1%	D:2%
89	A:13%	B:77%	C:6%	D:4%
90	A:2%	B:4%	C:89%	D:0%
91	A:2%	B:5%	C:92%	D:1%
92	A:4%	B:71%	C:12%	D:13%
93	A:2%	B:5%	C:92%	D:1%
94	A:1%	B:91%	C:2%	D:6%
95	A:7%	B:4%	C:89%	D:0%
96	A:2%	B:7%	C:81%	D:10%
97	A:95%	B:2%	C:1%	D:2%
98	A:2%	B:94%	C:3%	D:1%
99	A:2%	B:94%	C:3%	D:1%
100	A:81%	B:2%	C:5%	D:12%
101	A:2%	B:5%	C:92%	D:1%
102	A:2%	B:5%	C:92%	D:1%
103	A:2%	B:7%	C:0%	D:91%
104	A:9%	B:13%	C:9%	D:69%
105	A:2%	B:5%	C:92%	D:1%
106	A:95%	B:2%	C:1%	D:2%
107	A:13%	B:11%	C:67%	D:9%
108	A:2%	B:94%	C:3%	D:1%
109	A:2%	B:7%	C:0%	D:91%
110	A:2%	B:7%	C:0%	D:91%
111	A:7%	B:4%	C:89%	D:0%
112	A:87%	B:5%	C:2%	D:6%
113	A:2%	B:5%	C:92%	D:1%
114	A:2%	B:94%	C:3%	D:1%
115	A:95%	B:2%	C:1%	D:2%
116	A:2%	B:7%	C:3%	D:88%
117	A:2%	B:94%	C:3%	D:1%
118	A:2%	B:94%	C:3%	D:1%
119	A:95%	B:2%	C:1%	D:2%
120	A:2%	B:94%	C:3%	D:1%
121	A:2%	B:7%	C:0%	D:91%
122	A:95%	B:2%	C:1%	D:2%
123	A:2%	B:5%	C:92%	D:1%
124	A:2%	B:7%	C:0%	D:91%
125	A:2%	B:5%	C:92%	D:1%
126	A:2%	B:5%	C:92%	D:1%
127	A:2%	B:94%	C:3%	D:1%
128	A:2%	B:7%	C:0%	D:91%
129	A:2%	B:7%	C:0%	D:91%
130	A:2%	B:7%	C:0%	D:91%
131	A:74%	B:5%	C:7%	D:14%
132	A:2%	B:94%	C:3%	D:1%
133	A:2%	B:7%	C:0%	D:91%
134	A:2%	B:94%	C:3%	D:1%
135	A:2%	B:5%	C:92%	D:1%
136	A:1%	B:91%	C:2%	D:6%
137	A:95%	B:2%	C:1%	D:2%
138	A:2%	B:5%	C:92%	D:1%
139	A:15%	B:11%	C:8%	D:66%
140	A:2%	B:5%	C:92%	D:1%
141	A:15%	B:65%	C:6%	D:14%
142	A:2%	B:5%	C:92%	D:1%
143	A:95%	B:2%	C:1%	D:2%
144	A:2%	B:7%	C:0%	D:91%

145	A:2%	B:94%	C:3%	D:1%
146	A:95%	B:2%	C:1%	D:2%
147	A:95%	B:2%	C:1%	D:2%
148	A:2%	B:7%	C:0%	D:91%
149	A:2%	B:7%	C:0%	D:91%
150	A:2%	B:94%	C:3%	D:1%
151	A:2%	B:94%	C:3%	D:1%
152	A:13%	B:77%	C:6%	D:4%
153	A:95%	B:2%	C:1%	D:2%
154	A:2%	B:94%	C:3%	D:1%
155	A:2%	B:94%	C:3%	D:1%
156	A:2%	B:94%	C:3%	D:1%
157	A:4%	B:7%	C:87%	D:2%
158	A:2%	B:5%	C:92%	D:1%
159	A:2%	B:7%	C:0%	D:91%
160	A:2%	B:94%	C:3%	D:1%
161	A:6%	B:83%	C:4%	D:7%
162	A:95%	B:2%	C:1%	D:2%
163	A:2%	B:94%	C:3%	D:1%
164	A:2%	B:7%	C:0%	D:91%
165	A:2%	B:7%	C:3%	D:88%
166	A:95%	B:2%	C:1%	D:2%
167	A:7%	B:4%	C:89%	D:0%
168	A:2%	B:5%	C:92%	D:1%
169	A:95%	B:2%	C:1%	D:2%
170	A:2%	B:94%	C:3%	D:1%
171	A:2%	B:5%	C:92%	D:1%
172	A:82%	B:3%	C:14%	D:1%

£300

1	A:2%	B:5%	C:92%	D:1%
2	A:95%	B:2%	C:1%	D:2%
3	A:95%	B:2%	C:1%	D:2%
4	A:62%	B:16%	C:13%	D:4%
5	A:95%	B:2%	C:1%	D:2%
6	A:2%	B:94%	C:3%	D:1%
7	A:14%	B:37%	C:5%	D:44%
8	A:2%	B:94%	C:3%	D:1%
9	A:62%	B:16%	C:13%	D:9%
10	A:2%	B:7%	C:0%	D:91%
11	A:2%	B:5%	C:92%	D:1%
12	A:2%	B:94%	C:3%	D:1%
13	A:13%	B:77%	C:6%	D:4%
14	A:14%	B:1%	C:16%	D:69%
15	A:2%	B:94%	C:3%	D:1%
16	A:6%	B:83%	C:4%	D:7%
17	A:2%	B:5%	C:92%	D:1%
18	A:2%	B:94%	C:3%	D:1%
19	A:8%	B:7%	C:22%	D:63%
20	A:95%	B:2%	C:1%	D:2%
21	A:1%	B:12%	C:4%	D:83%
22	A:2%	B:5%	C:92%	D:1%
23	A:2%	B:7%	C:0%	D:91%
24	A:2%	B:7%	C:0%	D:91%
25	A:95%	B:2%	C:1%	D:2%
26	A:2%	B:94%	C:3%	D:1%
27	A:2%	B:5%	C:92%	D:1%
28	A:2%	B:7%	C:0%	D:91%
29	A:2%	B:7%	C:0%	D:91%
30	A:2%	B:7%	C:0%	D:91%
31	A:95%	B:2%	C:1%	D:2%
32	A:2%	B:7%	C:0%	D:91%
33	A:2%	B:7%	C:0%	D:91%
34	A:1%	B:12%	C:4%	D:83%
35	A:1%	B:12%	C:4%	D:83%
36	A:6%	B:83%	C:4%	D:7%
37	A:2%	B:5%	C:92%	D:1%
38	A:3%	B:80%	C:12%	D:0%
39	A:2%	B:7%	C:0%	D:91%
40	A:95%	B:2%	C:1%	D:2%
41	A:2%	B:5%	C:92%	D:1%
42	A:2%	B:94%	C:3%	D:1%
43	A:2%	B:94%	C:3%	D:1%
44	A:2%	B:5%	C:92%	D:1%
45	A:2%	B:5%	C:92%	D:1%
46	A:2%	B:7%	C:0%	D:91%
47	A:6%	B:3%	C:81%	D:10%
48	A:95%	B:2%	C:1%	D:2%
49	A:2%	B:94%	C:3%	D:1%
50	A:95%	B:2%	C:1%	D:2%

ASK THE AUDIENCE

51	A:2%	B:5%	C:92%	D:1%
52	A:2%	B:5%	C:92%	D:1%
53	A:95%	B:2%	C:1%	D:2%
54	A:2%	B:7%	C:0%	D:91%
55	A:2%	B:94%	C:3%	D:1%
56	A:2%	B:94%	C:3%	D:1%
57	A:2%	B:94%	C:3%	D:1%
58	A:2%	B:7%	C:0%	D:91%
59	A:2%	B:5%	C:92%	D:1%
60	A:2%	B:94%	C:3%	D:1%
61	A:2%	B:7%	C:0%	D:91%
62	A:2%	B:5%	C:92%	D:1%
63	A:95%	B:2%	C:1%	D:2%
64	A:2%	B:7%	C:0%	D:91%
65	A:2%	B:5%	C:92%	D:1%
66	A:15%	B:65%	C:6%	D:14%
67	A:95%	B:2%	C:1%	D:2%
68	A:2%	B:7%	C:0%	D:91%
69	A:62%	B:5%	C:25%	D:8%
70	A:95%	B:2%	C:1%	D:2%
71	A:2%	B:7%	C:0%	D:91%
72	A:2%	B:7%	C:0%	D:91%
73	A:2%	B:7%	C:0%	D:91%
74	A:6%	B:83%	C:4%	D:7%
75	A:2%	B:7%	C:0%	D:91%
76	A:2%	B:94%	C:3%	D:1%
77	A:4%	B:7%	C:87%	D:2%
78	A:2%	B:94%	C:3%	D:1%
79	A:2%	B:5%	C:92%	D:1%
80	A:2%	B:5%	C:92%	D:1%
81	A:2%	B:94%	C:3%	D:1%
82	A:13%	B:77%	C:6%	D:4%
83	A:18%	B:3%	C:2%	D:77%
84	A:13%	B:11%	C:67%	D:9%
85	A:2%	B:7%	C:0%	D:91%
86	A:2%	B:94%	C:3%	D:1%
87	A:2%	B:5%	C:92%	D:1%
88	A:95%	B:2%	C:1%	D:2%
89	A:95%	B:2%	C:1%	D:2%
90	A:9%	B:13%	C:9%	D:69%
91	A:87%	B:4%	C:2%	D:2%
92	A:95%	B:2%	C:1%	D:2%
93	A:9%	B:2%	C:83%	D:6%
94	A:67%	B:22%	C:5%	D:6%
95	A:2%	B:7%	C:0%	D:91%
96	A:14%	B:1%	C:16%	D:69%
97	A:95%	B:2%	C:1%	D:2%
98	A:4%	B:7%	C:87%	D:2%
99	A:10%	B:22%	C:3%	D:65%
100	A:12%	B:67%	C:7%	D:14%
101	A:95%	B:2%	C:1%	D:2%
102	A:2%	B:7%	C:0%	D:91%
103	A:2%	B:5%	C:92%	D:1%
104	A:2%	B:5%	C:92%	D:1%
105	A:95%	B:2%	C:1%	D:2%
106	A:2%	B:5%	C:92%	D:1%
107	A:95%	B:2%	C:1%	D:2%
108	A:82%	B:3%	C:14%	D:1%
109	A:95%	B:2%	C:1%	D:2%
110	A:95%	B:2%	C:1%	D:2%
111	A:95%	B:2%	C:1%	D:2%
112	A:95%	B:2%	C:1%	D:2%
113	A:87%	B:4%	C:2%	D:7%
114	A:2%	B:7%	C:0%	D:91%
115	A:2%	B:5%	C:92%	D:1%
116	A:95%	B:2%	C:1%	D:2%
117	A:2%	B:7%	C:0%	D:91%
118	A:2%	B:94%	C:3%	D:1%
119	A:2%	B:5%	C:92%	D:1%
120	A:2%	B:7%	C:3%	D:88%
121	A:82%	B:3%	C:14%	D:1%
122	A:2%	B:7%	C:0%	D:91%
123	A:2%	B:94%	C:3%	D:1%
124	A:2%	B:5%	C:92%	D:1%
125	A:14%	B:1%	C:83%	D:2%
126	A:2%	B:94%	C:3%	D:1%
127	A:22%	B:63%	C:14%	D:1%
128	A:60%	B:5%	C:12%	D:23%
129	A:2%	B:7%	C:0%	D:91%
130	A:2%	B:94%	C:3%	D:1%
131	A:87%	B:4%	C:2%	D:7%
132	A:2%	B:5%	C:92%	D:1%
133	A:2%	B:7%	C:0%	D:91%
134	A:2%	B:7%	C:0%	D:91%
135	A:95%	B:2%	C:1%	D:2%
136	A:2%	B:5%	C:92%	D:1%

137	A:2%	B:94%	C:3%	D:1%	151	A:2%	B:5%	C:92%	D:1%
138	A:2%	B:7%	C:0%	D:91%	152	A:2%	B:7%	C:0%	D:91%
139	A:2%	B:5%	C:92%	D:1%	153	A:2%	B:94%	C:3%	D:1%
140	A:2%	B:94%	C:3%	D:1%	154	A:2%	B:7%	C:0%	D:91%
141	A:2%	B:7%	C:0%	D:91%	155	A:2%	B:5%	C:92%	D:1%
142	A:2%	B:94%	C:3%	D:1%	156	A:2%	B:94%	C:3%	D:1%
143	A:95%	B:2%	C:1%	D:2%	157	A:14%	B:1%	C:83%	D:2%
144	A:95%	B:2%	C:1%	D:2%	158	A:2%	B:5%	C:92%	D:1%
145	A:95%	B:2%	C:1%	D:2%	159	A:2%	B:94%	C:3%	D:1%
146	A:2%	B:94%	C:3%	D:1%	160	A:95%	B:2%	C:1%	D:2%
147	A:10%	B:5%	C:6%	D:79%	161	A:7%	B:4%	C:89%	D:0%
148	A:2%	B:7%	C:3%	D:88%	162	A:95%	B:2%	C:1%	D:2%
149	A:95%	B:2%	C:1%	D:2%	163	A:2%	B:94%	C:3%	D:1%
150	A:2%	B:94%	C:3%	D:1%	164	A:2%	B:94%	C:3%	D:1%

£500

1	A:95%	B:2%	C:1%	D:2%	26	A:2%	B:5%	C:92%	D:1%
2	A:6%	B:83%	C:4%	D:7%	27	A:13%	B:11%	C:67%	D:9%
3	A:95%	B:2%	C:1%	D:2%	28	A:3%	B:76%	C:12%	D:9%
4	A:8%	B:11%	C:6%	D:75%	29	A:87%	B:4%	C:2%	D:7%
5	A:4%	B:71%	C:12%	D:13%	30	A:87%	B:4%	C:2%	D:7%
6	A:95%	B:2%	C:1%	D:2%	31	A:2%	B:94%	C:3%	D:1%
7	A:8%	B:11%	C:6%	D:75%	32	A:72%	B:21%	C:3%	D:4%
8	A:13%	B:11%	C:67%	D:9%	33	A:2%	B:7%	C:0%	D:91%
9	A:87%	B:4%	C:2%	D:2%	34	A:12%	B:65%	C:13%	D:10%
10	A:2%	B:94%	C:3%	D:1%	35	A:7%	B:2%	C:8%	D:83%
11	A:87%	B:4%	C:2%	D:7%	36	A:95%	B:2%	C:1%	D:2%
12	A:3%	B:76%	C:12%	D:9%	37	A:12%	B:65%	C:13%	D:10%
13	A:2%	B:7%	C:0%	D:91%	38	A:2%	B:7%	C:0%	D:91%
14	A:9%	B:11%	C:59%	D:21%	39	A:2%	B:94%	C:3%	D:1%
15	A:6%	B:83%	C:4%	D:7%	40	A:2%	B:94%	C:3%	D:1%
16	A:2%	B:5%	C:92%	D:1%	41	A:18%	B:3%	C:2%	D:77%
17	A:57%	B:23%	C:6%	D:14%	42	A:4%	B:71%	C:12%	D:13%
18	A:2%	B:94%	C:3%	D:1%	43	A:95%	B:2%	C:1%	D:2%
19	A:87%	B:4%	C:2%	D:7%	44	A:87%	B:4%	C:2%	D:7%
20	A:4%	B:11%	C:72%	D:13%	45	A:2%	B:7%	C:0%	D:91%
21	A:3%	B:76%	C:12%	D:9%	46	A:13%	B:11%	C:67%	D:9%
22	A:8%	B:11%	C:6%	D:75%	47	A:2%	B:5%	C:92%	D:1%
23	A:2%	B:5%	C:92%	D:1%	48	A:2%	B:7%	C:3%	D:88%
24	A:2%	B:5%	C:92%	D:1%	49	A:4%	B:7%	C:87%	D:2%
25	A:2%	B:7%	C:0%	D:91%	50	A:62%	B:16%	C:13%	D:9%

ASK THE AUDIENCE

51	A:10%	B:2%	C:75%	D:13%
52	A:81%	B:2%	C:5%	D:12%
53	A:2%	B:94%	C:3%	D:1%
54	A:7%	B:2%	C:8%	D:83%
55	A:95%	B:2%	C:1%	D:2%
56	A:2%	B:94%	C:3%	D:1%
57	A:6%	B:83%	C:4%	D:7%
58	A:2%	B:7%	C:7%	D:88%
59	A:2%	B:94%	C:3%	D:1%
60	A:3%	B:76%	C:12%	D:9%
61	A:3%	B:76%	C:12%	D:9%
62	A:6%	B:83%	C:4%	D:7%
63	A:81%	B:2%	C:5%	D:12%
64	A:12%	B:65%	C:13%	D:10%
65	A:9%	B:11%	C:59%	D:21%
66	A:2%	B:7%	C:3%	D:88%
67	A:2%	B:7%	C:81%	D:10%
68	A:2%	B:5%	C:92%	D:1%
69	A:2%	B:7%	C:0%	D:91%
70	A:95%	B:2%	C:1%	D:2%
71	A:4%	B:12%	C:9%	D:75%
72	A:2%	B:5%	C:92%	D:1%
73	A:2%	B:5%	C:92%	D:1%
74	A:2%	B:2%	C:8%	D:83%
75	A:6%	B:83%	C:4%	D:7%
76	A:12%	B:65%	C:13%	D:10%
77	A:2%	B:94%	C:3%	D:1%
78	A:13%	B:11%	C:67%	D:9%
79	A:81%	B:2%	C:5%	D:12%
80	A:87%	B:4%	C:2%	D:7%
81	A:95%	B:2%	C:1%	D:2%
82	A:2%	B:2%	C:0%	D:91%
83	A:26%	B:67%	C:3%	D:4%
84	A:4%	B:2%	C:16%	D:73%
85	A:60%	B:5%	C:12%	D:23%
86	A:26%	B:1%	C:68%	D:5%
87	A:95%	B:2%	C:1%	D:2%
88	A:7%	B:4%	C:89%	D:0%
89	A:2%	B:7%	C:0%	D:91%
90	A:2%	B:7%	C:3%	D:88%
91	A:5%	B:65%	C:9%	D:21%
92	A:2%	B:7%	C:0%	D:91%
93	A:5%	B:62%	C:13%	D:20%
94	A:14%	B:1%	C:83%	D:2%
95	A:62%	B:16%	C:13%	D:9%
96	A:2%	B:94%	C:3%	D:1%
97	A:72%	B:21%	C:3%	D:4%
98	A:2%	B:5%	C:92%	D:1%
99	A:87%	B:4%	C:2%	D:7%
100	A:2%	B:7%	C:0%	D:91%
101	A:2%	B:7%	C:81%	D:10%
102	A:6%	B:83%	C:4%	D:7%
103	A:67%	B:22%	C:5%	D:6%
104	A:13%	B:11%	C:67%	D:9%
105	A:2%	B:94%	C:3%	D:1%
106	A:5%	B:62%	C:13%	D:20%
107	A:2%	B:7%	C:8%	D:83%
108	A:2%	B:7%	C:81%	D:10%
109	A:2%	B:94%	C:3%	D:1%
110	A:8%	B:7%	C:22%	D:63%
111	A:2%	B:94%	C:3%	D:1%
112	A:2%	B:5%	C:92%	D:1%
113	A:12%	B:65%	C:13%	D:10%
114	A:2%	B:5%	C:92%	D:1%
115	A:81%	B:2%	C:5%	D:12%
116	A:14%	B:1%	C:16%	D:69%
117	A:14%	B:1%	C:83%	D:2%
118	A:7%	B:2%	C:8%	D:83%
119	A:2%	B:7%	C:0%	D:91%
120	A:6%	B:83%	C:4%	D:7%
121	A:2%	B:5%	C:92%	D:1%
122	A:15%	B:11%	C:8%	D:66%
123	A:6%	B:83%	C:4%	D:7%
124	A:8%	B:11%	C:6%	D:75%
125	A:2%	B:7%	C:0%	D:91%
126	A:62%	B:16%	C:13%	D:9%
127	A:2%	B:7%	C:0%	D:91%
128	A:2%	B:94%	C:3%	D:1%
129	A:87%	B:4%	C:2%	D:7%
130	A:4%	B:11%	C:22%	D:13%
131	A:2%	B:7%	C:3%	D:88%
132	A:2%	B:7%	C:0%	D:91%
133	A:2%	B:94%	C:3%	D:1%
134	A:2%	B:5%	C:92%	D:1%
135	A:2%	B:94%	C:3%	D:1%
136	A:6%	B:83%	C:4%	D:7%

137	A:7%	B:2%	C:8%	D:83%
138	A:2%	B:5%	C:92%	D:1%
139	A:13%	B:11%	C:67%	D:9%
140	A:2%	B:5%	C:92%	D:1%
141	A:95%	B:2%	C:1%	D:2%
142	A:2%	B:7%	C:0%	D:91%
143	A:95%	B:2%	C:1%	D:2%
144	A:95%	B:2%	C:1%	D:2%
145	A:2%	B:5%	C:92%	D:1%
146	A:2%	B:5%	C:92%	D:1%
147	A:6%	B:83%	C:4%	D:7%
148	A:12%	B:65%	C:13%	D:10%
149	A:13%	B:77%	C:6%	D:4%
150	A:87%	B:4%	C:2%	D:7%
151	A:3%	B:80%	C:17%	D:0%
152	A:2%	B:7%	C:3%	D:88%
153	A:2%	B:7%	C:3%	D:88%
154	A:4%	B:71%	C:12%	D:13%
155	A:4%	B:12%	C:9%	D:75%
156	A:62%	B:5%	C:25%	D:8%

£1,000

1	A:95%	B:2%	C:1%	D:2%
2	A:78%	B:4%	C:2%	D:16%
3	A:2%	B:5%	C:92%	D:1%
4	A:74%	B:5%	C:7%	D:14%
5	A:95%	B:2%	C:1%	D:2%
6	A:4%	B:7%	C:87%	D:2%
7	A:5%	B:0%	C:82%	D:13%
8	A:2%	B:7%	C:81%	D:10%
9	A:2%	B:94%	C:3%	D:1%
10	A:15%	B:11%	C:8%	D:66%
11	A:14%	B:1%	C:16%	D:69%
12	A:6%	B:83%	C:4%	D:7%
13	A:87%	B:4%	C:2%	D:7%
14	A:15%	B:11%	C:8%	D:66%
15	A:16%	B:81%	C:1%	D:2%
16	A:14%	B:1%	C:83%	D:2%
17	A:2%	B:94%	C:3%	D:1%
18	A:95%	B:2%	C:1%	D:2%
19	A:2%	B:7%	C:0%	D:91%
20	A:81%	B:2%	C:5%	D:12%
21	A:87%	B:5%	C:2%	D:6%
22	A:95%	B:2%	C:1%	D:2%
23	A:2%	B:7%	C:0%	D:91%
24	A:2%	B:7%	C:0%	D:91%
25	A:2%	B:7%	C:0%	D:91%
26	A:81%	B:2%	C:5%	D:12%
27	A:3%	B:76%	C:12%	D:9%
28	A:2%	B:7%	C:3%	D:88%
29	A:13%	B:11%	C:67%	D:9%
30	A:2%	B:94%	C:3%	D:1%
31	A:2%	B:5%	C:92%	D:1%
32	A:14%	B:1%	C:16%	D:69%
33	A:2%	B:5%	C:92%	D:1%
34	A:82%	B:3%	C:14%	D:1%
35	A:62%	B:16%	C:13%	D:9%
36	A:87%	B:4%	C:2%	D:7%
37	A:2%	B:5%	C:92%	D:1%
38	A:13%	B:11%	C:67%	D:9%
39	A:12%	B:67%	C:9%	D:12%
40	A:87%	B:4%	C:2%	D:7%
41	A:2%	B:94%	C:3%	D:1%
42	A:6%	B:83%	C:4%	D:7%
43	A:2%	B:7%	C:0%	D:91%
44	A:87%	B:4%	C:2%	D:7%
45	A:12%	B:65%	C:13%	D:10%
46	A:4%	B:7%	C:87%	D:2%
47	A:16%	B:81%	C:1%	D:2%
48	A:2%	B:5%	C:92%	D:1%
49	A:6%	B:83%	C:4%	D:7%
50	A:2%	B:7%	C:0%	D:91%
51	A:6%	B:3%	C:81%	D:10%
52	A:6%	B:3%	C:81%	D:10%
53	A:2%	B:94%	C:3%	D:1%
54	A:13%	B:11%	C:67%	D:9%
55	A:72%	B:21%	C:3%	D:4%
56	A:87%	B:4%	C:2%	D:7%
57	A:12%	B:65%	C:13%	D:10%
58	A:4%	B:7%	C:87%	D:2%

ASK THE AUDIENCE

69	A:2%	B:94%	C:3%	D:1%
60	A:72%	B:21%	C:3%	D:4%
61	A:3%	B:76%	C:12%	D:9%
62	A:2%	B:7%	C:0%	D:91%
63	A:2%	B:5%	C:92%	D:1%
64	A:87%	B:4%	C:2%	D:7%
65	A:13%	B:11%	C:67%	D:9%
66	A:18%	B:3%	C:2%	D:77%
67	A:2%	B:7%	C:0%	D:91%
68	A:3%	B:76%	C:12%	D:9%
69	A:4%	B:11%	C:77%	D:13%
70	A:2%	B:7%	C:3%	D:88%
71	A:2%	B:7%	C:81%	D:10%
72	A:95%	B:2%	C:1%	D:2%
73	A:2%	B:7%	C:0%	D:91%
74	A:2%	B:7%	C:0%	D:91%
75	A:2%	B:94%	C:3%	D:1%
76	A:6%	B:83%	C:4%	D:7%
77	A:2%	B:94%	C:3%	D:1%
78	A:2%	B:7%	C:0%	D:91%
79	A:15%	B:11%	C:8%	D:66%
80	A:2%	B:5%	C:92%	D:1%
81	A:2%	B:7%	C:81%	D:10%
82	A:8%	B:11%	C:6%	D:75%
83	A:6%	B:83%	C:4%	D:7%
84	A:6%	B:83%	C:4%	D:7%
85	A:12%	B:67%	C:7%	D:14%
86	A:2%	B:7%	C:3%	D:88%
87	A:2%	B:94%	C:3%	D:1%
88	A:8%	B:11%	C:6%	D:75%
89	A:4%	B:2%	C:87%	D:2%
90	A:2%	B:94%	C:3%	D:1%
91	A:2%	B:7%	C:0%	D:91%
92	A:6%	B:83%	C:4%	D:7%
93	A:57%	B:23%	C:6%	D:14%
94	A:6%	B:83%	C:4%	D:7%
95	A:2%	B:5%	C:92%	D:1%
96	A:6%	B:83%	C:4%	D:7%
97	A:6%	B:3%	C:81%	D:10%
98	A:2%	B:94%	C:3%	D:1%
99	A:15%	B:11%	C:8%	D:66%
100	A:2%	B:94%	C:3%	D:1%
101	A:15%	B:11%	C:8%	D:66%
102	A:87%	B:4%	C:2%	D:7%
103	A:13%	B:11%	C:67%	D:9%
104	A:8%	B:2%	C:79%	D:11%
105	A:6%	B:83%	C:4%	D:2%
106	A:62%	B:16%	C:13%	D:9%
107	A:8%	B:11%	C:6%	D:75%
108	A:4%	B:11%	C:72%	D:13%
109	A:6%	B:83%	C:4%	D:7%
110	A:80%	B:4%	C:3%	D:13%
111	A:10%	B:22%	C:3%	D:65%
112	A:6%	B:4%	C:14%	D:76%
113	A:2%	B:7%	C:0%	D:91%
114	A:2%	B:7%	C:0%	D:91%
115	A:14%	B:1%	C:83%	D:2%
116	A:13%	B:11%	C:67%	D:9%
117	A:67%	B:22%	C:5%	D:6%
118	A:95%	B:2%	C:1%	D:2%
119	A:2%	B:5%	C:92%	D:1%
120	A:2%	B:94%	C:3%	D:1%
121	A:10%	B:22%	C:3%	D:65%
122	A:9%	B:11%	C:59%	D:21%
123	A:95%	B:2%	C:1%	D:2%
124	A:2%	B:94%	C:3%	D:1%
125	A:2%	B:94%	C:3%	D:1%
126	A:2%	B:5%	C:92%	D:1%
127	A:7%	B:4%	C:89%	D:0%
128	A:2%	B:5%	C:92%	D:1%
129	A:6%	B:83%	C:4%	D:7%
130	A:2%	B:94%	C:3%	D:1%
131	A:95%	B:2%	C:1%	D:2%
132	A:95%	B:2%	C:1%	D:2%
133	A:3%	B:76%	C:12%	D:9%
134	A:2%	B:94%	C:3%	D:1%
135	A:2%	B:94%	C:3%	D:1%
136	A:7%	B:4%	C:88%	D:0%
137	A:2%	B:7%	C:0%	D:91%
138	A:1%	B:12%	C:4%	D:83%
139	A:2%	B:5%	C:92%	D:1%
140	A:2%	B:94%	C:3%	D:1%
141	A:2%	B:94%	C:3%	D:1%
142	A:3%	B:76%	C:12%	D:9%
143	A:2%	B:94%	C:3%	D:1%
144	A:13%	B:11%	C:67%	D:9%

145	A:7%	B:4%	C:89%	D:0%
146	A:6%	B:3%	C:81%	D:10%
147	A:2%	B:7%	C:0%	D:91%
148	A:2%	B:94%	C:3%	D:1%

£2,000

1	A:67%	B:22%	C:5%	D:6%
2	A:6%	B:3%	C:81%	D:10%
3	A:2%	B:7%	C:0%	D:91%
4	A:8%	B:7%	C:22%	D:63%
5	A:81%	B:2%	C:5%	D:12%
6	A:3%	B:5%	C:92%	D:1%
7	A:95%	B:2%	C:1%	D:2%
8	A:7%	B:2%	C:8%	D:83%
9	A:6%	B:83%	C:4%	D:7%
10	A:2%	B:7%	C:81%	D:10%
11	A:6%	B:83%	C:4%	D:7%
12	A:6%	B:83%	C:4%	D:7%
13	A:62%	B:16%	C:13%	D:4%
14	A:2%	B:94%	C:3%	D:1%
15	A:14%	B:1%	C:83%	D:2%
16	A:4%	B:7%	C:87%	D:2%
17	A:87%	B:4%	C:2%	D:7%
18	A:2%	B:5%	C:92%	D:1%
19	A:95%	B:2%	C:1%	D:2%
20	A:95%	B:2%	C:1%	D:2%
21	A:12%	B:67%	C:7%	D:14%
22	A:2%	B:94%	C:3%	D:1%
23	A:13%	B:11%	C:67%	D:9%
24	A:2%	B:7%	C:0%	D:91%
25	A:95%	B:2%	C:1%	D:2%
26	A:4%	B:11%	C:72%	D:13%
27	A:52%	B:0%	C:27%	D:21%
28	A:12%	B:67%	C:7%	D:14%
29	A:2%	B:7%	C:81%	D:10%
30	A:57%	B:23%	C:6%	D:14%
31	A:13%	B:11%	C:67%	D:9%
32	A:3%	B:76%	C:12%	D:9%
33	A:2%	B:7%	C:3%	D:88%
34	A:2%	B:94%	C:3%	D:1%
35	A:95%	B:2%	C:1%	D:2%
36	A:8%	B:11%	C:6%	D:75%
37	A:2%	B:7%	C:0%	D:91%
38	A:2%	B:7%	C:0%	D:91%
39	A:2%	B:94%	C:3%	D:1%
40	A:95%	B:2%	C:1%	D:2%
41	A:87%	B:4%	C:2%	D:7%
42	A:95%	B:2%	C:1%	D:2%
43	A:3%	B:76%	C:12%	D:9%
44	A:2%	B:94%	C:3%	D:1%
45	A:87%	B:4%	C:2%	D:7%
46	A:2%	B:7%	C:3%	D:88%
47	A:13%	B:11%	C:67%	D:9%
48	A:13%	B:77%	C:6%	D:4%
49	A:4%	B:7%	C:16%	D:73%
50	A:16%	B:81%	C:1%	D:2%
51	A:6%	B:83%	C:4%	D:7%
52	A:87%	B:4%	C:2%	D:7%
53	A:62%	B:16%	C:13%	D:9%
54	A:2%	B:94%	C:3%	D:1%
55	A:2%	B:7%	C:3%	D:88%
56	A:87%	B:4%	C:2%	D:7%
57	A:3%	B:76%	C:12%	D:9%
58	A:81%	B:2%	C:5%	D:12%
59	A:81%	B:2%	C:5%	D:12%
60	A:95%	B:2%	C:1%	D:2%
61	A:2%	B:7%	C:3%	D:88%
62	A:22%	B:14%	C:63%	D:1%
63	A:2%	B:94%	C:3%	D:1%
64	A:7%	B:4%	C:89%	D:0%
65	A:7%	B:4%	C:89%	D:0%
66	A:9%	B:13%	C:9%	D:69%
67	A:95%	B:2%	C:1%	D:2%
68	A:60%	B:5%	C:12%	D:23%
69	A:5%	B:0%	C:82%	D:13%
70	A:62%	B:16%	C:13%	D:9%
71	A:87%	B:4%	C:2%	D:7%
72	A:5%	D:0%	C:82%	D:13%
73	A:4%	D:71%	C:12%	D:13%
74	A:2%	D:5%	C:92%	D:1%

75	A:2%	D:94%	C:3%	D:1%
76	A:4%	D:11%	C:72%	D:13%
77	A:87%	D:4%	C:2%	D:7%
78	A:12%	D:65%	C:13%	D:10%
79	A:8%	D:7%	C:22%	D:63%
80	A:2%	D:5%	C:92%	D:1%
81	A:2%	D:7%	C:0%	D:91%
82	A:2%	B:5%	C:92%	D:1%
83	A:9%	B:11%	C:59%	D:21%
84	A:15%	B:11%	C:8%	D:66%
85	A:4%	B:12%	C:9%	D:75%
86	A:12%	B:65%	C:13%	D:10%
87	A:2%	B:7%	C:3%	D:88%
88	A:87%	B:4%	C:2%	D:7%
89	A:15%	B:65%	C:6%	D:14%
90	A:95%	B:2%	C:1%	D:2%
91	A:13%	B:77%	C:6%	D:4%
92	A:60%	B:5%	C:12%	D:23%
93	A:2%	B:5%	C:92%	D:1%
94	A:67%	B:22%	C:5%	D:6%
95	A:4%	B:11%	C:72%	D:13%
96	A:87%	B:4%	C:2%	D:7%
97	A:3%	B:76%	C:12%	D:9%
98	A:5%	B:62%	C:13%	D:20%
99	A:62%	B:16%	C:13%	D:9%
100	A:12%	B:65%	C:13%	D:10%
101	A:61%	B:6%	C:8%	D:25%
102	A:6%	B:83%	C:4%	D:7%
103	A:67%	B:22%	C:5%	D:6%
104	A:5%	B:65%	C:9%	D:21%
105	A:5%	B:62%	C:13%	D:20%
106	A:5%	B:11%	C:66%	D:18%
107	A:18%	B:3%	C:2%	D:77%
108	A:12%	B:67%	C:9%	D:12%
109	A:2%	B:7%	C:81%	D:10%
110	A:62%	B:5%	C:25%	D:8%
111	A:2%	B:7%	C:0%	D:91%
112	A:5%	B:0%	C:82%	D:13%
113	A:5%	B:11%	C:66%	D:18%
114	A:2%	B:5%	C:92%	D:1%
115	A:5%	B:62%	C:13%	D:20%
116	A:2%	B:7%	C:3%	D:88%
117	A:15%	B:65%	C:6%	D:14%
118	A:87%	B:4%	C:2%	D:7%
119	A:9%	B:11%	C:59%	D:21%
120	A:6%	B:83%	C:4%	D:7%
121	A:18%	B:3%	C:2%	D:77%
122	A:5%	B:62%	C:13%	D:20%
123	A:2%	B:7%	C:81%	D:10%
124	A:14%	B:1%	C:83%	D:2%
125	A:2%	B:7%	C:3%	D:88%
126	A:2%	B:7%	C:0%	D:91%
127	A:3%	B:76%	C:12%	D:9%
128	A:26%	B:1%	C:68%	D:5%
129	A:9%	B:11%	C:59%	D:21%
130	A:3%	B:76%	C:12%	D:9%
131	A:14%	B:1%	C:16%	D:69%
132	A:16%	B:81%	C:1%	D:2%
133	A:9%	B:13%	C:9%	D:69%
134	A:62%	B:5%	C:25%	D:8%
135	A:5%	B:11%	C:66%	D:18%
136	A:5%	B:62%	C:13%	D:20%
137	A:2%	B:94%	C:3%	D:1%
138	A:4%	B:11%	C:72%	D:13%
139	A:3%	B:76%	C:12%	D:9%
140	A:2%	B:7%	C:3%	D:88%

£4,000

1	A:2%	B:5%	C:92%	D:1%
2	A:5%	B:62%	C:13%	D:20%
3	A:3%	B:80%	C:12%	D:0%
4	A:95%	B:2%	C:1%	D:2%
5	A:9%	B:11%	C:59%	D:21%
6	A:2%	B:7%	C:0%	D:91%
7	A:2%	B:5%	C:92%	D:1%
8	A:6%	B:83%	C:4%	D:7%
9	A:5%	B:62%	C:13%	D:20%
10	A:2%	B:5%	C:92%	D:1%
11	A:95%	B:2%	C:1%	D:2%
12	A:8%	B:7%	C:22%	D:63%

ASK THE AUDIENCE

13	A:2%	B:94%	C:3%	D:1%
14	A:4%	B:7%	C:87%	D:2%
15	A:95%	B:2%	C:1%	D:2%
16	A:95%	B:2%	C:1%	D:2%
17	A:13%	B:11%	C:67%	D:9%
18	A:4%	B:7%	C:16%	D:73%
19	A:8%	B:2%	C:79%	D:11%
20	A:62%	B:5%	C:25%	D:8%
21	A:2%	B:7%	C:3%	D:88%
22	A:2%	B:5%	C:92%	D:1%
23	A:14%	B:1%	C:16%	D:69%
24	A:2%	B:94%	C:3%	D:1%
25	A:2%	B:5%	C:92%	D:1%
26	A:2%	B:7%	C:0%	D:91%
27	A:2%	B:7%	C:0%	D:91%
28	A:9%	B:11%	C:59%	D:21%
29	A:2%	B:5%	C:92%	D:1%
30	A:95%	B:2%	C:1%	D:2%
31	A:2%	B:7%	C:0%	D:91%
32	A:8%	B:11%	C:6%	D:75%
33	A:6%	B:83%	C:4%	D:7%
34	A:9%	B:11%	C:59%	D:21%
35	A:6%	B:3%	C:81%	D:10%
36	A:77%	B:21%	C:3%	D:4%
37	A:9%	B:13%	C:9%	D:69%
38	A:5%	B:65%	C:9%	D:21%
39	A:16%	B:81%	C:1%	D:2%
40	A:82%	B:3%	C:14%	D:1%
41	A:5%	B:0%	C:82b%	D:13%
42	A:11%	B:81%	C:2%	D:6%
43	A:2%	B:7%	C:81%	D:10%
44	A:13%	B:11%	C:67%	D:2%
45	A:87%	B:4%	C:2%	D:7%
46	A:9%	B:11%	C:59%	D:21%
47	A:2%	B:5%	C:92%	D:1%
48	A:2%	B:5%	C:92%	D:1%
49	A:12%	B:65%	C:13%	D:10%
50	A:2%	B:94%	C:3%	D:1%
51	A:4%	B:39%	C:49%	D:8%
52	A:2%	B:7%	C:3%	D:88%
53	A:62%	B:16%	C:13%	D:9%
54	A:12%	B:65%	C:13%	D:10%
55	A:9%	B:11%	C:59%	D:21%
56	A:95%	B:2%	C:1%	D:2%
57	A:5%	B:62%	C:13%	D:20%
58	A:4%	B:71%	C:12%	D:13%
59	A:2%	B:94%	C:3%	D:1%
60	A:1%	B:12%	C:4%	D:83%
61	A:10%	B:2%	C:75%	D:13%
62	A:81%	B:2%	C:5%	D:12%
63	A:5%	B:65%	C:9%	D:21%
64	A:2%	B:7%	C:3%	D:88%
65	A:2%	B:94%	C:3%	D:1%
66	A:4%	B:71%	C:12%	D:13%
67	A:14%	B:37%	C:5%	D:44%
68	A:13%	B:11%	C:67%	D:9%
69	A:81%	B:2%	C:5%	D:12%
70	A:5%	B:0%	C:14%	D:81%
71	A:26%	B:1%	C:68%	D:5%
72	A:2%	D:7%	C:0%	D:91%
73	A:4%	D:39%	C:49%	D:8%
74	A:5%	D:62%	C:13%	D:20%
75	A:72%	D:21%	C:3%	D:4%
76	A:2%	D:7%	C:81%	D:10%
77	A:6%	D:83%	C:4%	D:7%
78	A:15%	D:11%	C:8%	D:66%
79	A:6%	D:2%	C:11%	D:81%
80	A:81%	D:2%	C:5%	D:12%
81	A:2%	D:7%	C:3%	D:88%
82	A:4%	B:11%	C:72%	D:13%
83	A:6%	B:83%	C:4%	D:2%
84	A:2%	B:7%	C:3%	D:88%
85	A:9%	B:11%	C:59%	D:21%
86	A:13%	B:11%	C:67%	D:9%
87	A:15%	B:11%	C:8%	D:66%
88	A:6%	B:3%	C:81%	D:10%
89	A:14%	B:1%	C:83%	D:2%
90	A:72%	B:21%	C:3%	D:4%
91	A:8%	B:7%	C:22%	D:63%
92	A:26%	B:1%	C:68%	D:5%
93	A:2%	B:5%	C:92%	D:1%
94	A:4%	B:39%	C:49%	D:8%
95	A:62%	B:5%	C:25%	D:8%
96	A:7%	B:2%	C:8%	D:83%
97	A:5%	B:62%	C:13%	D:20%
98	A:57%	B:23%	C:6%	D:14%

99	A:10%	B:22%	C:3%	D:65%
100	A:2%	B:94%	C:3%	D:1%
101	A:18%	B:3%	C:2%	D:77%
102	A:2%	B:7%	C:0%	D:91%
103	A:3%	B:76%	C:12%	D:9%
104	A:2%	B:7%	C:81%	D:10%
105	A:62%	B:16%	C:17%	D:9%
106	A:2%	B:94%	C:3%	D:1%
107	A:57%	B:23%	C:6%	D:14%
108	A:5%	B:0%	C:82%	D:13%
109	A:12%	B:65%	C:13%	D:10%
110	A:4%	B:11%	C:72%	D:13%
111	A:12%	B:67%	C:7%	D:14%
112	A:7%	B:2%	C:8%	D:83%
113	A:8%	B:2%	C:79%	D:11%
114	A:5%	B:62%	C:13%	D:20%
115	A:3%	B:76%	C:12%	D:9%
116	A:6%	B:83%	C:4%	D:2%
117	A:2%	B:7%	C:81%	D:10%
118	A:2%	B:94%	C:3%	D:1%
119	A:2%	B:7%	C:0%	D:91%
120	A:2%	B:94%	C:3%	D:1%
121	A:2%	B:5%	C:92%	D:1%
122	A:9%	B:13%	C:9%	D:69%
123	A:7%	B:4%	C:89%	D:0%
124	A:12%	B:67%	C:7%	D:14%
125	A:67%	B:22%	C:5%	D:6%
126	A:62%	B:16%	C:13%	D:9%
127	A:82%	B:4%	C:2%	D:7%
128	A:2%	B:94%	C:3%	D:1%
129	A:2%	B:5%	C:92%	D:1%
130	A:7%	B:2%	C:8%	D:83%
131	A:2%	B:94%	C:3%	D:1%
132	A:26%	B:1%	C:68%	D:5%

page 480

£8,000

1	A:15%	B:65%	C:6%	D:14%
2	A:11%	B:81%	C:2%	D:6%
3	A:17%	B:77%	C:6%	D:4%
4	A:16%	B:81%	C:1%	D:2%
5	A:15%	B:11%	C:8%	D:66%
6	A:2%	B:94%	C:3%	D:1%
7	A:13%	B:11%	C:67%	D:9%
8	A:12%	B:65%	C:13%	D:10%
9	A:7%	B:4%	C:89%	D:0%
10	A:67%	B:22%	C:5%	D:6%
11	A:3%	B:76%	C:12%	D:9%
12	A:7%	B:4%	C:89%	D:0%
13	A:22%	B:63%	C:14%	D:1%
14	A:6%	B:83%	C:4%	D:7%
15	A:62%	B:5%	C:25%	D:8%
16	A:2%	B:7%	C:3%	D:88%
17	A:87%	B:4%	C:2%	D:7%
18	A:5%	B:11%	C:66%	D:18%
19	A:2%	B:7%	C:3%	D:88%
20	A:3%	B:76%	C:12%	D:9%
21	A:6%	B:83%	C:4%	D:7%
22	A:31%	B:49%	C:7%	D:13%
23	A:12%	B:65%	C:13%	D:10%
24	A:8%	B:11%	C:6%	D:75%
25	A:95%	B:2%	C:1%	D:2%
26	A:72%	B:21%	C:3%	D:4%
27	A:14%	B:1%	C:16%	D:69%
28	A:2%	B:7%	C:0%	D:91%
29	A:2%	B:7%	C:0%	D:91%
30	A:2%	B:94%	C:3%	D:1%
31	A:5%	B:62%	C:13%	D:20%
32	A:13%	B:77%	C:6%	D:4%
33	A:2%	B:5%	C:92%	D:1%
34	A:31%	B:49%	C:7%	D:13%
35	A:13%	B:77%	C:6%	D:4%
36	A:8%	B:7%	C:22%	D:63%
37	A:6%	B:83%	C:4%	D:7%
38	A:2%	B:7%	C:0%	D:91%
39	A:2%	B:94%	C:3%	D:1%
40	A:87%	B:4%	C:2%	D:7%
41	A:5%	B:62%	C:13%	D:20%
42	A:7%	B:76%	C:6%	D:11%
43	A:47%	B:3%	C:24%	D:26%
44	A:82%	B:3%	C:14%	D:1%

ASK THE AUDIENCE

45	A:2%	B:7%	C:0%	D:91%
46	A:78%	B:4%	C:2%	D:16%
47	A:95%	B:2%	C:1%	D:2%
48	A:19%	B:65%	C:6%	D:14%
49	A:12%	B:67%	C:9%	D:12%
50	A:72%	B:21%	C:3%	D:4%
51	A:56%	B:3%	C:41%	D:0%
52	A:22%	B:63%	C:14%	D:1%
53	A:60%	B:5%	C:12%	D:23%
54	A:87%	B:4%	C:2%	D:7%
55	A:2%	B:7%	C:3%	D:88%
56	A:15%	B:65%	C:6%	D:14%
57	A:67%	B:22%	C:5%	D:6%
58	A:1%	B:44%	C:55%	D:0%
59	A:82%	B:3%	C:14%	D:1%
60	A:2%	B:5%	C:92%	D:1%
61	A:22%	B:63%	C:14%	D:1%
62	A:2%	B:7%	C:0%	D:91%
63	A:2%	B:94%	C:3%	D:1%
64	A:87%	B:4%	C:2%	D:7%
65	A:95%	B:2%	C:1%	D:2%
66	A:4%	B:39%	C:49%	D:8%
67	A:12%	B:67%	C:7%	D:14%
68	A:4%	B:71%	C:12%	D:13%
69	A:4%	B:71%	C:12%	D:13%
70	A:6%	B:3%	C:81%	D:10%
71	A:40%	B:39%	C:49%	D:8%
72	A:8%	D:11%	C:6%	D:75%
73	A:6%	D:4%	C:14%	D:76%
74	A:87%	D:4%	C:2%	D:7%
75	A:2%	D:94%	C:3%	D:1%
76	A:2%	D:5%	C:92%	D:1%
77	A:12%	D:67%	C:7%	D:14%
78	A:2%	D:7%	C:81%	D:10%
79	A:31%	D:49%	C:7%	D:13%
80	A:14%	D:1%	C:83%	D:2%
81	A:6%	D:83%	C:4%	D:7%
82	A:47%	B:3%	C:24%	D:26%
83	A:13%	B:11%	C:67%	D:9%
84	A:57%	B:23%	C:6%	D:14%
85	A:5%	B:11%	C:66%	D:18%
86	A:2%	B:94%	C:3%	D:1%
87	A:81%	B:2%	C:5%	D:12%
88	A:7%	B:76%	C:6%	D:11%
89	A:17%	B:67%	C:7%	D:14%
90	A:82%	B:3%	C:14%	D:1%
91	A:3%	B:76%	C:12%	D:9%
92	A:2%	B:7%	C:3%	D:88%
93	A:15%	B:11%	C:8%	D:66%
94	A:18%	B:3%	C:2%	D:77%
95	A:15%	B:11%	C:8%	D:66%
96	A:2%	B:7%	C:0%	D:91%
97	A:2%	B:7%	C:81%	D:10%
98	A:8%	B:11%	C:6%	D:75%
99	A:2%	B:7%	C:0%	D:91%
100	A:1%	B:12%	C:4%	D:83%
101	A:18%	B:3%	C:7%	D:77%
102	A:15%	B:11%	C:8%	D:66%
103	A:9%	B:11%	C:59%	D:21%
104	A:22%	B:63%	C:14%	D:1%
105	A:2%	B:5%	C:92%	D:1%
106	A:4%	B:39%	C:49%	D:8%
107	A:9%	B:11%	C:59%	D:21%
108	A:95%	B:2%	C:1%	D:2%
109	A:14%	B:1%	C:83%	D:2%
110	A:13%	B:11%	C:67%	D:9%
111	A:12%	B:65%	C:13%	D:10%
112	A:6%	B:83%	C:4%	D:7%
113	A:9%	B:11%	C:59%	D:21%
114	A:12%	B:65%	C:13%	D:1%
115	A:2%	B:7%	C:0%	D:91%
116	A:81%	B:2%	C:5%	D:12%
117	A:2%	B:94%	C:3%	D:1%
118	A:95%	B:2%	C:1%	D:2%
119	A:14%	B:1%	C:83%	D:12%
120	A:2%	B:5%	C:92%	D:1%
121	A:2%	B:5%	C:92%	D:1%
122	A:95%	B:2%	C:1%	D:2%
123	A:2%	B:5%	C:92%	D:1%
124	A:6%	B:83%	C:4%	D:7%

ASK THE AUDIENCE

£16,000

1	A:62%	B:5%	C:25%	D:8%
2	A:57%	B:23%	C:6%	D:14%
3	A:74%	B:5%	C:2%	D:14%
4	A:9%	B:11%	C:59%	D:21%
5	A:20%	B:5%	C:92%	D:1%
6	A:6%	B:2%	C:11%	D:81%
7	A:67%	B:22%	C:5%	D:6%
8	A:12%	B:65%	C:13%	D:10%
9	A:9%	B:11%	C:59%	D:21%
10	A:67%	B:22%	C:5%	D:6%
11	A:26%	B:1%	C:68%	D:5%
12	A:2%	B:94%	C:3%	D:1%
13	A:6%	B:4%	C:14%	D:76%
14	A:9%	B:11%	C:59%	D:21%
15	A:5%	B:62%	C:13%	D:20%
16	A:18%	B:3%	C:2%	D:77%
17	A:15%	B:65%	C:6%	D:14%
18	A:4%	B:39%	C:49%	D:8%
19	A:2%	B:94%	C:3%	D:1%
20	A:2%	B:7%	C:0%	D:91%
21	A:95%	B:2%	C:1%	D:2%
22	A:2%	B:94%	C:3%	D:1%
23	A:2%	B:5%	C:92%	D:1%
24	A:7%	B:4%	C:89%	D:0%
25	A:8%	B:2%	C:79%	D:11%
26	A:2%	B:94%	C:3%	D:1%
27	A:95%	B:2%	C:1%	D:2%
28	A:4%	B:11%	C:72%	D:13%
29	A:2%	B:94%	C:3%	D:1%
30	A:95%	B:2%	C:1%	D:2%
31	A:2%	B:7%	C:0%	D:91%
32	A:13%	B:77%	C:6%	D:4%
33	A:2%	B:5%	C:92%	D:1%
34	A:2%	B:94%	C:3%	D:1%
35	A:95%	B:2%	C:1%	D:2%
36	A:67%	B:22%	C:5%	D:6%
37	A:72%	B:21%	C:3%	D:4%
38	A:4%	B:39%	C:49%	D:8%
39	A:7%	B:4%	C:89%	D:0%
40	A:9%	B:11%	C:59%	D:21%
41	A:13%	B:11%	C:67%	D:9%
42	A:6%	B:3%	C:81%	D:10%
43	A:95%	B:2%	C:1%	D:2%
44	A:2%	B:94%	C:3%	D:1%
45	A:13%	B:11%	C:67%	D:9%
46	A:3%	B:76%	C:12%	D:9%
47	A:16%	B:2%	C:9%	D:73%
48	A:9%	B:11%	C:59%	D:21%
49	A:9%	B:11%	C:59%	D:21%
50	A:78%	B:4%	C:2%	D:16%
51	A:87%	B:4%	C:2%	D:7%
52	A:81%	B:2%	C:5%	D:12%
53	A:5%	B:62%	C:13%	D:20%
54	A:2%	B:7%	C:0%	D:91%
55	A:82%	B:3%	C:14%	D:1%
56	A:95%	B:2%	C:1%	D:2%
57	A:3%	B:76%	C:12%	D:9%
58	A:2%	B:7%	C:81%	D:10%
59	A:12%	B:67%	C:7%	D:14%
60	A:81%	B:2%	C:5%	D:12%
61	A:2%	B:7%	C:3%	D:88%
62	A:4%	B:7%	C:16%	D:73%
63	A:95%	B:2%	C:1%	D:2%
64	A:13%	B:11%	C:67%	D:9%
65	A:81%	B:2%	C:5%	D:12%
66	A:5%	B:11%	C:66%	D:18%
67	A:62%	B:5%	C:25%	D:8%
68	A:4%	B:39%	C:49%	D:8%
69	A:9%	B:11%	C:59%	D:21%
70	A:22%	B:63%	C:14%	D:1%
71	A:61%	B:6%	C:8%	D:25%
72	A:4%	D:11%	C:72%	D:13%
73	A:5%	D:0%	C:82%	D:13%
74	A:9%	D:11%	C:59%	D:21%
75	A:8%	D:7%	C:22%	D:63%
76	A:61%	D:6%	C:8%	D:25%
77	A:8%	D:7%	C:22%	D:63%
78	A:10%	D:22%	C:3%	D:65%
79	A:16%	D:81%	C:1%	D:2%
80	A:26%	D:67%	C:3%	D:4%
81	A:7%	D:2%	C:8%	D:83%
82	A:2%	B:7%	C:81%	D:10%
83	A:4%	B:7%	C:87%	D:2%
84	A:72%	B:21%	C:3%	D:4%

ASK THE AUDIENCE

85	A:2%	B:94%	C:3%	D:1%	101	A:47%	B:3%	C:24%	D:26%
86	A:6%	B:83%	C:4%	D:2%	102	A:10%	B:22%	C:3%	D:65%
87	A:8%	B:7%	C:22%	D:63%	103	A:22%	B:63%	C:14%	D:1%
88	A:4%	B:39%	C:49%	D:8%	104	A:22%	B:63%	C:14%	D:1%
89	A:15%	B:65%	C:6%	D:14%	105	A:52%	B:0%	C:22%	D:21%
90	A:18%	B:3%	C:2%	D:77%	106	A:3%	B:76%	C:12%	D:9%
91	A:81%	B:2%	C:5%	D:12%	107	A:9%	B:11%	C:59%	D:21%
92	A:5%	B:62%	C:13%	D:20%	108	A:80%	B:4%	C:3%	D:13%
93	A:9%	B:11%	C:59%	D:21%	109	A:62%	B:5%	C:25%	D:8%
94	A:10%	B:22%	C:3%	D:65%	110	A:47%	B:3%	C:24%	D:26%
95	A:4%	B:39%	C:49%	D:8%	111	A:5%	B:65%	C:9%	D:21%
96	A:26%	B:10%	C:68%	D:5%	112	A:16%	B:81%	C:1%	D:2%
97	A:56%	B:3%	C:41%	D:0%	113	A:5%	B:62%	C:13%	D:20%
98	A:95%	B:2%	C:1%	D:2%	114	A:5%	B:11%	C:66%	D:18%
99	A:3%	B:80%	C:17%	D:0%	115	A:12%	B:67%	C:9%	D:12%
100	A:2%	B:94%	C:3%	D:1%	116	A:2%	B:94%	C:3%	D:1%

£32,000

1	A:3%	B:9%	C:0%	D:88%	24	A:91%	B:3%	C:0%	D:6%
2	A:3%	B:88%	C:3%	D:6%	25	A:0%	B:84%	C:3%	D:13%
3	A:0%	B:6%	C:0%	D:94%	26	A:9%	B:3%	C:0%	D:88%
4	A:75%	B:0%	C:19%	D:6%	27	A:28%	B:53%	C:16%	D:3%
5	A:6%	B:3%	C:91%	D:0%	28	A:3%	B:0%	C:0%	D:97%
6	A:3%	B:88%	C:3%	D:6%	29	A:0%	B:3%	C:97%	D:0%
7	A:6%	B:6%	C:88%	D:0%	30	A:0%	B:9%	C:75%	D:16%
8	A:94%	B:6%	C:0%	D:0%	31	A:82%	B:3%	C:6%	D:9%
9	A:28%	B:13%	C:53%	D:6%	32	A:0%	B:3%	C:97%	D:0%
10	A:22%	B:6%	C:69%	D:3%	33	A:0%	B:3%	C:0%	D:97%
11	A:0%	B:25%	C:50%	D:25%	34	A:0%	B:34%	C:0%	D:66%
12	A:0%	B:0%	C:0%	D:100%	35	A:75%	B:13%	C:6%	D:6%
13	A:6%	B:85%	C:6%	D:3%	36	A:0%	B:3%	C:94%	D:3%
14	A:0%	B:0%	C:100%	D:0%	37	A:3%	B:6%	C:3%	D:88%
15	A:0%	B:6%	C:94%	D:0%	38	A:0%	B:3%	C:97%	D:0%
16	A:16%	B:84%	C:0%	D:0%	39	A:100%	B:0%	C:0%	D:0%
17	A:3%	B:0%	C:97%	D:0%	40	A:0%	B:0%	C:3%	D:97%
18	A:6%	B:0%	C:0%	D:94%	41	A:0%	B:100%	C:0%	D:0%
19	A:0%	B:3%	C:94%	D:3%	42	A:3%	B:97%	C:0%	D:0%
20	A:3%	B:0%	C:97%	D:0%	43	A:22%	B:53%	C:25%	D:0%
21	A:81%	B:13%	C:3%	D:3%	44	A:3%	B:0%	C:94%	D:3%
22	A:0%	B:12%	C:0%	D:88%	45	A:0%	B:100%	C:0%	D:0%
23	A:6%	B:0%	C:91%	D:3%	46	A:0%	B:0%	C:100%	D:0%

47	A:22%	B:50%	C:9%	D:19%
48	A:0%	B:3%	C:91%	D:6%
49	A:9%	B:0%	C:69%	D:22%
50	A:0%	B:3%	C:0%	D:97%
51	A:3%	B:0%	C:97%	D:0%
52	A:13%	B:16%	C:22%	D:49%
53	A:0%	B:97%	C:0%	D:3%
54	A:0%	B:100%	C:0%	D:0%
55	A:0%	B:6%	C:60%	D:34%
56	A:100%	B:0%	C:0%	D:0%
57	A:0%	B:3%	C:0%	D:97%
58	A:94%	B:6%	C:0%	D:0%
59	A:6%	B:3%	C:91%	D:0%
60	A:9%	B:91%	C:0%	D:0%
61	A:22%	B:72%	C:6%	D:0%
62	A:22%	B:9%	C:50%	D:19%
63	A:88%	B:3%	C:9%	D:0%
64	A:0%	B:100%	C:0%	D:0%
65	A:91%	B:0%	C:6%	D:3%
66	A:12%	B:0%	C:88%	D:0%
67	A:84%	B:3%	C:0%	D:13%
68	A:81%	B:0%	C:6%	D:13%
69	A:3%	B:3%	C:3%	D:91%
70	A:0%	B:0%	C:97%	D:3%
71	A:91%	B:0%	C:0%	D:9%
72	A:63%	B:9%	C:19%	D:9%
73	A:25%	B:66%	C:0%	D:9%
74	A:0%	B:3%	C:3%	D:94%
75	A:3%	B:0%	C:94%	D:3%
76	A:0%	B:3%	C:88%	D:9%
77	A:3%	B:97%	C:0%	D:0%
78	A:0%	B:100%	C:0%	D:0%
79	A:3%	B:3%	C:0%	D:94%
80	A:100%	B:0%	C:0%	D:0%
81	A:0%	B:0%	C:97%	D:3%
82	A:0%	B:19%	C:65%	D:16%
83	A:0%	B:0%	C:94%	D:6%
84	A:34%	B:28%	C:38%	D:0%
85	A:13%	B:34%	C:50%	D:3%
86	A:0%	B:97%	C:3%	D:0%
87	A:0%	B:0%	C:100%	D:0%
88	A:0%	B:3%	C:84%	D:13%
89	A:59%	B:25%	C:0%	D:16%
90	A:0%	B:9%	C:91%	D:0%
91	A:0%	B:6%	C:94%	D:0%
92	A:0%	B:19%	C:0%	D:81%
93	A:22%	B:62%	C:13%	D:3%
94	A:3%	B:6%	C:0%	D:91%
95	A:6%	B:3%	C:0%	D:91%
96	A:6%	B:41%	C:0%	D:53%
97	A:28%	B:66%	C:3%	D:3%
98	A:0%	B:97%	C:0%	D:3%
99	A:94%	B:0%	C:3%	D:3%
100	A:3%	B:81%	C:13%	D:3%
101	A:9%	B:82%	C:6%	D:3%
102	A:3%	B:50%	C:28%	D:19%
103	A:6%	B:0%	C:75%	D:19%
104	A:3%	B:28%	C:38%	D:31%
105	A:0%	B:41%	C:59%	D:0%
106	A:13%	B:9%	C:59%	D:19%
107	A:3%	B:34%	C:60%	D:3%
108	A:9%	B:91%	C:0%	D:0%

£64,000

1	A:89%	B:11%	C:0%	D:0%
2	A:8%	B:39%	C:3%	D:50%
3	A:3%	B:0%	C:91%	D:6%
4	A:75%	B:19%	C:3%	D:3%
5	A:8%	B:42%	C:36%	D:14%
6	A:88%	B:6%	C:0%	D:6%
7	A:28%	B:31%	C:19%	D:22%
8	A:3%	B:8%	C:50%	D:39%
9	A:17%	B:8%	C:50%	D:25%
10	A:6%	B:33%	C:39%	D:22%
11	A:3%	B:53%	C:38%	D:6%
12	A:0%	B:91%	C:3%	D:6%
13	A:83%	B:8%	C:6%	D:3%
14	A:8%	B:6%	C:8%	D:78%
15	A:64%	B:25%	C:3%	D:8%
16	A:14%	B:14%	C:72%	D:0%

ASK THE AUDIENCE

17	A:3%	B:11%	C:3%	D:83%
18	A:22%	B:45%	C:8%	D:25%
19	A:41%	B:3%	C:31%	D:25%
20	A:22%	B:0%	C:3%	D:75%
21	A:97%	B:3%	C:0%	D:0%
22	A:0%	B:0%	C:0%	D:100%
23	A:0%	B:44%	C:3%	D:53%
24	A:17%	B:8%	C:0%	D:75%
25	A:8%	B:65%	C:19%	D:8%
26	A:0%	B:0%	C:0%	D:100%
27	A:14%	B:6%	C:74%	D:6%
28	A:14%	B:25%	C:11%	D:50%
29	A:86%	B:8%	C:3%	D:3%
30	A:89%	B:0%	C:0%	D:11%
31	A:3%	B:94%	C:0%	D:3%
32	A:0%	B:94%	C:3%	D:3%
33	A:0%	B:0%	C:0%	D:100%
34	A:0%	B:97%	C:0%	D:3%
35	A:35%	B:31%	C:31%	D:3%
36	A:3%	B:19%	C:78%	D:0%
37	A:91%	B:6%	C:3%	D:0%
38	A:97%	B:3%	C:0%	D:0%
39	A:0%	B:3%	C:3%	D:94%
40	A:59%	B:14%	C:19%	D:8%
41	A:97%	B:0%	C:3%	D:0%
42	A:97%	B:3%	C:0%	D:0%
43	A:17%	B:14%	C:58%	D:11%
44	A:14%	B:83%	C:3%	D:0%
45	A:8%	B:14%	C:19%	D:59%
46	A:0%	B:89%	C:0%	D:11%
47	A:0%	B:19%	C:3%	D:78%
48	A:83%	B:3%	C:14%	D:0%
49	A:11%	B:0%	C:89%	D:0%
50	A:11%	B:6%	C:80%	D:3%
51	A:39%	B:0%	C:3%	D:58%
52	A:80%	B:14%	C:6%	D:0%
53	A:14%	B:0%	C:0%	D:86%
54	A:11%	B:31%	C:17%	D:41%
55	A:22%	B:31%	C:28%	D:19%
56	A:14%	B:0%	C:83%	D:3%
57	A:19%	B:31%	C:44%	D:6%
58	A:0%	B:14%	C:33%	D:53%
59	A:8%	B:3%	C:86%	D:3%
60	A:39%	B:31%	C:8%	D:22%
61	A:6%	B:11%	C:83%	D:0%
62	A:8%	B:89%	C:0%	D:3%
63	A:6%	B:77%	C:17%	D:0%
64	A:19%	B:64%	C:6%	D:11%
65	A:71%	B:6%	C:17%	D:6%
66	A:52%	B:17%	C:14%	D:17%
67	A:19%	B:73%	C:0%	D:8%
68	A:22%	B:11%	C:28%	D:39%
69	A:42%	B:8%	C:28%	D:22%
70	A:6%	B:0%	C:86%	D:8%
71	A:0%	B:14%	C:83%	D:3%
72	A:17%	B:11%	C:28%	D:44%
73	A:6%	B:17%	C:19%	D:58%
74	A:8%	B:47%	C:28%	D:17%
75	A:50%	B:8%	C:14%	D:28%
76	A:25%	B:61%	C:0%	D:14%
77	A:17%	B:19%	C:25%	D:39%
78	A:58%	B:6%	C:11%	D:25%
79	A:28%	B:36%	C:11%	D:25%
80	A:6%	B:14%	C:36%	D:44%
81	A:0%	B:66%	C:28%	D:6%
82	A:6%	B:17%	C:25%	D:52%
83	A:91%	B:3%	C:6%	D:0%
84	A:28%	B:58%	C:14%	D:0%
85	A:16%	B:39%	C:6%	D:39%
86	A:11%	B:36%	C:3%	D:50%
87	A:3%	B:72%	C:11%	D:14%
88	A:47%	B:33%	C:14%	D:6%
89	A:31%	D:32%	C:6%	D:31%
90	A:28%	B:55%	C:11%	D:6%
91	A:53%	B:0%	C:11%	D:36%
92	A:60%	B:3%	C:31%	D:6%
93	A:42%	B:44%	C:6%	D:8%
94	A:6%	B:42%	C:19%	D:33%
95	A:42%	B:16%	C:0%	D:42%
96	A:0%	B:94%	C:6%	D:0%
97	A:6%	B:14%	C:72%	D:8%
98	A:59%	B:19%	C:14%	D:8%
99	A:3%	B:3%	C:6%	D:88%
100	A:28%	B:31%	C:33%	D:8%

ASK THE AUDIENCE

£125,000

1	A:26%	B:26%	C:37%	D:11%	43	A:16%	B:5%	C:74%	D:5%
2	A:32%	B:5%	C:42%	D:21%	44	A:5%	B:0%	C:95%	D:0%
3	A:5%	B:63%	C:21%	D:11%	45	A:11%	B:21%	C:26%	D:42%
4	A:16%	B:79%	C:0%	D:5%	46	A:5%	B:11%	C:31%	D:53%
5	A:21%	B:0%	C:79%	D:0%	47	A:21%	B:58%	C:16%	D:5%
6	A:0%	B:89%	C:11%	D:0%	48	A:58%	B:21%	C:5%	D:16%
7	A:0%	B:32%	C:68%	D:0%	49	A:11%	B:26%	C:5%	D:58%
8	A:16%	B:42%	C:0%	D:42%	50	A:11%	B:52%	C:37%	D:0%
9	A:11%	B:74%	C:0%	D:15%	51	A:53%	B:16%	C:5%	D:26%
10	A:0%	B:95%	C:5%	D:0%	52	A:5%	B:31%	C:43%	D:21%
11	A:42%	B:48%	C:5%	D:5%	53	A:59%	B:31%	C:5%	D:5%
12	A:42%	B:47%	C:11%	D:0%	54	A:63%	B:5%	C:11%	D:21%
13	A:84%	B:0%	C:0%	D:16%	55	A:16%	B:53%	C:0%	D:31%
14	A:26%	B:11%	C:47%	D:16%	56	A:5%	B:0%	C:79%	D:16%
15	A:53%	B:26%	C:21%	D:0%	57	A:21%	B:48%	C:26%	D:5%
16	A:58%	B:16%	C:26%	D:0%	58	A:5%	B:16%	C:37%	D:42%
17	A:0%	B:74%	C:16%	D:10%	59	A:16%	B:37%	C:42%	D:5%
18	A:74%	B:5%	C:21%	D:0%	60	A:0%	B:0%	C:100%	D:0%
19	A:5%	B:37%	C:37%	D:21%	61	A:26%	B:0%	C:5%	D:69%
20	A:31%	B:38%	C:0%	D:31%	62	A:5%	B:5%	C:79%	D:11%
21	A:64%	B:0%	C:31%	D:5%	63	A:0%	B:90%	C:5%	D:5%
22	A:0%	B:89%	C:11%	D:0%	64	A:0%	B:53%	C:16%	D:31%
23	A:0%	B:37%	C:42%	D:21%	65	A:5%	B:5%	C:16%	D:74%
24	A:16%	B:5%	C:5%	D:74%	66	A:0%	B:11%	C:84%	D:5%
25	A:5%	B:5%	C:85%	D:5%	67	A:21%	B:52%	C:11%	D:16%
26	A:0%	B:0%	C:0%	D:100%	68	A:16%	B:5%	C:58%	D:21%
27	A:53%	B:47%	C:0%	D:0%	69	A:32%	B:21%	C:21%	D:26%
28	A:0%	B:21%	C:74%	D:5%	70	A:0%	B:11%	C:11%	D:78%
29	A:0%	B:0%	C:0%	D:100%	71	A:5%	B:48%	C:31%	D:16%
30	A:89%	B:0%	C:0%	D:11%	72	A:11%	B:0%	C:89%	D:0%
31	A:21%	B:0%	C:16%	D:63%	73	A:53%	B:21%	C:5%	D:21%
32	A:0%	B:95%	C:0%	D:5%	74	A:31%	B:5%	C:0%	D:64%
33	A:0%	B:11%	C:0%	D:89%	75	A:16%	B:5%	C:31%	D:48%
34	A:5%	B:53%	C:31%	D:11%	76	A:5%	B:43%	C:21%	D:31%
35	A:0%	B:100%	C:0%	D:0%	77	A:11%	B:37%	C:31%	D:21%
36	A:0%	B:89%	C:0%	D:11%	78	A:21%	B:16%	C:16%	D:47%
37	A:0%	B:0%	C:100%	D:0%	79	A:5%	B:69%	C:0%	D:26%
38	A:0%	B:100%	C:0%	D:0%	80	A:79%	B:5%	C:11%	D:5%
39	A:0%	B:0%	C:89%	D:11%	81	A:58%	B:0%	C:26%	D:16%
40	A:0%	B:0%	C:5%	D:95%	82	A:5%	B:0%	C:95%	D:0%
41	A:84%	B:0%	C:11%	D:5%	83	A:0%	B:0%	C:0%	D:100%
42	A:0%	B:0%	C:0%	D:100%	84	A:32%	B:26%	C:26%	D:16%

85	A:21%	B:57%	C:11%	D:11%	89	A:5%	B:47%	C:32%	D:16%
86	A:16%	B:42%	C:16%	D:26%	90	A:0%	B:95%	C:0%	D:5%
87	A:26%	B:53%	C:16%	D:5%	91	A:0%	B:11%	C:11%	D:78%
88	A:21%	B:21%	C:32%	D:26%	92	A:11%	B:21%	C:57%	D:11%

£250,000

1	A:4%	B:7%	C:89%	D:0%	36	A:86%	B:0%	C:14%	D:0%
2	A:0%	B:4%	C:96%	D:0%	37	A:46%	B:7%	C:43%	D:4%
3	A:25%	B:7%	C:50%	D:18%	38	A:0%	B:86%	C:14%	D:0%
4	A:18%	B:71%	C:11%	D:0%	39	A:4%	B:42%	C:25%	D:29%
5	A:89%	B:11%	C:0%	D:0%	40	A:96%	B:0%	C:4%	D:0%
6	A:0%	B:0%	C:100%	D:0%	41	A:0%	B:100%	C:0%	D:0%
7	A:7%	B:7%	C:11%	D:75%	42	A:42%	B:46%	C:12%	D:0%
8	A:0%	B:82%	C:11%	D:7%	43	A:43%	B:0%	C:0%	D:57%
9	A:0%	B:21%	C:4%	D:75%	44	A:89%	B:4%	C:7%	D:0%
10	A:21%	B:11%	C:50%	D:18%	45	A:14%	B:4%	C:7%	D:75%
11	A:25%	B:14%	C:43%	D:18%	46	A:4%	B:60%	C:11%	D:25%
12	A:25%	B:14%	C:18%	D:43%	47	A:4%	B:81%	C:11%	D:4%
13	A:29%	B:18%	C:24%	D:29%	48	A:4%	B:75%	C:0%	D:21%
14	A:7%	B:7%	C:82%	D:4%	49	A:92%	B:4%	C:4%	D:0%
15	A:89%	B:0%	C:7%	D:4%	50	A:43%	B:7%	C:4%	D:46%
16	A:29%	B:46%	C:14%	D:11%	51	A:32%	B:25%	C:29%	D:14%
17	A:79%	B:7%	C:7%	D:7%	52	A:18%	B:53%	C:0%	D:29%
18	A:25%	B:54%	C:21%	D:0%	53	A:0%	B:21%	C:21%	D:58%
19	A:0%	B:4%	C:28%	D:68%	54	A:14%	B:51%	C:21%	D:14%
20	A:18%	B:18%	C:53%	D:11%	55	A:53%	B:14%	C:4%	D:29%
21	A:0%	B:53%	C:36%	D:11%	56	A:0%	B:14%	C:86%	D:0%
22	A:0%	B:43%	C:39%	D:18%	57	A:28%	B:36%	C:18%	D:18%
23	A:85%	B:7%	C:4%	D:4%	58	A:39%	B:4%	C:18%	D:39%
24	A:14%	B:43%	C:39%	D:4%	59	A:54%	B:7%	C:7%	D:32%
25	A:0%	B:0%	C:100%	D:0%	60	A:75%	B:7%	C:14%	D:4%
26	A:72%	B:14%	C:0%	D:14%	61	A:18%	B:57%	C:11%	D:14%
27	A:7%	B:7%	C:75%	D:11%	62	A:61%	B:7%	C:0%	D:32%
28	A:4%	B:64%	C:4%	D:28%	63	A:7%	B:0%	C:82%	D:11%
29	A:0%	B:4%	C:4%	D:92%	64	A:4%	B:4%	C:92%	D:0%
30	A:86%	B:0%	C:14%	D:0%	65	A:25%	B:36%	C:39%	D:0%
31	A:54%	B:21%	C:25%	D:0%	66	A:11%	B:0%	C:89%	D:0%
32	A:85%	B:11%	C:4%	D:0%	67	A:58%	B:21%	C:14%	D:7%
33	A:74%	B:11%	C:4%	D:11%	68	A:32%	B:14%	C:18%	D:36%
34	A:14%	B:11%	C:4%	D:71%	69	A:0%	B:86%	C:7%	D:7%
35	A:29%	B:31%	C:29%	D:11%	70	A:68%	B:11%	C:14%	D:7%

71	A:11%	B:18%	C:50%	D:21%
72	A:0%	B:4%	C:92%	D:4%
73	A:21%	B:43%	C:4%	D:32%
74	A:18%	B:46%	C:4%	D:32%
75	A:11%	B:7%	C:4%	D:78%
76	A:0%	B:89%	C:7%	D:4%
77	A:78%	B:0%	C:11%	D:11%
78	A:11%	B:7%	C:61%	D:21%
79	A:18%	B:21%	C:7%	D:54%
80	A:14%	B:18%	C:39%	D:29%
81	A:7%	B:82%	C:7%	D:4%
82	A:0%	B:14%	C:21%	D:65%
83	A:11%	B:25%	C:57%	D:7%
84	A:0%	B:4%	C:96%	D:0%

£500,000

1	A:46%	B:20%	C:3%	D:31%
2	A:6%	B:14%	C:54%	D:26%
3	A:37%	B:3%	C:60%	D:0%
4	A:23%	B:29%	C:6%	D:42%
5	A:9%	B:43%	C:34%	D:14%
6	A:0%	B:88%	C:6%	D:6%
7	A:3%	B:88%	C:6%	D:3%
8	A:9%	B:3%	C:20%	D:68%
9	A:37%	B:9%	C:31%	D:23%
10	A:0%	B:29%	C:11%	D:60%
11	A:37%	B:40%	C:6%	D:17%
12	A:23%	B:17%	C:43%	D:17%
13	A:60%	B:9%	C:14%	D:17%
14	A:11%	B:18%	C:60%	D:11%
15	A:28%	B:37%	C:9%	D:26%
16	A:14%	B:23%	C:60%	D:3%
17	A:3%	B:9%	C:62%	D:26%
18	A:49%	B:31%	C:6%	D:14%
19	A:14%	B:11%	C:64%	D:11%
20	A:37%	B:23%	C:29%	D:11%
21	A:20%	B:20%	C:14%	D:46%
22	A:17%	B:29%	C:11%	D:43%
23	A:3%	B:75%	C:11%	D:11%
24	A:11%	B:9%	C:49%	D:31%
25	A:37%	B:11%	C:23%	D:29%
26	A:20%	B:17%	C:3%	D:60%
27	A:9%	B:54%	C:23%	D:14%
28	A:72%	B:14%	C:11%	D:3%
29	A:34%	B:29%	C:11%	D:26%
30	A:46%	B:26%	C:17%	D:11%
31	A:31%	B:20%	C:26%	D:23%
32	A:26%	B:37%	C:11%	D:26%
33	A:26%	B:0%	C:63%	D:11%
34	A:70%	B:29%	C:1%	D:0%
35	A:57%	B:6%	C:0%	D:37%
36	A:9%	B:60%	C:14%	D:17%
37	A:9%	B:51%	C:17%	D:23%
38	A:29%	B:17%	C:9%	D:45%
39	A:29%	B:26%	C:26%	D:19%
40	A:3%	B:3%	C:74%	D:20%
41	A:11%	B:3%	C:17%	D:69%
42	A:40%	B:31%	C:20%	D:9%
43	A:17%	B:3%	C:17%	D:63%
44	A:9%	B:65%	C:6%	D:20%
45	A:3%	B:54%	C:3%	D:40%
46	A:6%	B:17%	C:6%	D:71%
47	A:46%	B:31%	C:23%	D:0%
48	A:0%	B:83%	C:3%	D:14%
49	A:62%	B:26%	C:3%	D:9%
50	A:3%	B:88%	C:6%	D:3%
51	A:9%	B:17%	C:74%	D:0%
52	A:43%	B:17%	C:29%	D:11%
53	A:9%	B:65%	C:9%	D:17%
54	A:31%	B:41%	C:11%	D:17%
55	A:57%	B:23%	C:9%	D:11%
56	A:26%	B:68%	C:3%	D:3%
57	A:3%	B:20%	C:54%	D:23%
58	A:11%	B:40%	C:29%	D:20%
59	A:15%	B:11%	C:29%	D:45%
60	A:6%	B:14%	C:31%	D:49%
61	A:9%	B:51%	C:6%	D:34%
62	A:26%	B:31%	C:23%	D:20%
63	A:23%	B:26%	C:45%	D:6%
64	A:17%	B:54%	C:23%	D:6%
65	A:24%	B:31%	C:31%	D:14%
66	A:17%	B:46%	C:6%	D:31%

67	A:14%	B:37%	C:3%	D:46%	72	A:11%	B:17%	C:49%	D:23%
68	A:29%	B:11%	C:37%	D:23%	73	A:40%	B:34%	C:23%	D:3%
69	A:20%	B:46%	C:28%	D:6%	74	A:20%	B:6%	C:9%	D:65%
70	A:9%	B:0%	C:71%	D:20%	75	A:6%	B:20%	C:51%	D:23%
71	A:49%	B:14%	C:23%	D:14%	76	A:94%	B:0%	C:0%	D:6%

£1 MILLION

1	A:41%	B:41%	C:11%	D:7%	35	A:4%	B:0%	C:18%	D:78%
2	A:18%	B:4%	C:52%	D:26%	36	A:7%	B:49%	C:11%	D:33%
3	A:26%	B:15%	C:48%	D:11%	37	A:11%	B:33%	C:19%	D:37%
4	A:22%	B:56%	C:18%	D:4%	38	A:33%	B:30%	C:7%	D:30%
5	A:15%	B:70%	C:4%	D:11%	39	A:7%	B:74%	C:4%	D:15%
6	A:30%	B:26%	C:37%	D:7%	40	A:11%	B:33%	C:37%	D:19%
7	A:22%	B:44%	C:30%	D:4%	41	A:36%	B:19%	C:30%	D:15%
8	A:19%	B:19%	C:56%	D:6%	42	A:63%	B:26%	C:4%	D:7%
9	A:11%	B:30%	C:7%	D:52%	43	A:26%	B:37%	C:37%	D:0%
10	A:0%	B:74%	C:22%	D:4%	44	A:4%	B:4%	C:70%	D:22%
11	A:7%	B:93%	C:0%	D:0%	45	A:37%	B:15%	C:22%	D:26%
12	A:25%	B:15%	C:30%	D:30%	46	A:7%	B:4%	C:74%	D:15%
13	A:11%	B:11%	C:30%	D:48%	47	A:44%	B:19%	C:33%	D:4%
14	A:22%	B:49%	C:7%	D:22%	48	A:4%	B:14%	C:26%	D:56%
15	A:41%	B:7%	C:48%	D:4%	49	A:15%	B:44%	C:4%	D:37%
16	A:22%	B:60%	C:7%	D:11%	50	A:33%	B:0%	C:4%	D:63%
17	A:33%	B:52%	C:4%	D:11%	51	A:4%	B:18%	C:4%	D:74%
18	A:15%	B:22%	C:48%	D:15%	52	A:30%	B:55%	C:11%	D:4%
19	A:4%	B:22%	C:15%	D:59%	53	A:26%	B:7%	C:19%	D:48%
20	A:7%	B:52%	C:19%	D:22%	54	A:37%	B:30%	C:33%	D:0%
21	A:4%	B:33%	C:59%	D:4%	55	A:45%	B:11%	C:33%	D:11%
22	A:22%	B:60%	C:7%	D:11%	56	A:22%	B:15%	C:26%	D:37%
23	A:59%	B:33%	C:4%	D:4%	57	A:37%	B:15%	C:33%	D:15%
24	A:11%	B:30%	C:52%	D:7%	58	A:33%	B:19%	C:33%	D:15%
25	A:52%	B:0%	C:7%	D:41%	59	A:22%	B:56%	C:7%	D:15%
26	A:22%	B:70%	C:0%	D:8%	60	A:15%	B:33%	C:37%	D:15%
27	A:30%	B:19%	C:36%	D:15%	61	A:7%	B:26%	C:19%	D:48%
28	A:15%	B:19%	C:11%	D:55%	62	A:15%	B:33%	C:15%	D:37%
29	A:22%	B:19%	C:44%	D:15%	63	A:22%	B:34%	C:22%	D:22%
30	A:30%	B:22%	C:15%	D:33%	64	A:4%	B:22%	C:67%	D:7%
31	A:33%	B:45%	C:0%	D:22%	65	A:4%	B:22%	C:67%	D:7%
32	A:48%	B:26%	C:26%	D:0%	66	A:29%	B:19%	C:19%	D:33%
33	A:19%	B:40%	C:19%	D:22%	67	A:22%	B:19%	C:26%	D:33%
34	A:30%	B:4%	C:66%	D:0%	68	A:22%	B:55%	C:19%	D:4%

Answers

Fastest Finger First

1	BDAC	2	CABD	3	ADBC	4	BDCA	5	BDCA
6	DCBA	7	DBAC	8	ADCB	9	BDAC	10	ACDB
11	BACD	12	DCBA	13	DBCA	14	BADC	15	BCDA
16	DABC	17	DBCA	18	BCDA	19	CBAD	20	BCAD
21	BDAC	22	ADCB	23	DBCA	24	ADCB	25	BCDA
26	BDCA	27	DCBA	28	ABDC	29	DBCA	30	BCAD
31	DABC	32	DBAC	33	BACD	34	CBDA	35	BDCA
36	CBAD	37	CDBA	38	DBAC	39	CBAD	40	ABDC
41	BACD	42	BACD	43	DCAB	44	DCAB	45	ADBC
46	DCBA	47	BCDA	48	ADBC	49	ABDC	50	ABCD
51	ADCB	52	DACB	53	CBAD	54	DBAC	55	BDAC
56	ADBC	57	BDCA	58	CDAB	59	DABC	60	BCDA
61	CBDA	62	DACB	63	BDAC	64	BDCA	65	DBCA
66	ACBD	67	ADCB	68	BCAD	69	ACBD	70	ACBD
71	DCBA	72	BDCA	73	ADCB	74	CADB	75	CBAD
76	DBCA	77	DBCA	78	ACDB	79	ADBC	80	DBAC
81	DACB	82	CADB	83	ACDB	84	DCBA	85	BDCA
86	CBAD	87	CABD	88	ABDC	89	CBDA	90	DABC
91	CDAB	92	BCDA	93	CADB	94	BADC	95	DABC
96	DCBA	97	BCDA	98	CDBA	99	DABC	100	CADB
101	ADBC	102	BDAC	103	DBCA	104	CADB	105	ADBC
106	DABC	107	CDAB	108	BACD	109	ABDC	110	DCBA
111	ABDC	112	DCAB	113	ABDC	114	ABCD	115	BDCA
116	CBDA	117	CADB	118	ABDC	119	BADC	120	DABC
121	BDAC	122	DCBA	123	BDAC	124	CDBA	125	BDCA
126	ABCD	127	DCBA	128	DCAB	129	BACD	130	ABDC
131	BDAC	132	DCBA	133	DBCA	134	CDAB	135	DACB
136	BACD	137	ACBD	138	ACBD	139	ADBC	140	BCDA
141	DBCA	142	ADCB	143	DCAB	144	BACD	145	ABCD
146	ADBC	147	DABC	148	DABC	149	DABC	150	BCAD

If you answered correctly, well done! Turn to page 41 to play for £100!

ANSWERS

£100

1 A	2 A	3 C	4 B	5 B	6 B	7 C
8 C	9 B	10 C	11 B	12 D	13 B	14 B
15 C	16 B	17 A	18 C	19 C	20 D	21 C
22 B	23 C	24 B	25 B	26 D	27 B	28 C
29 A	30 C	31 B	32 B	33 A	34 B	35 C
36 C	37 A	38 D	39 C	40 B	41 B	42 C
43 D	44 C	45 D	46 A	47 C	48 C	49 B
50 D	51 C	52 A	53 D	54 C	55 D	56 D
57 D	58 C	59 A	60 A	61 D	62 C	63 C
64 A	65 C	66 A	67 B	68 C	69 A	70 A
71 D	72 A	73 B	74 C	75 B	76 A	77 D
78 D	79 D	80 D	81 B	82 A	83 B	84 C
85 B	86 D	87 D	88 C	89 C	90 A	91 C
92 D	93 C	94 B	95 C	96 C	97 A	98 D
99 B	100 C	101 A	102 D	103 C	104 B	105 A
106 B	107 A	108 D	109 D	110 C	111 B	112 B
113 A	114 C	115 B	116 C	117 A	118 D	119 C
120 A	121 B	122 C	123 A	124 A	125 B	126 C
127 A	128 C	129 C	130 B	131 B	132 B	133 C
134 D	135 C	136 B	137 A	138 C	139 A	140 B
141 D	142 D	143 D	144 A	145 D	146 A	147 A
148 B	149 D	150 D	151 A	152 B	153 A	154 A
155 A	156 D	157 C	158 A	159 C	160 A	161 A
162 B	163 A	164 B	165 B	166 C	167 C	168 A
169 A	170 B	171 A	172 A	173 B	174 A	175 B
176 A	177 B	178 B	179 C	180 B		

If you have won £100, well done! Turn to page 79 to play for £200!

£200

1 A	2 C	3 B	4 C	5 A	6 B	7 B
8 A	9 D	10 D	11 D	12 C	13 B	14 B
15 D	16 A	17 C	18 A	19 C	20 C	21 C
22 A	23 C	24 C	25 C	26 D	27 B	28 A
29 C	30 C	31 D	32 B	33 A	34 C	35 C
36 C	37 A	38 A	39 D	40 A	41 D	42 B
43 A	44 D	45 B	46 A	47 A	48 C	49 B
50 D	51 B	52 D	53 D	54 D	55 C	56 D
57 C	58 D	59 B	60 C	61 A	62 D	63 D
64 C	65 C	66 D	67 A	68 C	69 D	70 A
71 D	72 B	73 D	74 A	75 D	76 D	77 D
78 B	79 A	80 D	81 B	82 A	83 C	84 C

ANSWERS

85 B	86 A	87 C	88 A	89 B	90 C	91 C
92 B	93 C	94 B	95 C	96 C	97 A	98 B
99 B	100 A	101 C	102 C	103 D	104 D	105 C
106 A	107 C	108 B	109 D	110 D	111 C	112 A
113 C	114 B	115 A	116 D	117 B	118 B	119 A
120 B	121 D	122 A	123 C	124 D	125 C	126 C
127 B	128 D	129 D	130 D	131 A	132 B	133 D
134 B	135 C	136 B	137 A	138 C	139 D	140 C
141 B	142 C	143 A	144 D	145 B	146 A	147 A
148 D	149 D	150 B	151 B	152 B	153 A	154 B
155 B	156 B	157 C	158 C	159 D	160 B	161 B
162 A	163 B	164 D	165 D	166 A	167 C	168 C
169 A	170 B	171 C	172 A			

If you have won £200, well done! Turn to page 115 to play for £300!

£300

1 C	2 A	3 A	4 A	5 A	6 B	7 D
8 B	9 A	10 D	11 C	12 B	13 B	14 D
15 B	16 B	17 C	18 B	19 D	20 A	21 D
22 C	23 D	24 D	25 A	26 B	27 C	28 D
29 D	30 D	31 A	32 D	33 D	34 D	35 D
36 B	37 C	38 B	39 D	40 A	41 C	42 B
43 B	44 C	45 C	46 D	47 C	48 A	49 B
50 A	51 C	52 C	53 A	54 D	55 B	56 B
57 B	58 D	59 C	60 B	61 D	62 C	63 A
64 D	65 C	66 B	67 A	68 D	69 A	70 A
71 D	72 D	73 D	74 B	75 D	76 B	77 C
78 B	79 C	80 C	81 B	82 B	83 D	84 C
85 D	86 B	87 C	88 A	89 A	90 D	91 A
92 A	93 C	94 A	95 D	96 D	97 A	98 C
99 D	100 B	101 A	102 D	103 C	104 C	105 A
106 C	107 A	108 A	109 A	110 A	111 A	112 A
113 A	114 D	115 C	116 A	117 D	118 B	119 C
120 D	121 A	122 D	123 B	124 C	125 C	126 B
127 B	128 A	129 D	130 B	131 A	132 C	133 D
134 D	135 A	136 C	137 B	138 D	139 C	140 B
141 D	142 B	143 A	144 A	145 A	146 B	147 D
148 D	149 A	150 B	151 C	152 D	153 B	154 D
155 C	156 B	157 C	158 C	159 B	160 A	161 C
162 A	163 B	164 B				

If you have won £300, well done! Turn to page 149 to play for £500!

ANSWERS

£500

1 A	2 B	3 A	4 D	5 B	6 A	7 D
8 C	9 A	10 B	11 A	12 B	13 D	14 C
15 B	16 C	17 A	18 B	19 A	20 C	21 B
22 D	23 C	24 C	25 D	26 C	27 C	28 B
29 A	30 A	31 B	32 A	33 D	34 B	35 D
36 A	37 B	38 D	39 B	40 B	41 D	42 B
43 A	44 A	45 D	46 C	47 C	48 D	49 C
50 A	51 C	52 A	53 B	54 D	55 A	56 B
57 B	58 D	59 B	60 B	61 B	62 B	63 A
64 B	65 C	66 D	67 C	68 C	69 D	70 A
71 D	72 C	73 C	74 D	75 B	76 B	77 B
78 C	79 A	80 A	81 A	82 D	83 B	84 D
85 A	86 C	87 A	88 C	89 D	90 D	91 B
92 D	93 B	94 C	95 A	96 B	97 A	98 C
99 A	100 D	101 C	102 B	103 A	104 C	105 B
106 B	107 D	108 C	109 B	110 D	111 B	112 C
113 B	114 C	115 A	116 D	117 C	118 D	119 D
120 B	121 C	122 D	123 B	124 D	125 D	126 A
127 D	128 B	129 A	130 C	131 D	132 D	133 B
134 C	135 B	136 B	137 D	138 C	139 C	140 C
141 A	142 D	143 A	144 A	145 C	146 C	147 B
148 B	149 B	150 A	151 B	152 D	153 D	154 B
155 D	156 A					

If you have won £500, well done! Turn to page 183 to play for £1,000!

£1,000

1 A	2 A	3 C	4 A	5 A	6 C	7 C
8 C	9 B	10 D	11 D	12 B	13 A	14 D
15 B	16 C	17 B	18 A	19 D	20 A	21 A
22 A	23 D	24 D	25 D	26 A	27 B	28 D
29 C	30 B	31 C	32 D	33 C	34 A	35 A
36 A	37 C	38 C	39 B	40 A	41 B	42 B
43 D	44 A	45 B	46 C	47 B	48 C	49 B
50 D	51 C	52 C	53 B	54 C	55 A	56 A
57 B	58 C	59 B	60 A	61 B	62 B	63 C
64 A	65 C	66 D	67 D	68 B	69 C	70 D
71 C	72 A	73 D	74 D	75 B	76 B	77 B
78 D	79 D	80 C	81 C	82 D	83 B	84 B
85 B	86 D	87 B	88 D	89 C	90 B	91 D
92 B	93 A	94 B	95 C	96 B	97 C	98 B
99 D	100 B	101 D	102 A	103 C	104 C	105 B

106 A	107 D	108 C	109 B	110 A	111 D	112 D
113 D	114 D	115 C	116 C	117 A	118 A	119 C
120 B	121 D	122 C	123 A	124 B	125 B	126 C
127 C	128 C	129 B	130 B	131 A	132 A	133 B
134 B	135 B	136 C	137 D	138 D	139 C	140 B
141 B	142 B	143 B	144 C	145 C	146 C	147 D
148 B						

If you have won £1,000, well done! Turn to page 215 to play for £2,000!

£2,000

1 A	2 C	3 D	4 D	5 A	6 C	7 A
8 D	9 B	10 C	11 B	12 B	13 A	14 B
15 C	16 C	17 A	18 C	19 A	20 A	21 B
22 B	23 C	24 D	25 A	26 C	27 A	28 B
29 C	30 A	31 A	32 B	33 D	34 B	35 A
36 D	37 D	38 D	39 B	40 A	41 A	42 A
43 B	44 B	45 A	46 D	47 C	48 B	49 D
50 B	51 B	52 A	53 A	54 B	55 D	56 A
57 B	58 A	59 B	60 A	61 D	62 C	63 B
64 C	65 C	66 D	67 A	68 A	69 C	70 A
71 A	72 C	73 B	74 C	75 B	76 C	77 A
78 B	79 D	80 C	81 D	82 C	83 C	84 D
85 D	86 B	87 D	88 A	89 B	90 A	91 B
92 A	93 C	94 A	95 C	96 A	97 B	98 B
99 A	100 B	101 A	102 B	103 A	104 B	105 B
106 C	107 D	108 B	109 C	110 A	111 D	112 C
113 C	114 C	115 B	116 D	117 B	118 A	119 C
120 B	121 D	122 B	123 C	124 C	125 D	126 D
127 B	128 C	129 C	130 B	131 D	132 B	133 D
134 A	135 C	136 B	137 B	138 C	139 B	140 D

If you have won £2,000, well done! Turn to page 245 to play for £4,000!

£4,000

1 C	2 B	3 B	4 A	5 C	6 D	7 C
8 B	9 B	10 C	11 A	12 D	13 B	14 C
15 A	16 A	17 C	18 D	19 C	20 A	21 D
22 C	23 D	24 B	25 C	26 D	27 D	28 C
29 C	30 A	31 D	32 D	33 B	34 C	35 C
36 A	37 D	38 B	39 B	40 A	41 C	42 B
43 C	44 C	45 A	46 C	47 C	48 C	49 B
50 B	51 C	52 D	53 A	54 B	55 C	56 A

57 B	58 B	59 B	60 D	61 C	62 A	63 B
64 D	65 B	66 B	67 D	68 C	69 A	70 D
71 C	72 D	73 C	74 B	75 A	76 C	77 B
78 D	79 D	80 A	81 D	82 C	83 B	84 D
85 C	86 C	87 D	88 C	89 C	90 A	91 D
92 C	93 C	94 C	95 A	96 D	97 B	98 A
99 D	100 B	101 D	102 D	103 B	104 C	105 A
106 B	107 A	108 C	109 B	110 C	111 B	112 D
113 C	114 B	115 B	116 B	117 C	118 B	119 D
120 B	121 C	122 D	123 C	124 B	125 A	126 A
127 A	128 B	129 C	130 D	131 B	132 C	

If you have won £4,000, well done! Turn to page 273 to play for £8,000!

£8,000

1 B	2 B	3 B	4 B	5 D	6 B	7 C
8 B	9 C	10 A	11 B	12 C	13 B	14 B
15 A	16 D	17 A	18 C	19 D	20 B	21 B
22 B	23 B	24 D	25 A	26 A	27 D	28 D
29 D	30 B	31 B	32 B	33 C	34 B	35 B
36 D	37 B	38 D	39 B	40 A	41 B	42 B
43 A	44 B	45 D	46 A	47 A	48 B	49 B
50 A	51 A	52 B	53 A	54 A	55 D	56 B
57 A	58 C	59 A	60 C	61 B	62 D	63 B
64 A	65 A	66 C	67 B	68 B	69 B	70 C
71 C	72 D	73 D	74 A	75 B	76 C	77 B
78 C	79 B	80 C	81 B	82 A	83 C	84 A
85 C	86 B	87 A	88 B	89 B	90 A	91 B
92 D	93 D	94 D	95 D	96 D	97 C	98 D
99 D	100 D	101 D	102 D	103 C	104 B	105 C
106 C	107 C	108 A	109 C	110 C	111 B	112 B
113 C	114 B	115 D	116 A	117 B	118 A	119 C
120 C	121 C	122 A	123 C	124 B		

If you have won £8,000, well done! Turn to page 299 to play for £16,000!

£16,000

1 A	2 A	3 A	4 C	5 C	6 D	7 A
8 B	9 C	10 A	11 C	12 B	13 D	14 C
15 B	16 D	17 B	18 C	19 B	20 D	21 A
22 B	23 C	24 C	25 C	26 B	27 A	28 C
29 B	30 A	31 D	32 C	33 C	34 B	35 A
36 A	37 A	38 C	39 C	40 C	41 C	42 C

43 A	44 B	45 C	46 B	47 D	48 C	49 C
50 A	51 A	52 A	53 B	54 D	55 A	56 A
57 B	58 C	59 B	60 A	61 D	62 D	63 A
64 C	65 A	66 C	67 A	68 C	69 C	70 B
71 A	72 C	73 C	74 C	75 D	76 A	77 D
78 D	79 B	80 B	81 D	82 C	83 C	84 A
85 B	86 B	87 D	88 C	89 B	90 D	91 A
92 B	93 C	94 D	95 C	96 C	97 A	98 A
99 B	100 B	101 A	102 D	103 B	104 A	105 A
106 B	107 C	108 A	109 A	110 A	111 B	112 B
113 B	114 C	115 B	116 B			

If you have won £16,000, well done! Turn to page 325 to play for £32,000!

£32,000

1 D	2 B	3 D	4 A	5 C	6 B	7 C
8 A	9 C	10 C	11 C	12 D	13 B	14 C
15 C	16 B	17 C	18 D	19 C	20 C	21 A
22 D	23 C	24 A	25 B	26 D	27 B	28 D
29 C	30 C	31 A	32 C	33 D	34 D	35 A
36 C	37 D	38 C	39 A	40 D	41 B	42 B
43 C	44 C	45 B	46 C	47 B	48 C	49 C
50 D	51 C	52 C	53 B	54 B	55 C	56 A
57 D	58 A	59 C	60 B	61 B	62 C	63 A
64 B	65 A	66 C	67 A	68 A	69 D	70 C
71 A	72 A	73 B	74 D	75 C	76 C	77 B
78 B	79 D	80 A	81 C	82 D	83 C	84 C
85 C	86 B	87 C	88 C	89 A	90 C	91 C
92 D	93 B	94 D	95 C	96 D	97 B	98 B
99 A	100 B	101 B	102 C	103 C	104 D	105 B
106 C	107 B	108 C				

If you have won £32,000, well done! Turn to page 349 to play for £64,000!

£64,000

1 A	2 D	3 C	4 A	5 B	6 A	7 D
8 C	9 C	10 C	11 B	12 B	13 A	14 D
15 A	16 C	17 D	18 A	19 A	20 D	21 A
22 D	23 B	24 D	25 B	26 D	27 C	28 D
29 A	30 A	31 B	32 B	33 D	34 B	35 A
36 C	37 A	38 A	39 D	40 A	41 A	42 A
43 C	44 B	45 D	46 B	47 D	48 A	49 C
50 C	51 D	52 A	53 D	54 B	55 B	56 C

57	C	58	D	59	C	60	A	61	C	62	B	63	C
64	B	65	A	66	A	67	B	68	C	69	A	70	C
71	C	72	D	73	D	74	B	75	D	76	B	77	C
78	D	79	B	80	C	81	B	82	C	83	A	84	A
85	D	86	B	87	B	88	A	89	B	90	B	91	A
92	A	93	A	94	B	95	D	96	B	97	C	98	A
99	D	100	C										

If you have won £64,000, well done! Turn to page 371 to play for £125,000!

£125,000

1	C	2	A	3	B	4	B	5	C	6	B	7	C
8	B	9	B	10	B	11	A	12	A	13	A	14	C
15	B	16	C	17	B	18	C	19	D	20	B	21	C
22	B	23	C	24	D	25	C	26	D	27	B	28	C
29	D	30	A	31	D	32	B	33	D	34	C	35	B
36	B	37	C	38	B	39	C	40	D	41	A	42	D
43	C	44	C	45	A	46	C	47	B	48	A	49	D
50	B	51	A	52	C	53	A	54	A	55	D	56	C
57	A	58	C	59	C	60	C	61	D	62	C	63	B
64	C	65	D	66	C	67	B	68	D	69	A	70	D
71	D	72	C	73	B	74	D	75	D	76	D	77	B
78	C	79	B	80	A	81	A	82	C	83	D	84	A
85	B	86	C	87	A	88	D	89	B	90	B	91	D
92	C												

If you have won £125,000, well done! Turn to page 391 to play for £250,000!

£250,000

1	C	2	C	3	C	4	B	5	A	6	C	7	D
8	B	9	D	10	C	11	C	12	B	13	A	14	C
15	A	16	D	17	A	18	C	19	D	20	B	21	C
22	B	23	A	24	B	25	C	26	A	27	C	28	B
29	D	30	A	31	A	32	A	33	A	34	D	35	C
36	A	37	A	38	B	39	B	40	A	41	B	42	A
43	D	44	A	45	D	46	B	47	B	48	B	49	A
50	D	51	A	52	D	53	D	54	C	55	D	56	C
57	B	58	D	59	A	60	A	61	B	62	A	63	C
64	C	65	B	66	C	67	A	68	D	69	B	70	A
71	C	72	C	73	D	74	D	75	D	76	B	77	A
78	C	79	D	80	C	81	C	82	D	83	D	84	C

If you have won £250,000, well done! Turn to page 409 to play for £500,000!

ANSWERS

£500,000

1	A	2	C	3	C	4	B	5	A	6	B	7	B
8	D	9	B	10	D	11	D	12	C	13	A	14	C
15	B	16	A	17	C	18	D	19	C	20	B	21	D
22	A	23	B	24	C	25	A	26	D	27	C	28	A
29	A	30	D	31	D	32	A	33	C	34	A	35	C
36	B	37	A	38	D	39	A	40	C	41	D	42	C
43	D	44	B	45	A	46	A	47	A	48	B	49	A
50	B	51	C	52	D	53	C	54	A	55	A	56	B
57	B	58	C	59	D	60	C	61	B	62	B	63	C
64	D	65	C	66	B	67	D	68	C	69	B	70	C
71	D	72	C	73	B	74	D	75	C	76	A		

If you have won £500,000, well done! Turn to page 427 to play for £1 Million!

£1 MILLION

1	A	2	C	3	C	4	A	5	B	6	B	7	B
8	C	9	D	10	B	11	B	12	C	13	B	14	B
15	C	16	B	17	B	18	B	19	D	20	B	21	B
22	A	23	B	24	B	25	A	26	B	27	B	28	D
29	D	30	B	31	B	32	C	33	B	34	C	35	D
36	B	37	B	38	D	39	B	40	B	41	A	42	A
43	C	44	C	45	D	46	C	47	C	48	C	49	B
50	D	51	D	52	B	53	D	54	C	55	B	56	A
57	B	58	C	59	B	60	C	61	B	62	A	63	B
64	D	65	C	66	B	67	D	68	B				

If you have won £1,000,000, well done! You're a Millionaire!

Score sheets

Write your name and the names of any other contestants in the space provided. Shade in each of the boxes lightly with a pencil once you or one of your fellow contestants has won the amount in that box. If you or any of the other contestants answer a question incorrectly and are out of the game, use a soft eraser to rub out the relevant boxes so that the final score is showing.

SCORE SHEET

contestant's name		contestant's name	
....		....	
50:50		50:50	
15	£1 MILLION	15	£1 MILLION
14	£500,000	14	£500,000
13	£250,000	13	£250,000
12	£125,000	12	£125,000
11	£64,000	11	£64,000
10	£32,000	10	£32,000
9	£16,000	9	£16,000
8	£8,000	8	£8,000
7	£4,000	7	£4,000
6	£2,000	6	£2,000
5	£1,000	5	£1,000
4	£500	4	£500
3	£300	3	£300
2	£200	2	£200
1	£100	1	£100

SCORE SHEET

contestant's name ....

50:50 ☐ ☐ ☐

15	£1 MILLION
14	£500,000
13	£250,000
12	£125,000
11	£64,000
10	£32,000
9	£16,000
8	£8,000
7	£4,000
6	£2,000
5	£1,000
4	£500
3	£300
2	£200
1	£100

contestant's name ....

50:50 ☐ ☐ ☐

15	£1 MILLION
14	£500,000
13	£250,000
12	£125,000
11	£64,000
10	£32,000
9	£16,000
8	£8,000
7	£4,000
6	£2,000
5	£1,000
4	£500
3	£300
2	£200
1	£100

SCORE SHEET

contestant's name		contestant's name	
50:50 ☐ ☐ ☐		50:50 ☐ ☐ ☐	
15	£1 MILLION	15	£1 MILLION
14	£500,000	14	£500,000
13	£250,000	13	£250,000
12	£125,000	12	£125,000
11	£64,000	11	£64,000
10	£32,000	10	£32,000
9	£16,000	9	£16,000
8	£8,000	8	£8,000
7	£4,000	7	£4,000
6	£2,000	6	£2,000
5	£1,000	5	£1,000
4	£500	4	£500
3	£300	3	£300
2	£200	2	£200
1	£100	1	£100

SCORE SHEET

contestant's name		contestant's name	
....		....	
50:50		50:50	
15	£1 MILLION	15	£1 MILLION
14	£500,000	14	£500,000
13	£250,000	13	£250,000
12	£125,000	12	£125,000
11	£64,000	11	£64,000
10	£32,000	10	£32,000
9	£16,000	9	£16,000
8	£8,000	8	£8,000
7	£4,000	7	£4,000
6	£2,000	6	£2,000
5	£1,000	5	£1,000
4	£500	4	£500
3	£300	3	£300
2	£200	2	£200
1	£100	1	£100

SCORE SHEET

contestant's name		contestant's name	
....		....	
50:50		50:50	
15	£1 MILLION	15	£1 MILLION
14	£500,000	14	£500,000
13	£250,000	13	£250,000
12	£125,000	12	£125,000
11	£64,000	11	£64,000
10	£32,000	10	£32,000
9	£16,000	9	£16,000
8	£8,000	8	£8,000
7	£4,000	7	£4,000
6	£2,000	6	£2,000
5	£1,000	5	£1,000
4	£500	4	£500
3	£300	3	£300
2	£200	2	£200
1	£100	1	£100

SCORE SHEET

contestant's name		contestant's name	
50:50 ☐ ☐ ☐		50:50 ☐ ☐ ☐	
15	£1 MILLION	15	£1 MILLION
14	£500,000	14	£500,000
13	£250,000	13	£250,000
12	£125,000	12	£125,000
11	£64,000	11	£64,000
10	£32,000	10	£32,000
9	£16,000	9	£16,000
8	£8,000	8	£8,000
7	£4,000	7	£4,000
6	£2,000	6	£2,000
5	£1,000	5	£1,000
4	£500	4	£500
3	£300	3	£300
2	£200	2	£200
1	£100	1	£100

SCORE SHEET

contestant's name		contestant's name	
50:50 ☐ ☐ ☐		50:50 ☐ ☐ ☐	
15	£1 MILLION	15	£1 MILLION
14	£500,000	14	£500,000
13	£250,000	13	£250,000
12	£125,000	12	£125,000
11	£64,000	11	£64,000
10	£32,000	10	£32,000
9	£16,000	9	£16,000
8	£8,000	8	£8,000
7	£4,000	7	£4,000
6	£2,000	6	£2,000
5	£1,000	5	£1,000
4	£500	4	£500
3	£300	3	£300
2	£200	2	£200
1	£100	1	£100

SCORE SHEET

contestant's name		contestant's name	
50:50 ☐ ☐ ☐		50:50 ☐ ☐ ☐	
15	£1 MILLION	15	£1 MILLION
14	£500,000	14	£500,000
13	£250,000	13	£250,000
12	£125,000	12	£125,000
11	£64,000	11	£64,000
10	£32,000	10	£32,000
9	£16,000	9	£16,000
8	£8,000	8	£8,000
7	£4,000	7	£4,000
6	£2,000	6	£2,000
5	£1,000	5	£1,000
4	£500	4	£500
3	£300	3	£300
2	£200	2	£200
1	£100	1	£100

SCORE SHEET

contestant's name		contestant's name	
50:50		50:50	
15	£1 MILLION	15	£1 MILLION
14	£500,000	14	£500,000
13	£250,000	13	£250,000
12	£125,000	12	£125,000
11	£64,000	11	£64,000
10	£32,000	10	£32,000
9	£16,000	9	£16,000
8	£8,000	8	£8,000
7	£4,000	7	£4,000
6	£2,000	6	£2,000
5	£1,000	5	£1,000
4	£500	4	£500
3	£300	3	£300
2	£200	2	£200
1	£100	1	£100

SCORE SHEET

contestant's name	contestant's name
....	....
50:50 ☐ ☐ ☐	50:50 ☐ ☐ ☐

15	£1 MILLION	15	£1 MILLION
14	£500,000	14	£500,000
13	£250,000	13	£250,000
12	£125,000	12	£125,000
11	£64,000	11	£64,000
10	£32,000	10	£32,000
9	£16,000	9	£16,000
8	£8,000	8	£8,000
7	£4,000	7	£4,000
6	£2,000	6	£2,000
5	£1,000	5	£1,000
4	£500	4	£500
3	£300	3	£300
2	£200	2	£200
1	£100	1	£100

S C O R E   S H E E T

contestant's name

....

50:50

15	£1 MILLION
14	£500,000
13	£250,000
12	£125,000
11	£64,000
10	£32,000
9	£16,000
8	£8,000
7	£4,000
6	£2,000
5	£1,000
4	£500
3	£300
2	£200
1	£100

contestant's name

....

50:50

15	£1 MILLION
14	£500,000
13	£250,000
12	£125,000
11	£64,000
10	£32,000
9	£16,000
8	£8,000
7	£4,000
6	£2,000
5	£1,000
4	£500
3	£300
2	£200
1	£100

SCORE SHEET

contestant's name

....

50:50

15	£1 MILLION
14	£500,000
13	£250,000
12	£125,000
11	£64,000
10	£32,000
9	£16,000
8	£8,000
7	£4,000
6	£2,000
5	£1,000
4	£500
3	£300
2	£200
1	£100

contestant's name

....

50:50

15	£1 MILLION
14	£500,000
13	£250,000
12	£125,000
11	£64,000
10	£32,000
9	£16,000
8	£8,000
7	£4,000
6	£2,000
5	£1,000
4	£500
3	£300
2	£200
1	£100

SCORE SHEET

contestant's name

....

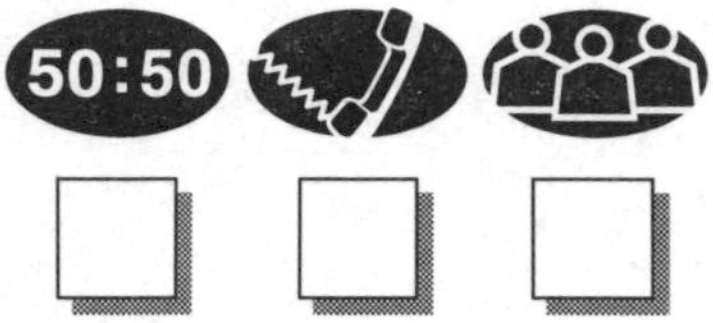

15	£1 MILLION
14	£500,000
13	£250,000
12	£125,000
11	£64,000
10	£32,000
9	£16,000
8	£8,000
7	£4,000
6	£2,000
5	£1,000
4	£500
3	£300
2	£200
1	£100

contestant's name

....

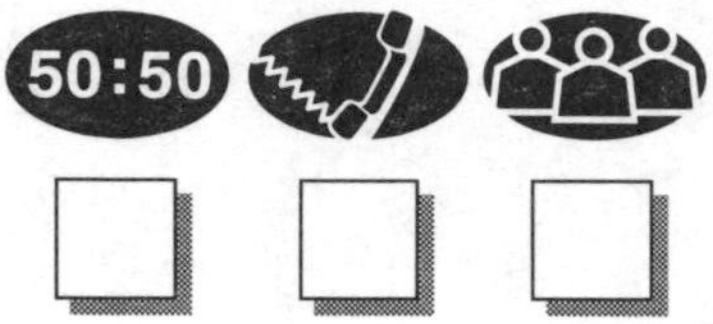

15	£1 MILLION
14	£500,000
13	£250,000
12	£125,000
11	£64,000
10	£32,000
9	£16,000
8	£8,000
7	£4,000
6	£2,000
5	£1,000
4	£500
3	£300
2	£200
1	£100

SCORE SHEET

contestant's name		contestant's name	
50:50 ☐ ☐ ☐		50:50 ☐ ☐ ☐	
15	£1 MILLION	15	£1 MILLION
14	£500,000	14	£500,000
13	£250,000	13	£250,000
12	£125,000	12	£125,000
11	£64,000	11	£64,000
10	£32,000	10	£32,000
9	£16,000	9	£16,000
8	£8,000	8	£8,000
7	£4,000	7	£4,000
6	£2,000	6	£2,000
5	£1,000	5	£1,000
4	£500	4	£500
3	£300	3	£300
2	£200	2	£200
1	£100	1	£100

SCORE SHEET

contestant's name		contestant's name	
15	£1 MILLION	15	£1 MILLION
14	£500,000	14	£500,000
13	£250,000	13	£250,000
12	£125,000	12	£125,000
11	£64,000	11	£64,000
10	£32,000	10	£32,000
9	£16,000	9	£16,000
8	£8,000	8	£8,000
7	£4,000	7	£4,000
6	£2,000	6	£2,000
5	£1,000	5	£1,000
4	£500	4	£500
3	£300	3	£300
2	£200	2	£200
1	£100	1	£100

SCORE SHEET

contestant's name		contestant's name	
....		....	
50:50		50:50	
15	£1 MILLION	15	£1 MILLION
14	£500,000	14	£500,000
13	£250,000	13	£250,000
12	£125,000	12	£125,000
11	£64,000	11	£64,000
10	£32,000	10	£32,000
9	£16,000	9	£16,000
8	£8,000	8	£8,000
7	£4,000	7	£4,000
6	£2,000	6	£2,000
5	£1,000	5	£1,000
4	£500	4	£500
3	£300	3	£300
2	£200	2	£200
1	£100	1	£100

SCORE SHEET

contestant's name		contestant's name	
50:50 ☐	☐ ☐	50:50 ☐	☐ ☐
15	£1 MILLION	15	£1 MILLION
14	£500,000	14	£500,000
13	£250,000	13	£250,000
12	£125,000	12	£125,000
11	£64,000	11	£64,000
10	£32,000	10	£32,000
9	£16,000	9	£16,000
8	£8,000	8	£8,000
7	£4,000	7	£4,000
6	£2,000	6	£2,000
5	£1,000	5	£1,000
4	£500	4	£500
3	£300	3	£300
2	£200	2	£200
1	£100	1	£100

SCORE SHEET

contestant's name		contestant's name	
....		....	
50:50 ☐ / ☐ / ☐		50:50 ☐ / ☐ / ☐	
15	£1 MILLION	15	£1 MILLION
14	£500,000	14	£500,000
13	£250,000	13	£250,000
12	£125,000	12	£125,000
11	£64,000	11	£64,000
10	£32,000	**10**	£32,000
9	£16,000	9	£16,000
8	£8,000	8	£8,000
7	£4,000	7	£4,000
6	£2,000	6	£2,000
5	£1,000	**5**	£1,000
4	£500	4	£500
3	£300	3	£300
2	£200	2	£200
1	£100	1	£100

SCORE SHEET

contestant's name

....

50:50

15	£1 MILLION
14	£500,000
13	£250,000
12	£125,000
11	£64,000
10	£32,000
9	£16,000
8	£8,000
7	£4,000
6	£2,000
5	£1,000
4	£500
3	£300
2	£200
1	£100

contestant's name

....

50:50

15	£1 MILLION
14	£500,000
13	£250,000
12	£125,000
11	£64,000
10	£32,000
9	£16,000
8	£8,000
7	£4,000
6	£2,000
5	£1,000
4	£500
3	£300
2	£200
1	£100

SCORE SHEET

	contestant's name		contestant's name ....
	50:50		50:50
15	£1 MILLION	15	£1 MILLION
14	£500,000	14	£500,000
13	£250,000	13	£250,000
12	£125,000	12	£125,000
11	£64,000	11	£64,000
10	£32,000	10	£32,000
9	£16,000	9	£16,000
8	£8,000	8	£8,000
7	£4,000	7	£4,000
6	£2,000	6	£2,000
5	£1,000	5	£1,000
4	£500	4	£500
3	£300	3	£300
2	£200	2	£200
1	£100	1	£100

SCORE SHEET

contestant's name

....

50:50

15	£1 MILLION
14	£500,000
13	£250,000
12	£125,000
11	£64,000
10	£32,000
9	£16,000
8	£8,000
7	£4,000
6	£2,000
5	£1,000
4	£500
3	£300
2	£200
1	£100

contestant's name

....

50:50

15	£1 MILLION
14	£500,000
13	£250,000
12	£125,000
11	£64,000
10	£32,000
9	£16,000
8	£8,000
7	£4,000
6	£2,000
5	£1,000
4	£500
3	£300
2	£200
1	£100

SCORE SHEET

	contestant's name		contestant's name
	50:50		50:50
15	£1 MILLION	15	£1 MILLION
14	£500,000	14	£500,000
13	£250,000	13	£250,000
12	£125,000	12	£125,000
11	£64,000	11	£64,000
10	£32,000	10	£32,000
9	£16,000	9	£16,000
8	£8,000	8	£8,000
7	£4,000	7	£4,000
6	£2,000	6	£2,000
5	£1,000	5	£1,000
4	£500	4	£500
3	£300	3	£300
2	£200	2	£200
1	£100	1	£100

SCORE SHEET

contestant's name		contestant's name	
....		....	
50:50 ☐ ☐ ☐		50:50 ☐ ☐ ☐	
15	£1 MILLION	15	£1 MILLION
14	£500,000	14	£500,000
13	£250,000	13	£250,000
12	£125,000	12	£125,000
11	£64,000	11	£64,000
10	£32,000	10	£32,000
9	£16,000	9	£16,000
8	£8,000	8	£8,000
7	£4,000	7	£4,000
6	£2,000	6	£2,000
5	£1,000	5	£1,000
4	£500	4	£500
3	£300	3	£300
2	£200	2	£200
1	£100	1	£100

SCORE SHEET

contestant's name

....

50:50

15	£1 MILLION
14	£500,000
13	£250,000
12	£125,000
11	£64,000
10	£32,000
9	£16,000
8	£8,000
7	£4,000
6	£2,000
5	£1,000
4	£500
3	£300
2	£200
1	£100

contestant's name

....

50:50

15	£1 MILLION
14	£500,000
13	£250,000
12	£125,000
11	£64,000
10	£32,000
9	£16,000
8	£8,000
7	£4,000
6	£2,000
5	£1,000
4	£500
3	£300
2	£200
1	£100

SCORE SHEET

contestant's name		contestant's name	
50:50 ☐	☐ ☐	50:50 ☐	☐ ☐
15	£1 MILLION	15	£1 MILLION
14	£500,000	14	£500,000
13	£250,000	13	£250,000
12	£125,000	12	£125,000
11	£64,000	11	£64,000
10	£32,000	10	£32,000
9	£16,000	9	£16,000
8	£8,000	8	£8,000
7	£4,000	7	£4,000
6	£2,000	6	£2,000
5	£1,000	5	£1,000
4	£500	4	£500
3	£300	3	£300
2	£200	2	£200
1	£100	1	£100

SCORE SHEET

contestant's name	....	contestant's name	....
50:50	☐ ☐ ☐	50:50	☐ ☐ ☐
15	£1 MILLION	15	£1 MILLION
14	£500,000	14	£500,000
13	£250,000	13	£250,000
12	£125,000	12	£125,000
11	£64,000	11	£64,000
10	£32,000	**10**	£32,000
9	£16,000	9	£16,000
8	£8,000	8	£8,000
7	£4,000	7	£4,000
6	£2,000	6	£2,000
5	£1,000	**5**	£1,000
4	£500	4	£500
3	£300	3	£300
2	£200	2	£200
1	£100	1	£100

SCORE SHEET

contestant's name

....

50:50

15	£1 MILLION
14	£500,000
13	£250,000
12	£125,000
11	£64,000
10	£32,000
9	£16,000
8	£8,000
7	£4,000
6	£2,000
5	£1,000
4	£500
3	£300
2	£200
1	£100

contestant's name

....

50:50

15	£1 MILLION
14	£500,000
13	£250,000
12	£125,000
11	£64,000
10	£32,000
9	£16,000
8	£8,000
7	£4,000
6	£2,000
5	£1,000
4	£500
3	£300
2	£200
1	£100